PHP 7 Zend Certification Study Guide

Ace the ZCE 2017-PHP Exam

Andrew Beak

Apress®

PHP 7 Zend Certification Study Guide

Andrew Beak
Grafham, Cambridgeshire, United Kingdom

ISBN-13 (pbk): 978-1-4842-3245-3 ISBN-13 (electronic): 978-1-4842-3246-0
https://doi.org/10.1007/978-1-4842-3246-0

Library of Congress Control Number: 2017960936

Cover image by Freepik (`www.freepik.com`)

Managing Director: Welmoed Spahr
Editorial Director: Todd Green
Acquisitions Editor: Nikhil Karkal
Development Editor: James Markham
Technical Reviewer: Nico Loubser
Coordinating Editor: Prachi Mehta
Copy Editor: Kezia Endsley

Distributed to the book trade worldwide by Springer Science+Business Media New York, 233 Spring Street, 6th Floor, New York, NY 10013. Phone 1-800-SPRINGER, fax (201) 348-4505, e-mail orders-ny@springer-sbm.com, or visit `www.springeronline.com`. Apress Media, LLC is a California LLC and the sole member (owner) is Springer Science + Business Media Finance Inc (SSBM Finance Inc). SSBM Finance Inc is a **Delaware** corporation.

For information on translations, please e-mail rights@apress.com, or visit http://www.apress.com/rights-permissions.

Apress titles may be purchased in bulk for academic, corporate, or promotional use. eBook versions and licenses are also available for most titles. For more information, reference our Print and eBook Bulk Sales web page at http://www.apress.com/bulk-sales.

Any source code or other supplementary material referenced by the author in this book is available to readers on GitHub via the book's product page, located at www.apress.com/978-1-4842-3245-3. For more detailed information, please visit http://www.apress.com/source-code.

Printed on acid-free paper

For Duckems, Beastly, and Bratface
for whom I'd change the world if I had the source code

Contents

About the Author

Andrew Beak is a software architect responsible for the cloud platform of an Internet television company. He is a ZCE and has over six years of professional experience working in PHP. He has been the technical lead for teams in South Africa and the United Kingdom. His enjoyment for writing coupled with his interest in empowering staff inspired him to write this book. He has also written a book on scaling PHP and published a series of video courses focused on the Zend examinations.

About the Technical Reviewer

Nico Loubser is the lead software developer and team lead in a company that specializes in the payment industry, with a degree in information systems. He has been working in PHP since PHP 3.8, as well as working in numerous industries, and is a serious PHP 7 enthusiast.

Introduction

Welcome to what I hope is an accessible reference that helps you quickly find and learn relevant facts about the PHP language. I'm writing it with the following readers in mind:

- Intermediate PHP programmers with two or three years of experience who are hoping to sit for the Zend 2017 certification exams in the PHP 7.1 language.

- Programmers who are proficient in another language but want a quick reference book to dive into PHP.

This book is specifically not an introduction to programming and no attempt is made to introduce basic topics such as what a variable is. It is purely a reference to learn the idiosyncrasies of PHP and serve as a guide toward certifying.

Additionally, it does not intend to replace the PHP manual but rather to focus the reader's attention on aspects of PHP relevant to the Zend certification exams. To that end, I make liberal use of footnotes linking to manual pages and other reference pages.

This guide cannot possibly cover the full depth of the PHP manual,[1] and you cannot consider yourself prepared until you have worked through the manual pages. It is essential to follow the footnote links, read the page, and even follow some links through the PHP manual related to the topic.

This book focuses on PHP 7.1 and in order to keep focused on the exam syllabus does not attempt to exhaustively explain what features are available in which version of PHP. You can assume that if a feature is referenced in this book then it is available in PHP 7.1.

You won't need to know when a feature was introduced into PHP, but you will need to know what features are deprecated in PHP 7.1. I've tried to keep that in mind when giving information about the availability of a feature.

Wherever possible, I'll flag where something has changed from PHP 5.6, especially where it is not backward compatible.

This book tries to avoid having an opinion about coding standards such as PSR2, but it is strongly recommended that a practicing developer learn these in parallel. You won't be asked about them on the exam and so I won't teach them here.

Some paragraphs in this book are marked up with symbols, as explained next.

---

[1]https://php.net/

■ **Caution** These paragraphs draw your attention to something that might be counter-intuitive or a part of PHP weirdness.

■ **Note** These paragraphs deserve special attention.

■ **Tip** These paragraphs draw your attention to potential exam questions.

The Zend Certification Syllabus

Zend certification is one of the few industry certifications that is widely recognized as an established benchmark for proficiency in PHP. Part of why this certification is so well respected is that it is not easy to attain. To pass your exam, you need to have an in-depth knowledge of a wide area of topics in PHP programming.

This book aims to highlight the topics that are important in the certification examination. I've included a bunch of quizzes that test the topics, and if you notice any gaps in your knowledge, you should make sure to go carefully through the relevant sections in the manual.

The actual exam consists of about 70 questions drawn from a pool. Questions will vary in difficulty and will sometimes require you to apply the principles from more than one area of the syllabus to solve them.

There are ten topics covered in the examination. Zend places varying amount of importance to the topics in the exam. You can find a list of exam topics on the Zend web site.

You'll notice that this guide has a chapter for each of the topics in the list:

Very Important	Average Importance	Lower Importance
PHP basics	Functions	Databases and SQL
Object-Oriented PHP	Web Features	Data Format and Types
Security	Strings	Input-Output
	Arrays	
	Error Handling	

The sections on PHP basics, object-oriented programming, and security are regarded as being the most important and are given the most weight in the exam.

There are a lot of tricky questions in the PHP Basics section, so don't be fooled by the inclusion of the word "basics" in the topic title. It's one of the three most important topics in the exam syllabus, so don't skimp on the time you spend finding the gaps in your knowledge.

The sections on databases, data formats and types, and input-output are considered less important. You'll still need to know them, however, as exam questions will often rely on a broad knowledge of PHP and may require you to apply knowledge from different topics.

The exam has a mixture of multiple choice and free text questions. You'll be required to code short snippets to answer some questions.

Although you won't be required to have an encyclopedic knowledge of the PHP manual, you will be asked questions about function parameters, what function to use in a particular situation, common classes, exceptions, and other elements of PHP.

Unless they note otherwise, all questions assume that you are working with PHP 7.1 that has been configured with the recommended settings. You can assume that error display is set on and that error reporting is set to E_ALL.

You can mark questions for review and come back to them later. Don't spend more time than is allocated to a question; That just makes the following questions more difficult because you have less time!

Finally, there is no negative marking in the exam. You won't be penalized for an incorrect answer, so taking a guess works in your favor.

CHAPTER 1

■ ■ ■

PHP Basics

Introduction

This chapter focuses on the nitty gritty details of PHP as a language. This is a big chapter and it covers one of the most important aspects of the exam. The best advice that I can give is not to skim over it. There are a lot of places where PHP has some peculiarities and even with a few years of experience you might not have encountered them all.

Basic Language Features

All statements in PHP must be terminated with a semicolon. An exception to this is if the statement happens to be the last statement before a closing tag.

Whitespace has no semantic meaning in PHP. There is no need to line code up, but most coding standards enforce this to improve code readability. Whitespace may not appear in the middle of function names, variable names, or keywords.

Multiple statements are allowed on a single line.

Code blocks are denoted by the brace symbols { }.

PHP language construct and function names are not case-sensitive, but variable and constant names are.

```
<?php
ECHO "Hello World"; // works
$variable = "Hello World";
echo $VARIABLE; // won't work
```

Inserting PHP into Web Pages

Although PHP is a general scripting language and can be used for other purposes, it is most commonly deployed as a server-side scripting language used for building web pages.

The PHP parser does not parse anything that is not included in the tags that indicate PHP script. Content outside of PHP tags is simply output without inspection. This allows PHP to be embedded in HTML.

© Andrew Beak 2017
A. Beak, *PHP 7 Zend Certification Study Guide*,
https://doi.org/10.1007/978-1-4842-3246-0_1

There are several ways to delimit PHP script, but only the first two in this table are commonly used:

Type	Open	Close	Note
Standard	`<?php`	`?>`	
Echo	`<?=`	`?>`	
Short	`<?`	`?>`	Deprecated
Script	`<script language="php">`	`</script>`	Do not use
ASP	`<%`	`%>`	Deprecated

The echo tag allows you to easily echo a PHP variable and the shortened tag makes your HTML document easier to read. It is commonly used in templates where you want to output several values into various positions on a page. Using the short syntax keeps your template code much neater.

Its usage is easiest to understand when it's shown along with the equivalent in standard opening codes. The following two tags are identical:

```
<?= $variable ?>
<?php echo $variable ?>
```

■ **Note**   The echo statement is the last statement before a closing tag and so it does not need a semicolon to terminate it.

You can use PHP logic between opening and closing tags, as in this example:

```
Balance:
<?php
if ($bankBalance > 0): ?>
<p class="black">
<?php else: ?>
<p class="red">
<?php endif; ?>
<?= $bankBalance?>
</p>
```

Let's step through the code:

1. The PHP parser will output Balance: without evaluating it because it is not in the PHP tags.

2. The PHP tag then checks if the balance is greater than zero and terminates. The `<p class="black">` tag is only output if that condition is true; otherwise, the `<p class="red">` tag is output.

3. We use the echo tag syntax to output the $bankBalance variable.

4. Finally, the closing paragraph tag is output without being parsed because the PHP script has been closed.

■ **Note** This approach will also work using the curly brace syntax of an if statement.

It is quite common in PHP programs to omit the closing tag ?> in a file. This is acceptable to the parser and is a useful way to prevent problems with newline characters appearing after the closing tag.

These newline characters are sent as output by the PHP interpreter and could interfere with the HTTP headers or cause other unintended side-effects. By not closing the script in a PHP file, you prevent the chance of newline characters being sent.

■ **Tip** It is a common coding standard to require that the closing tag is omitted in included files, but this is not a PHP requirement.

Language Constructs

Language constructs are different from functions in that they are baked right into the language.

Language constructs can be understood directly by the parser and do not need to be broken down. Functions, on the other hand, are mapped and simplified to a set of language constructs before they are parsed.

Language constructs are not functions, and so cannot be used as a callback function. They follow rules that are different from functions when it comes to parameters and the use of parentheses.

For example, echo doesn't always need parentheses when you call it and, if you call it with more than one argument, then you can't use parentheses.

```php
<?php
// one parameter, no brackets
echo "hello\r\n";
// two parameters, brackets (syntax error)
//echo('hello', 'world');
// two parameters, no brackets
echo 'hello', 'world';
```

Furthermore, echo does not return a value, whereas every function will always return a value (or null).

The PHP Manual page on reserved keywords[1] has a complete list, but here are some of the constructs that you should be familiar with:

Construct	Used For
assert	Debug command to test a condition and do something if it is not true.
echo	Outputting a value to stdout.
print	Outputting a value to stdout.
exit	Optionally outputting a message and terminating the program.
die	This is an alias for exit.
return	Terminates a function and returns control to the calling scope, or if called in the global scope, terminates the program.
include	Includes a file and evaluates it. PHP will issue a warning if the file is not found or cannot be read.
include_once	If you specify include_once then PHP will make sure that it includes the file only once.
require	PHP will include a file and evaluate it. If the file is not found or cannot be read, then a fatal error will be generated.
require_once	As for include_once, but a fatal error will be generated instead of a warning.
eval	The argument is evaluated as PHP and affects the calling scope.
empty	Returns a Boolean value depending on whether the variable is empty or not. Empty variables include null variables, empty strings, arrays with no elements, numeric values of 0, a string value of 0, and Boolean values of false.
isset	Returns true if the variable has been set and false otherwise.
unset	Clears a variable.
list	Assigns multiple variables at one time from an array.

One possible tricky exam question that might come up is in understanding the small difference between print and echo. The echo construct does not return a value, not even null, and so is not suitable for use inside an expression. The print construct will however return a value.

The reason not to use include_once() and require_once() all the time is a performance issue. PHP tracks a list of files that has been included to support the functionality of these functions. This requires memory so these functions are rather used when they are necessary and not in favor of include or require.

---

[1]https://php.net/manual/en/reserved.php

Comments

There are three styles to mark comments:

```php
<?php
# Perl style comments
// C style comments
/*
   Multiline comment
*/
```

API documentation can additionally conform to external standards such as those used by the PHPDocumentor project.[2] This tool examines your API style comments and automatically creates documentation for you.

API documentation looks very similar to multiline comments:

```php
<?php
/**
      API documentation has two asterisks, this is not a PHP
      syntax distinction, but is just a convention.
*/
```

Representing Numbers

There are four ways in which an integer may be expressed in a PHP script:

Notation	Example	Note
Decimal	1234	
Binary	0b10011010010	Identified by leading 0b or 0B
Octal	02322	Identified by leading 0
Hexadecimal	0x4D2	Identified by leading 0x or 0X

Floating point numbers (called doubles in some other languages) can be expressed either in standard decimal format or in exponential format.

Form	Example
Decimal	123.456
Exponential	0.123456e3 or 0.123456E3

---

[2]https://www.phpdoc.org/

5

■ **Note** The letter "e" in the exponential form is case-insensitive, as are the other letters used in the integer formats.

Variables

In this section, I'm going to be focusing on how PHP handles variables. I'm assuming that you've had enough experience with PHP that I don't need to explain what variables are or how to use them. We'll be looking at the various types of variables PHP offers, how to change the type of a variable, and how to check if a variable is set or not.

Variable Types

PHP is a loosely typed language. It is important not to think that PHP variables don't have a type. They most definitely do, it's just that they may change type during runtime and don't need their type to be declared explicitly when initialized.

PHP will implicitly cast the variable to the data type required for an operation. For example, if an operation requires a number, such as the addition (+) operation, then PHP will convert the operands into a numeric format.

You'll be introduced to type juggling in the "Casting Variables" section and you'll need to know the rules PHP follows when changing a variable type. For now, you just need to know that PHP variables have a type, that type can change, and although you can explicitly change the type PHP does this implicitly for you.

PHP has three categories of variable—scalars, composite, and resources. A scalar variable is one that can only hold one value at a time. Composite variables can contain several values at a time.

A resource variable points to something not native to PHP like a handle provided by the OS to a file or a database connection. These variables cannot be cast.

Finally, PHP has the null type, which is used for variables that have not had a value set to them. You can also assign the null value to a variable, but you cannot cast to a null type in PHP 7.1.

Scalar Types

There are four scalar types:

Type	Alias	Contains
Boolean	bool	True or False
Integer	int	A signed numeric integer
Float		A signed numeric double or float data
String		An ordered collection of binary data

Some types have aliases. For example, consider this code that shows that bool is an alias for boolean:

```php
<?php
$a = (boolean)true;
$b = (bool)true;
var_dump($a === $b); // bool(true)
```

Strings in PHP are not simply a list of characters. Internally PHP strings contain information about their length and are not null terminated. This means that they may contain binary information such as an image file that has been read from disk. In other words, PHP strings are binary safe.

Composite Types

There are two composite types: arrays and objects. Each of these has its own section in this book.

Casting Variables

This is a very important section of understanding PHP and even very experienced developers may not be aware of some of the rules that PHP uses to cast variables.

PHP implicitly casts variables to the type required to perform an operation.

It is also possible to explicitly cast variables using one of two options:

- Use a casting operator

- Use a PHP function

Casting operators are used by putting the name of the data type you want to cast into brackets before the variable name. For example:

```php
<?php
$a = '123';        // $a is a string
$a = (int)$a;      // $a is now an integer
$a = (bool)$a;     // $a is now Boolean and is true
```

You can cast a variable to null, as in the following example, but this behavior is deprecated in PHP 7.2 so you shouldn't do it even though PHP 7.1 supports it.

```php
<?php
$a = "Hello World";
$a = (unset)$a; // Deprecated in PHP 7.2
var_dump($a);   // NULL
```

There are also PHP functions that will convert a variable to a data type. These are named in a way that is self-documenting: floatval, intval, strval, and boolval.

Additionally, the intdiv function will potentially cast a double to an integer when it returns the integer result of dividing two integers.

You can also call the settype function on a variable that takes the desired data type as a second argument.

There are some rules that need to be remembered regarding how variables are cast in PHP. You should read the manual page on type juggling[3] carefully, because there are many trips and traps in type juggling. Also make sure that you read the pages linked to from the type juggling page.

Instead of exhaustively listing the rules, I'll focus on some of the rules that may be counter-intuitive or are commonly mistaken.

Casting from float to integer does not round the value up or down, but rather truncates the decimal portion.

```php
<?php
$a = 1234.56;
echo (int)$a;      // 1234 (not 1235)
$a = -1234.56
echo (int)$a;      // -1234
```

Some general rules for casting to Boolean are that:

- Empty arrays and strings are cast to false.

- Strings always evaluate to Boolean true unless they have a value that's considered "empty" by PHP.

- Strings containing numbers evaluate to true if the number is not zero. Recall that such strings return false when the empty() function is called on them.

- Any integer (or float) that is non-zero is true, so negative numbers are true.

Objects can have the magic method __toString() defined on them. This can be overloaded if you want to have a custom way to cast your object to string. We look at this in the section on "Casting Objects to String".

Converting a string to a number results in 0 unless the string begins with valid numeric data (see the PHP Manual[4] for more detail). By default, the variable type of the cast number will be integer, unless an exponent or decimal point is encountered, in which case it will be a float.

---

[3]https://php.net/manual/en/language.types.type-juggling.php
[4]https://secure.php.net/manual/en/language.types.string.php#language.types.string.conversion

Here is an example script that shows some string conversions:

```php
<?php
$examples = [
    "12 o clock",
    "Half past 12",
    "12.30",
    "7.2e2 minutes after midnight"
];
foreach ($examples as $example) {
    $result = 0 + $example;
    var_dump($result);
}

/*
This outputs:
    int(12)
    int(0)
    double(12.3)
    double(720)
*/
```

Floats and Integers

Be very careful when casting between floats and integers. The PHP Manual[5] has a very good example of how internal implementation details of numeric types can have counter-intuitive results:

```php
<?php
echo (int) ( (0.1+0.7) * 10 ); // 7
echo (int) ( (0.1+0.5) * 10);  // 6
```

One would expect the first example to display 8, but in fact the internal floating-point representation is just slightly less than 8.

When PHP converts a floating point number to integer it rounds toward zero, so it becomes 7.

The reason behind this is that some numbers are rational in base 10 but are irrational in base 2. Although 0.7 can be expressed as a rational number in base 10, when expressed in base 2 it is irrational. Because there are a limited number of bits available to store the number, it is inevitable that some loss of precision will occur.

PHP integers are always signed. The range of values that an integer can take will depend on the system PHP is running on.

---

[5]https://secure.php.net/manual/en/language.types.integer.php

9

You can determine the size of an integer in bytes at runtime by querying the constant PHP_INT_SIZE. The constants PHP_INT_MAX and PHP_INT_MIN will give you the maximum and minimum values that can be stored in an integer, respectively. There are similar constants for other numeric types. They are listed in the PHP Manual page on reserved constants.[6]

■ **Caution**   You should not rely on floats precision up to the last digit.

You should avoid testing floats directly for equality and rather test if they are the same up to a given degree of precision, as in this example:

```php
<?php
$pi = 3.14159625;
$indiana = 3.2;
$epsilon = 0.00001; // degree of error

if(abs($pi - $indiana) < $epsilon) {
    echo "Those values look the same to me";
} else {
    echo "Those values are different";
}
```

This code is checking if the values are the same to five degrees of precision. This script will output Those values are different because the difference is greater than the degree of error that we defined.

Naming Variables

PHP variables begin with the dollar symbol $ and PHP variable names adhere to the following rules:

- Names are case sensitive

- Names may contain letters, numbers, and the underscore character

- Names may not begin with a number

Coding conventions differ on the use of camelCase, StudlyCase, or snake_case, but all of these formats are valid PHP variable name formats.

---

[6]https://php.net/manual/en/reserved.constants.php

PHP also allows for variable variable names. This is best illustrated by example:

```php
<?php
$a = 'foo';
$$a = 'bar'; // $a is 'foo', so variable $foo is set
echo $foo;    // bar
```

PHP 7 will always evaluate access strictly left to right. Older versions had a complicated set of rules to determine how it would evaluate this sort of syntax. Happily, PHP 7 is simpler and consistent and I won't worry about explaining older versions.

Here is a more complicated example that illustrates how PHP evaluates from left to right:

```php
<?php
$a = 'foo';
$$a['bar'] = 'Murky code';
// this assert passes
assert($$a['bar'] === $foo['bar']);
var_dump($foo);

/*
    array(1) {
      ["bar"]=>
      array(1) {
        ["baz"]=>
        string(10) "Murky code"
      }
    }
*/
```

There are several caveats to using variable variable names. They could impact on your code security and can also make your code a little murky to read.

Checking If a Variable Has Been Set

The command isset() will return true if a variable has been set and false otherwise. It is preferable to use this function instead of checking if the variable is null because it won't cause PHP to generate a warning.

The command empty() will return true if a variable is not set and will not generate a warning. This is not a bulletproof way to test if a variable is set.

■ **Note**   Remember that the string "o" is considered empty, but is actually set.

Variables become unset when they become out of scope and you can use the command unset() to manually clear a variable. We'll see later in the book that the garbage collector is responsible for freeing up the memory allocated to variables that have been unset.

Constants

Constants[7] are similar to variables but are immutable. They have the same naming rules as variables, but by convention will have uppercase names.

They can be defined using the define[8] function as shown:

```php
<?php
define('PI', 3.142);
echo PI;
define('UNITS', ['MILES_CONVERSION' => 1.6, 'INCHES_CONVERSION' => '2.54']);
echo "5km in miles is " . 5 * UNITS['MILES_CONVERSION'];
/*
  3.1425km in miles is 8
*/
```

The third parameter of define is optional and indicates whether the constant name is case sensitive or not.

You can also use the const keyword to define constants. Constants can only contain arrays or scalar values and not resources or objects.

```php
<?php
const UNITS = ['MILES_CONVERSION' => 1.6,
               'INCHES_CONVERSION' => '2.54'];
echo "5km in miles is " . 5 * UNITS['MILES_CONVERSION'];
/*
  5km in miles is 8
*/
```

Only the const keyword can be used to create a namespaced constant, as in this example where we create constants in the "Foo" namespace and then try to reference them in the "Bar" namespace.

```php
<?php
namespace Foo;
const AVOCADO = 6.02214086;
// using define() will generate a warning
define(MOLE, 'hill');

namespace Bar;
echo \Foo\AVOCADO;
// referencing the constant we tried to define() results in a fatal error
echo \Foo\MOLE;
```

---

[7]https://php.net/manual/en/language.constants.syntax.php
[8]https://php.net/manual/en/function.define.php

You cannot assign a variable to a constant.

You can use static scalar values to define a constant, like this:

```
const STORAGE_PATH = __DIR__ . '/storage';
```

■ **Note**   Note the use of the "magic" constant __DIR__ that is set by PHP at runtime and contains the path that the script resides in on the file system. These constants are discussed in the section "Magic Constants".

The constant() function[9] is used to retrieve the value of a constant.

```
<?php
const MILES_CONVERSION = 1.6;
echo 'There are ' . constant('MILES_CONVERSION') . ' miles in a kilometer';
/*
  There are 1.6 miles in a kilometer
*/
```

Superglobals

PHP has several superglobals[10] that are available automatically to the script. Superglobals are available in every scope.

You can alter the values of superglobals, but it's generally suggested to rather assign a locally scoped variable to the superglobal and modify that. You need to know what each of the superglobals stores.

Suberglobal	Stores
$GLOBALS	An array of variables that exist in the global scope.
$_SERVER	An array of information about paths, headers, and other information relevant to the server environment.
$_GET	Variables sent in a GET request.
$_POST	Variables sent in a POST request.
$_FILES	An associative array of files that were uploaded as part of a POST request.
$_COOKIE	An associative array of variables passed to the current script via HTTP cookies.

(continued)

---

[9]https://php.net/manual/en/function.constant.php
[10]https://php.net/manual/en/language.variables.superglobals.php

Superglobal	Stores
$_SESSION	An associative array containing session variables available to the current script.
$_REQUEST	POST, GET, and COOKIE request variables.
$_ENV	An associative array of variables passed to the current script via the environment method.

The $_SERVER superglobal has many keys, and you should be familiar with them. The PHP Manual[11] has a list of them and you should make sure that you've read the manual page and understood all of the keys.

■ **Tip**   Note that the $_SERVER['argv'] contains arguments sent to the script, which is distinct from $_ENV. Knowledge of this level of detail is required for the certification exam.

Magic Constants

Magic constants are those which PHP provides automatically to every running script. There are quite a lot of reserved constants[12] and you will need to know the error constants, as well as the commonly used predefined constants.[13]

Constant	Contains
__LINE__	The current line number of the PHP script being executed
__FILE__	The fully resolved (including symlinks) name and path of the file being executed
__CLASS__	The name of the class being executed
__METHOD__	The name of the class method being executed
__FUNCTION__	The name of the function being executed
__TRAIT__	The namespace and name of the trait that the code is running in
__NAMESPACE__	The current namespace

■ **Note**   The value of these magic constants changes depending on where you use it.

---

[11]https://php.net/manual/en/reserved.variables.server.php
[12]https://secure.php.net/manual/en/reserved.constants.php
[13]https://secure.php.net/manual/en/language.constants.predefined.php

Operators

Arithmetic

You should recognize the arithmetic functions:

Operation	Example	Description
Addition	1 + 2.3	
Subtraction	4 – 5	
Division	6 / 7	
Multiplication	8 * 9	
Modulus	10 % 11	Gives the remainder of dividing 10 by 11
Power	12 ** 13	Raises 12 to the power of 13

These arithmetic operators take two arguments and so are called *binary*.

The unary operators following take only one argument and their placement before or after the variable changes how they work. There are two unary operators in PHP, namely prefix and postfix. They are named for whether the operator appears before or after the variable that it affects.

- If the operator appears before the variable (prefix), then the interpreter will first evaluate it and then return the changed variable.

- If the operator appears after the variable (postfix), then the interpreter will return the variable as it was before the statement executed and then increment the variable.

Let's show their effects on a variable $a that we initialize to 1 and then operate on:

Command	Output	Value of $a Afterwards	Description
$a = 1;		1	
echo $a++;	1	2	Postfix
echo ++$a;	3	3	Prefix
echo $a--;	3	2	Postfix
echo --$a;	1	1	Prefix

Logic Operators

PHP uses both symbol and word form logic operators. The symbol form operators are C-based.

Operator	Example	True When
and	$a and $b	Both $a and $b evaluate true
and	$a && $b	
or	$a or $b	Either $a or $b evaluate true
or	$a || $b	
xor	$a xor $b	One of (but not both) $a or $b is True
xor	$a ^ $b	
not	!$a	$a is not true (false)

It is best practice not to mix the word form (e.g., and) and the symbol (e.g., &&) in the same comparison, as the operators have different precedence. It's safest to stick to using the symbol form exclusively.

In this example, we see that operator precedence[14] results in the variables $truth and $pravda not being the same even though we're performing the "same" logical operator to derive them.

This happens because the logical operators and and or have lower priority than the equality operator =.

```php
<?php
$a = true;
$b = false;
$truth = $a and $b;   // true
$pravda = $a && $b;   // false
assert($truth === $pravda);
/*
    Warning: assert(): assert($truth === $pravda) failed
*/
```

Ternary Operator

PHP implements the ternary operator in the same format as other C-ancestor languages. The general format is as follows:

```
condition ? expression1 : expression2;
```

If condition is true, then expression1 will be evaluated; otherwise expression2 is evaluated.

---

[14]https://php.net/manual/en/language.operators.precedence.php

Here is an example that checks the condition of isset($a) and assigns the string value 'true' or 'false' to $b accordingly.

```php
<?php
$a = 'foo';
$b = (isset($a)) ? 'true' : 'false';
echo $b;    // true
```

The syntax above is identical to the following if statement:

```php
<?php
$a = 'foo';
if (isset($a)) {
   $b = 'true';
} else {
   $b = 'false';
}
echo $b;    // true
```

If the true value is omitted in the ternary operator, then the statement is evaluated as the expression, as follows:

```php
<?php
$a = true;
$b = $a ?: 'foo';
echo $b;    // 1
```

This shortened version of the ternary operator is not suitable for testing if a variable exists, as the interpreter will throw a warning in this case.

Null Coalescing Operator

The null coalescing operator is just a special case of the ternary operator. It allows you to neaten up the syntax used when you're using isset to assign a default value to a variable.

```php
<?php
// Long form ternary syntax
$sortDirection = (isset($_GET['sort_dir'])) ? $_GET['sort_dir'] : 'ASC';

// Equivalent syntax using the null coalescing operator
$sortDirection = $_GET['sort_dir'] ?? 'ASC';

// The null-coalesce operator can be chained
$sortDirection = $_GET['sort_dir'] ?? $defaultSortDir ?? 'ASC';

// The Elvis operator raises E_NOTICE if the GET variable is not set
$sortDirection = $_GET['sort_dir'] ?: 'ASC';
```

It is preferable to use the null-coalescing operator over Elvis because the null-coalescing operator doesn't raise a notice error if the variable is not set.

Spaceship

The spaceship operator is used to compare two different values and is particularly useful for writing callbacks for the sorting functions that we'll be looking at later.

It returns -1, 0, or 1 when the left operand is respectively less than, equal to, or greater than the right.

Operation	Value
1 <=> 0	1
1 <=> 1	0
1 <=> 2	-1
'apples' <=> 'Bananas'	1
'Apples' <=> 'bananas'	-1

The spaceship operator uses the standard PHP comparison rules.

We'll see why there is this surprising difference in the string comparison in the section on "Strings" later.

Bitwise

Bitwise operators work on the bits of integers represented in binary form. Using them on a different variable type will cause PHP to cast the variable to integer before operating on it.

There are three standard logical bitwise operators:

Operator	Operation	Description
&	Bitwise AND	The result will have a bit set if both of the operands bits were set
|	Bitwise OR	If one or both of the operands have a bit set then the result will have that bit set
^	Bitwise XOR	If one and only one of the operands (not both) has the bit set then the result will have the bit set.

The result of a bitwise operator will be the value that has its bits set according to these rules. In other words, the bit in each position of the operands is evaluated against the corresponding bit in the same position of the other operand.

It's easier to consider the binary representations of numbers when using these operators. You can calculate the binary representation of the result by comparing bits (from right to left) and then converting to decimal when you're done.

Let's look at 50 & 25 as an example. I've put the binary representations in comments in the three rows. You can see that I calculated the binary representation of $c by checking whether the bit in that position is set in $a and in $b. In this case, only one such bit is true in both positions.

```php
<?php
$a = 50;          // 0b110010
$b = 25;          // 0b011001
$c = 50 & 25;     // 0b010000
echo $c;          // 16
```

Here is a tabular format that might make it easier to follow. I'm placing the bits from each number in columns. The row marked "operation" shows the comparison that happens—for every position the bits from the two values have the logical "and" operator applied to them.

Value/Operator	Bits in Each Position					
50	1	1	0	0	1	0
25	0	1	1	0	0	1
Operation	1 and 0	1 and 1	0 and 1	0 and 0	1 and 0	0 and 1
Result	0	1	0	0	0	0

When we echo out the result. PHP gives us the integer value and you can quickly confirm that the binary representation you evaluated matches it, because 2 raised to the power of 4 is 16.

Bit Shifting

PHP also has operators to shift bits left and right. The effect of these operators is to shift the bit pattern of the value either left or right while inserting bits set to 0 in the newly created empty spaces.

To understand how these operators work, picture your number represented in binary form and then all the 1s and 0s being stepped to the left or right.

The following table shows shifting bits, one to the right and one to the left.

Operation	Operation	Result in Binary	Result in Decimal
50		00110010	
50 >> 1	Shift Right	00011001	25
50 << 1	Shift Left	01100100	100

I've included enough leading zeroes in the binary forms to make it easier to see the pattern of what's happening.

You can see that when we shifted to the right, the right-hand bit was "lost". When we shift left, we insert new bits that are set to 0 on the right.

It's important to be cautious when using bitwise operations to perform calculations, as the integer overflow size may vary between the different environments that PHP is deployed on.

For example, although a 64-bit system will have the same result for both operations, on a 32-bit integer system they will not:

```php
<?php
$x = 1;
echo $x << 32;
echo $x * pow(2, 32);
```

The first line will echo 0 as shifting left 32 bits will fill the 32-bit integer with 0 bits. The second line will use the maths library and output the correct value of 2 raised to the power of 32.

■ **Tip**   If you want to experiment with binary operators, you'll find the base_convert() function extremely useful. For example, to output the binary representation of the decimal number 50, you could echo base_convert(50, 10, 2) . PHP_EOL;.

Bitwise NOT

You won't need to know the details of the mathematics behind this operator, so don't spend too much time worrying about the details. If you understand the effect it has on the bits, you should be ready to answer questions about it.

PHP uses the ~ (tilde) symbol for bitwise NOT. The effect of this operator is to flip the bits in a value—if a bit is set it becomes unset, and if it were not set it becomes set.

This is best understood by example:

	Bits					
50	1	1	0	0	1	0
~ (NOT)	0	0	1	1	0	1

The value (in decimal) of the result is -51.

Just for enrichment purposes, you could read up on Wikipedia about two's complement.[15] It is chiefly used to get to a binary representation of a negative number.

---

[15]https://en.wikipedia.org/wiki/Two%27s_complement

Assignment Operators

PHP uses the = symbol as an assignment operator. The following line sets the value of $a to 123.

```php
<?php
$a = 123;
```

The assignment operator can be combined with just about all the binary and arithmetic operators. This syntax serves as a shortcut that is best shown by providing an example of equivalent statements:

```php
<?php
$a += 345;    // equivalent to $a = $a + 345;
$a .= 'foo';  // equivalent to $a = $a . 'foo';
```

The result of any assignment expression is the value of the variable following the assignment.

A fairly common typing error is to mistakenly forget the second = symbol in an equality check. Consider the following example where we're using the assignment operator in the if statement where we intended to use the equality operator.

```php
<?php
$foo = "hello";
if ($foo = "world") {
  echo "matches";
} else {
  echo "does not match";
}
```

Had this been an equality operator, the if statement would be false and the script would output "does not match". However, because we're assigning the string "world" to the variable $foo, the result is the value "world", which when cast to Boolean is true (see "Casting Variables").

Some coding conventions use what is called the "Yoda Condition" to assist with this error. It uses the fact that PHP will not let you change the value of a constant. If you always place the constant on the left of an equality comparison, you'll be warned if you mistype the operator. Whether the cost of code readability is worth it is a matter of personal style.

Reference Operator

By default, PHP assigns all scalar variables by value.

PHP has optimizations to make assignment by value faster than assigning by reference (see the section on "Memory Management"), but if you want to assign by reference, you can use the & operator as follows:

```php
<?php
$a = 1;
$b = &$a;   // assign by reference
$b += 5;
echo $a;   // 6
```

PHP always assigns objects by reference; if you try to explicitly create it by reference, PHP will generate a parse error.

```php
<?php
class MyClass {}
// Parse error: syntax error, unexpected 'new'
$a = &new MyClass;
```

Comparison Operators

PHP uses the following comparison operators:

Operator	Description
>	Greater than
>=	Greater than or equal to
<	Less than
<=	Less than or equal to
<>	Not equal
==	Equivalence; values are equivalent if cast to the same variable type
===	Identity; values must be of the same data type and have the same value
!=	Not equivalent
!==	Not identical

It is important to understand the difference between an equivalent comparison and an identity comparison:

- Operands are equivalent if they can be cast to a common data type and have the same value.

- Operands are identical if they share the same data type and have the same value.

Arrays are equivalent if they have the same key and value pairs. They are identical if they have the same key and value pairs, in the same order, and the key-value are of the same type.

When using comparison operators on arrays, the count of their keys is used to determine which is greater or lesser.

When compared to a scalar variable, both an object and an array will be considered greater than the scalar.

```php
<?php
$a = [1];
$b = 100;
echo $a <=> $b; // 1
```

Be careful when using comparison operators on strings, or when using them on mismatching variable types. See the section on "Casting Variables" for more information.

Two More Operators

PHP provides an operator to suppress error messages. This will work only if the library that the function is based on uses PHP standard error reporting.

```php
<?php
// Error messages will be suppressed
$dbConnection = @mysqli_connect(...);
```

It's bad practice to suppress PHP errors with the @ operator. It is better to use PHP settings to suppress errors in your production environment and to allow your development environment to display errors. Having code that fails silently without producing an error makes debugging much more difficult than it needs to be.

The last operator we will discuss is the backtick operator. It is not commonly used and is equivalent to calling the shell_exec() command. In the following example, the variable $a will contain the name of the user running the PHP interpreter.

```php
<?php
// This is the equivalent of echo shell_exec('whoami');
echo `whoami`;
```

In a web environment this will probably be www-data. This is the default for Nginx and Apache, but from the command line will be the name of the user who is logged in.

Control Structures

Control structures allow you to analyze variables and then choose a direction for your program to flow in. In this section, we're going to be looking at several different sorts of control structures and how they're implemented in PHP.

Conditional Structures

PHP supports if, else, elseif, switch, and ternary conditional structures.

If structures look like this:

```php
<?php
if (condition) {
  // statements to execute
} elseif (second condition) {
  // statements to execute
} else {
  // statements to execute
}
```

Note that the space between else and if in the elseif is optional.

If statements may be nested.

The switch statement looks like this:

```php
<?php
switch ($value) {
  case '10' :
    // statements to execute
    break;
  case '20'  :
    // statements to execute
    break;
  case '30' :
    // statements to execute
    break;
  default:
    // statements to execute
    break;
}
```

Once a case matches the value, the statements in the code block will be executed until it reaches a break command.

If you omit the break command, then all the following statements in the switch will be executed until a break is hit even if the case does not match the value. This can be useful in some circumstances, but can also produce unintended outcomes if you forget to use the break statement.

To illustrate, consider this example:

```php
<?php
$value = 10;
switch ($value) {
    case '10' :
        echo "Value is 10";
        // no break statement
```

```
case '20'  :
    echo "Value is 20";
    break;
case '30'  :
    echo "Value is 30";
    break;
default:
    echo "Value is not 10,20, or 30";
    break;
}
// Value is 10Value is 20
```

■ **Note**   If you include case statements after the default case, they will not be checked.

Loops

PHP's most basic loop is the while loop. It has two forms, as shown:

```
<?php
while (expression) {
    // statements to execute
}

do {
    // statements to execute
} while (expression)
```

The difference between them is that in the first form, the expression is evaluated at the beginning of the loop and in the second form, it's evaluated at the end.

This means that if the expression is false, the while loop will not run at all in the first case but it will run at least once in the second case.

The for loop syntax shows the C roots of PHP and looks like this:

```
<?php
for ($i = 0; $i < 10; $i++) {
    // do something
}
```

As with C, the first statement is executed to initialize the loop. The second condition is evaluated at the beginning of each loop, and the last statement is executed at the end of each loop. The loop will continue to run until the condition evaluates as false.

To iterate over an array, you can use foreach, as follows:

```php
<?php
$arr = [
  'a' => 'one',
  'b' => 'two',
  'c' => 'three'
];

foreach ($arr as $value) {
    echo $value;   // one, two, three
}

foreach ($arr as $key => $value) {
    echo $key;     // a, b, c
    echo $value;   // one, two, three
}
```

Breaking Out of Loops

There are two ways to stop an iteration of a loop in PHP—break and continue.

Using continue has the effect of stopping the current iteration and allowing the loop to process the next evaluation condition. This allows you to let any further iterations to occur.

Using break has the effect of stopping the entire loop and no further iterations will occur.

The break statement takes an optional integer value that can be used to break out of multiple levels of a nested loop. If no value is specified, it defaults to 1.

Namespaces

Namespaces help you avoid naming collisions between libraries or other shared code. A namespace will encapsulate the items inside it so that they don't conflict with items declared elsewhere.

They can be used to avoid overly descriptive names for classes, to sub-divide a library into sections, or to limit the applicability of constants to one section of code.

Classes encapsulate code into instantiable units. Namespaces group functions, classes, and constants into spaces where their name is unique.

The namespace declaration must occur straight after the opening <?php tag and no other statements may precede it.

Namespaces affect constants, but you must declare them with the const keyword and not with define().

It is possible to have two namespaces in a file, but most coding standards will strongly discourage this. To accomplish this, you wrap the code for the namespace in braces, as in this example:

```php
<?php
namespace A {
  // this is in namespace A
}
namespace B {
  // this is in namespace B
}
namespace {
  // this is in the global namespace
}
```

■ **Note** This usage is not standard practice; in most cases a namespace declaration does not include the braces and all the statements in a file exist in only one namespace.

Fully Qualified Namespace Names

If you are working in a namespace, then the interpreter will assume that names are relative to the current namespace. Consider this class as a basis for the following examples:

```php
<?php
namespace MyApp\Helpers;

class Formatters
{
    public static function asCurrency($val) {
        // statement
    }
}
```

If we want to use this class from another namespace, we need to provide a fully qualified namespace, as in this example:

```php
<?php
// this file is in a different namespace
namespace MyApp\Lib;

// we must specify the full path to the namespace that the class is in
echo MyApp\Helpers\Formatters::asCurrency(10);
```

Alternatively, you may use the use statement to import a namespace so that you don't have to use the long format all the time:

```php
<?php
// this file is in a different namespace
namespace MyApp\Lib;

// the "use" keyword imports the namespace
use MyApp\Helpers\Formatters;
// we no longer have to provide a full reference
echo Formatters::asCurrency(10);
```

You may precede a name with a backslash to indicate that you intend to use the global namespace, as in this example:

```php
<?php
namespace MyApp;

throw new \Exception('Global namespace');
```

In this example, if we had not indicated the global scope with the backslash, the interpreter would look for a class called Exception within the MyApp namespace.

Configuration

I can highly recommend that you do some practical work to configure PHP. You can set up a virtual machine on your computer[16] and install Linux[17] on it, which will give you hands-on experience.

There are several Windows and Mac packages that offer an all-in-one configuration for PHP, but you should make sure that you find the config files and go through them.

Where Settings May Be Set or Changed

PHP offers a flexible configuration strategy whereby base configuration settings may be overridden by user configuration files and even at runtime by PHP itself.

It's best to refer to the manual for this. Duplicating it here will only result in stale information. Refer to the following links:

> https://secure.php.net/manual/en/configuration.
> changes.modes.php

> https://secure.php.net/manual/en/ini.list.php

---

[16]http://www.oracle.com/technetwork/server-storage/virtualbox/downloads/index.html
[17]https://www.ubuntu.com/download/server

Php.ini

The PHP.ini file defines the configuration for each PHP environment. An environment here refers to how PHP is run—for example by command shell, as an FPM process, or within Apache2 as a module.

Each environment will have a directory off the main configuration directory, which is /etc/php/7.0/ by default on Ubuntu.

Windows machines use the registry to store the location of the php.ini. The actual key name varies between versions of PHP, but will follow a pattern similar to this: HKEY_LOCAL_MACHINE\SOFTWARE\PHP. If a Windows machine is unable to find it in the location specified by the Registry, it will fall back to looking for the file in a number of default locations, including the Windows system directory.

In addition to the php.ini file, it is possible to specify a directory that PHP will scan for additional configuration files. You can use the php_ini_scanned_files() function to obtain a list of the files that were included, as well as the order of inclusion.

The config file is read whenever the server (apache) or process (fpm/cli) starts. This means that if you make a change to the PHP configuration, you will need to reload your Apache2 server or restart the fpm service. In contrast, changes to the CLI configuration will take effect the next time you run PHP from the shell.

It is possible to use OS environment variables in your PHP.ini file, using syntax like this:

```
; PHP_MEMORY_LIMIT is taken from environment
memory_limit = ${PHP_MEMORY_LIMIT}
```

User INI Files

PHP checks these files when it is operating in FastCGI mode (PHP 5.3+). This is the case when you're using the fpm module, but not in CLI or Apache2.

PHP will first check for these files in the directory that the script is running in and work backward up to the document root. The document root is configured in your host file and is reflected in the $_SERVER['DOCUMENT_ROOT'] variable.

These INI files will override the settings in php.ini, but will only affect settings that are flagged as PHP_INI_PERDIR or PHP_INI_USER. Refer to the previous link for a list of settings and where they may be changed.

The main configuration file has two directives that pertain to user INI files. The first, user_ini_filename, governs the name of the file that PHP looks for.

The second, user_cache_ttl, governs how often the user file is read from disk.

Apache Version of INI Files

If you are using Apache, then you can use .htaccess to manage user INI settings. They are searched for in the same method as the fastcgi files are.

You must set the AllowOverride setting in your vhost config to true in any directories that you want the .htaccess file to be read.

Performance

A great deal of PHP performance issues relate to the deployment environment, which is beyond the scope of this reference.

One potential deployment issue with performance worth mentioning in the context of the Zend examination is using the xdebug extension in production. As the name suggests, this extension is for debugging and should not be installed in production.

Another deployment concern is in keeping your PHP version up to date. PHP is constantly improving its performance and it's a good idea to migrate your code to keep up with new PHP versions.

■ **Tip** Using the latest version of PHP is a good way to improve performance. PHP 7 is about 30% (in my tests) faster than PHP 5 and some people claim it is even faster. PHP 7.2 is faster than PHP 7.1.

When considering performance for the Zend examination, we focus on memory management and the opcode cache.

Memory Management

Optimizing memory performance in PHP requires some understanding of how the language's internal data type representation works.

PHP uses a container called a zval to store variables. The zval container contains four pieces of information:

Piece	Description
Value	The value the variable is set to.
Type	The data type of the variable.
Is_ref	A Boolean value indicating whether this variable is part of a reference set. Remember that variables can be assigned by reference. This Boolean value helps PHP decide if a particular variable is a normal variable or if it is a reference to another variable.
Refcount	This is a counter that tracks how many variable names point to this particular zval container. This refcount is incremented when we declare a new variable to reference this one.

Variable names are referred to as symbols and are stored in a symbol table that is unique to the scope in which the variables occur.

Symbols Are Pointed to zval Containers

In the section on the reference operator, I mentioned that PHP has optimizations for assigning by value. PHP accomplishes this by only copying the value to a new zval when it changes, and initially pointing the new symbol to the same zval container. This mechanism is called "copy on write".[18]

Here is an example to illustrate:

```php
<?php
$a = "new string";
$b =& $a;
// the variable b points to the variable a
xdebug_debug_zval( 'a' );
xdebug_debug_zval( 'b' );
// change the string and see that the refcount is reset
$b = 'changed string';
xdebug_debug_zval( 'a' );
xdebug_debug_zval( 'b' );
```

The output of this script is as follows:

```
a: (refcount=2, is_ref=0)='new string'
b: (refcount=2, is_ref=0)='new string'
a: (refcount=1, is_ref=0)='new string'
b: (refcount=1, is_ref=0)='changed string'
```

We can see that until we change the value of $b it is referring to the same zval container as $a.

Arrays and Objects

Arrays and objects use their own symbol table, separate from the scalar variables. They also use zval containers, but creating an array or object will result in several containers being created.

Consider this example:

```php
<?php
$arr = ['name' => 'Bob', 'age' => 23 ];
xdebug_debug_zval( 'arr' );
```

The output from this script looks like this:

```
arr: (refcount=1, is_ref=0)=array (
      'name' => (refcount=1, is_ref=0)='Bob',
      'age' => (refcount=1, is_ref=0)=23)
```

---

[18]https://en.wikipedia.org/wiki/Copy-on-write

We can see that three zval containers are created, one for the array variable itself and one for each of its two values.

Just as for scalar variables, if we had a third member of the array with the same value as another member then instead of creating a new zval container PHP will increase the refcount and point the duplicate symbol to the same zval.

Memory Leaks in Arrays and Objects

Memory leaks can occur when a composite object includes a reference to itself as a member. This is more likely to occur in use-cases with objects because PHP always assigns objects by reference. Possibly, for example, in parent-child relationships such as might be found in an ORM model.

The PHP Manual has a series of diagrams explaining this on the refcounting basics page.[19] The problem occurs when you unset a composite object that has a reference to itself.

In this event, the symbol table is cleared of a reference to the zval structure that was used to contain the variable. PHP does not iterate through the composite object because this would result in recursion as it follows links to itself. This means that the member in the variable that is a reference to itself is not unset, and the zval container is not marked as free. There is no symbol pointing to this zval container and so the user cannot free the memory herself.

PHP will clear up these references at the end of the request. Remember that PHP is not intended to be a long-running language and is designed to be a text processor built for serving specific requests within the context of a web application.

Garbage Collection

The garbage collector clears circular references, which are those where a complex object contains a member that refers to itself.

PHP will initiate garbage collection when the root buffer is full or when the function gc_collect_cycles() is called.

The garbage collector will only cause a slowdown when it actually needs to do something. In smaller scripts where there is no leakage it won't cause a performance drop.

Garbage collection is likely to be of benefit in long-running scripts or those where a memory leak is repeatedly created, such as processing a very large amount of database records using ORM models that leak.

The Opcode Cache

PHP is compiled into a sequence of intermediate instructions that are executed in order by the runtime engine. These instructions are called opcodes or bytecodes and this process occurs every time the script is run.

---

[19]https://php.net/manual/en/features.gc.refcounting-basics.php

The bytecode is interpreted by the runtime engine; therefore, PHP is both precompiled and interpreted.

An opcode cache stores the converted instructions for a script. Subsequent calls to the script do not require the script to be interpreted prior to being run.

In 2013, Zend contributed their optimization engine to PHP. Known as *opcache*, it is baked into distributions of PHP as of version 5.5 and is probably the most commonly used PHP opcode cache.

■ **Note**   Opcache is built into PHP 7.1 and is enabled by default in your `php.ini`[20] settings.

Take note of the setting `opcache.revalidate_freq`. This determines the interval in seconds that PHP will scan for changes in the source file before recompiling it. You can set it to 0 to tell PHP to always scan for changes. PHP will not scan the file more than once per request.

In addition to the cache built into PHP, there are a number of third-party opcode caches available (see Wikipedia[21] if you're interested).

■ **Tip**   Using the opcode cache results in significant performance increases.

Extensions

PHP extensions extend on the functionality offered by the core language. A number of them are enabled by default into standard repository distributions of PHP. Other extensions need to be downloaded and installed manually.

PECL is a repository for PHP extensions. It provides an easy way to download and install extensions on Linux. Windows machines need to compile and install extensions manually, but usually they're distributed in a compiled form and you just need to edit your INI file to enable them.

PHP includes several extensions that cannot be removed from PHP with compilation flags. These extensions include core functionality such as reflection, arrays, date and time, SPL, and math. You should be able to rely on them being installed.

Installing an Extension

Extensions are enabled through the `php.ini` file using the "extension" setting to specify the filename of the extension, like this for `mcrypt`:

```
extension=mcrypt.so;
```

---

[20]https://github.com/php/php-src/blob/master/php.ini-production#L1763
[21]https://en.wikipedia.org/wiki/List_of_PHP_accelerators

You can set the extension directory with a setting in your php.ini file like so:

```
extension_dir = "/usr/lib/php5/20121212/mcrypt.so"
```

Different systems may provide convenient ways of installing and enabling extensions. PECL extensions can be installed using the pecl command-line utility.

Checking for Installed Extensions

The extensions installed will display if you call phpinfo() or if you use the more specific command get_loaded_extensions().

Running php -m from the shell will show a list of extensions installed.

You can check if an extension is loaded by calling extension_loaded(). This is recommended if you're using a function in an extension that is not loaded by default. Here is an example from the PHP Manual:

```php
<?php
if (!extension_loaded('gd')) {
    if (!dl('gd.so')) {
        exit;
    }
}
```

CHAPTER 1 QUIZ

Q1: Which of the following tags should you avoid using to include PHP in HTML?

```
<?php
```

```
<?
```

```
<?=
```

None of the above; these are all fine

Q2: Which of the following are NOT case sensitive in PHP? Choose all that apply.

Variable names

Class names

Namespaces

Function names

Q3: What will this script output?

```php
<?php
$a = "Hello";
$B = " world";
ECHO $a . $b;
```

Nothing; it won't run

Hello world

Hello

An error message because the variable b is not defined

An error message and the word "Hello"

Q4: What will this script output?

```php
<?php

function A() {
    try {
        b();
    } catch (Exception $e) {
        echo "Exception caught in " . __CLASS__;
    }
}

function B() {
    C();
}

try {
    A();
} catch (Error $e) {
    echo "Error caught in global scope: " . $e->getMessage();
}
```

Exception caught in A

Error caught in global scope: Call to undefined function C()

Error caught in global scope: Call to undefined function b()

None of the above

35

Q5: What will this script output?

```php
<?php

function A() {
    try {
        b();
    } catch (Exception $e) {
        echo "Exception caught in " . __CLASS__;
    }
}

function B() {
    echo 5 / "five";
}

try {
    A();
} catch (Error $e) {
    echo "Error caught in global scope: " . $e->getMessage();
}
```

Exception caught in A

Error caught in global scope: Call to undefined function C()

1

Error caught in global scope: Call to undefined function b()

None of the above

Q6: What will this script output?

```php
<?php

class MyException extends Exception {}
class ChildException extends MyException {}

try {
    throw new ChildException;
} catch (Exception $e) {
    echo "Caught Exception: " . get_class($e);
} catch (MyException $e) {
    echo "Caught MyException" . get_class($e);
}
```

Caught Exception: ChildException

Caught MyException: ChildException

Caught MyException: MyException

Nothing

An error message related to an uncaught exception

Q7: Which of the following settings can be configured at runtime using the ini_set() function?

output_buffering

memory_limit

max_execution_time

extension

Q8: What is the output of this script?

```php
<?php

$a = "apples" <=> "bananas";
$b = $a ?? $c ?? 10;
echo $b;
```

-1

0

1

10

apples

Q9: What is the output of this script?

```php
<?php
echo 10 <=> 10 << 1;
```

-1

0

1

10

Q10: What is the output of this script?

```php
<?php
define('A', 1);
const B = 2;
define('C', [A * A, B * B]);
echo(C[1]);
```

This will generate an error because constants can only hold scalar values.

This will generate an error because you cannot use define() to declare an array constant.

This will generate an error because you cannot use expressions or functions when declaring a constant.

1

2

4

CHAPTER 2

Functions

Functions are packages of code that can be used to execute a sequence of instructions. Any valid code can be used inside a function, including calls to other functions and classes.

In PHP, function names are case insensitive and can be referenced before they are defined, unless they are defined in a conditional code block. Functions can be built-in, provided by an extension, or user-defined. Functions are distinct from language constructs.

Arguments

Arguments to a function, also known as *parameters*, allow you to pass values into the function scope. Arguments are passed as a comma-separated list and are evaluated left to right.

Argument Type Declarations

You can specify what type of variable may be passed as an argument.

This is useful because PHP is a loosely typed language and if you specify exactly what sort of variable you expect, then your function is going to be more reliable and your code easier to read. Another advantage is that giving type hints helps your IDE to give you more meaningful hints.

If your function is called and the variable passed is the incorrect type, then PHP 7 will raise a TypeError exception.

To specify the type of argument that you are expecting, you add the type name in front of the argument definition, like this:

```php
<?php

// $itemName must be a string and $details must be an array
function addToShoppingCart(string $itemName, array $details) {}

/*
$paymentObject must be an object that either:
implements the PaymentProviderInterface interface,
```

© Andrew Beak 2017
A. Beak, *PHP 7 Zend Certification Study Guide*,
https://doi.org/10.1007/978-1-4842-3246-0_2

```
or is any child of a class that does
*/
function requestPayment(PaymentProviderInterface $paymentObject) {}

/*
$employee must be an object that is either:
an instance of the Employee class,
or is any child of a class that does
*/
function calculateWage(Employee $employee) {}

// $callback must be a callable
function performCalculation(callable $method) {}
```

In the previous example, I've shown that we can tell PHP to expect scalar variables, composite variables (arrays and objects), and callables. We discuss exactly what callables are a little later in this chapter.

The following table summarizes what types can be declared.

Type	Description
Class name or Interface	The parameter must be an instance of, or a child of, the specified class or interface.
`self`	The parameter must be an instance of the current class.
`array`	
`bool`	
`float`	
`int`	
`string`	
`iterable`	The parameter must be either an array or an `instanceof` traversable.
`callable`	The parameter must be a valid callable.

■ **Note** When I say "ancestor" class, I'm referring to any superclass of your class: the parent, the parent's parent, and so on. Likewise, I'm using the word "child" to denote a child, grandchild, great-grandchild, and so on.

You cannot use type aliases. For example, you cannot use boolean in place of bool as a type declaration; if you do so, PHP will expect an instance of a class called boolean, like this:

```php
<?php
function A(boolean $a) {var_dump($a);}
A(true);
// Fatal error: Uncaught TypeError: Argument 1 passed to A() must be an
instance of boolean, boolean given,
```

There are two ways that you can enforce scalar type hinting: coercive (default) and strict.

You configure the mode per file by placing a declare directive at the top of the file. This will affect the way that PHP enforces the function arguments as well as the function return type.

■ **Note** Setting strict mode is done per file.

In coercive mode, PHP will automatically try to cast variables of the wrong type to the expected type.

In the following example, the script outputs "string" because PHP silently casts the integer we pass to a string.

```php
<?php
function sayHello(string $name) {
    echo gettype($name);
}

sayHello(100); // string
```

If, however, we were to specify strict mode, then PHP will generate a TypeError, as in this example:

```php
<?php
declare(strict_types=1);
function sayHello(string $name) {
    echo gettype($name);
}

sayHello(100);
/*
Fatal error: Uncaught TypeError: Argument 1 passed to sayHello() must be of
the type string, integer given,
*/
```

Alternate Null Type Syntax

PHP 7.1 introduced a new way to type hint variables that may be null. You can prefix the type hint with a question mark to indicate that the variable may either be null or of the specified type. Here's an example:

```php
<?php

function myFunc(?MyObject $myObj)
{
    echo "hello world";
}
// this is allowed
myFunc(null);
// this produces a fatal error: Too few arguments
myFunc();
```

■ **Note**   The argument is not optional; you have to explicitly pass `null` or an object of the specified type.

Optional Arguments

You can specify a default value for a parameter that has the effect of making it optional.

■ **Note**   PHP 7 will throw an `ArgumentCountError`[1] if you do not supply all the mandatory parameters to a function. You can only omit passing parameters that are optional.

In the following example, if the user does not supply a message, the function assumes it will be world.

```php
<?php
function sayHi($message = 'world') {
    echo "Hello $message";
}
sayHi();
```

---

[1]We deal with this sort of error in Chapter 11 on error handling.

Overloading Functions

In other programming languages, overloading usually refers to declaring multiple functions with the same name but with differing quantities and types of arguments. PHP views overloading as providing the means to dynamically "create" properties and methods.

PHP will not let you redeclare the same function name. However, PHP does let you call a function with different arguments and offers you some functions to be able to access the arguments that a function was called with.

Here are three of these functions:

Function	Returns
func_num_args()	How many arguments were passed to the function
func_get_arg($num)	Parameter number $num (zero based)
func_get_args()	All parameters passed to the function as an array

Here is an example showing how a function can accept any number of parameters of any sort, and how you can access them:

```php
<?php
function myFunc() {
    foreach(func_get_args() as $arg => $value) {
        echo "$arg is $value" . PHP_EOL;
    }
}
myFunc('variable', 3, 'parameters');
/*
0 is variable
1 is 3
2 is parameters
*/
```

The following code illustrates an obscure difference between PHP 7 and PHP 5:

```php
<?php
function myFunc($data) {
    $data = 'Changed';
    echo func_get_arg(0);
}
```

In PHP 5, this outputs Variable, but in PHP 7, it outputs Changed. This shows that in PHP 7 if you change the value of an argument in a function, then the value returned by func_get_arg() will be the new value and not the original value.

Variadics

PHP 5.6 introduced variadics that explicitly accept a variable number of parameters. By using the ... token in your argument list, you specify that the function will accept a variable number of parameters.

The variadic parameters are made available in your function as an array.

If you are mixing normal fixed parameters with a variadic syntax, then the variadic parameter must be the last parameter in the list of parameters.

The PHP manual[2] has a very clear example that shows the interaction between compulsory, optional, and variadic parameters:

```php
<?php
function parameterTypeExample($required, $optional = null,
...$variadicParams) {
    printf('Required: %d; Optional: %d; number of variadic parameters:
%d'."\n",
        $required, $optional, count($variadicParams));
}

f(1);
f(1, 2);
f(1, 2, 3);
f(1, 2, 3, 4);
f(1, 2, 3, 4, 5);
```

This outputs:

```
$req: 1; $opt: 0; number of params: 0
$req: 1; $opt: 2; number of params: 0
$req: 1; $opt: 2; number of params: 1
$req: 1; $opt: 2; number of params: 2
$req: 1; $opt: 2; number of params: 3
```

Note that the variadic parameter is made available as an ordinary array $params.

References

By default, PHP passes arguments to functions by value, but it is possible to pass them by reference. You can do this by declaring the argument as a pass by reference, as in this example:

```php
<?php
function addOne(&$arg) {
    $arg++;
}
```

---

[2]https://secure.php.net/manual/en/migration56.new-features.php

```
$a = 0;
addOne($a);
echo $a; // 1
```

The & operator marks the parameter as being passed by reference. Changes to this parameter in the function will change the variable passed to it.

If a function argument is not defined as being a reference, then you cannot pass a reference in that argument.

This code will generate a fatal error:

```php
<?php
function addOne($arg) {
    $arg++;
}
$a = 0;
addOne(&$a); // fatal error as of PHP 5.4.0
echo $a;
```

Variable Functions

Variable functions are similar in concept to variable variable names. They're easiest to explain with a syntax example:

```php
<?php
function foo() {
    echo 'Foo';
}
$var = 'foo';
$var(); // calls foo()
```

We can see that if PHP encounters a variable name that has parentheses appended to it then it evaluates the variable. It then looks for a function that has a name matching this evaluation. If it finds a matching function, it is executed; otherwise, the normal error generation will occur.

■ **Note** Language constructs such as we saw earlier are not functions. You cannot use them as variable functions.

You can call any callable as a variable function. We'll discuss callables a little later in the "Callables, Lambdas, and Closures" section.

Returns

Using the `return` statement will prevent further code from executing in your function. If you `return` from the root scope, then your program will terminate.

```php
<?php
return "hello";
echo "This is never run";
```

PHP will return `NULL` if you do not specify a return value for your function using the `return` keyword.

In the "Generators" section, we deal with the `yield` keyword. These are similar enough to `returns` to mention in passing here, but important enough to have their own section later.

Generators let you write a function that will generate successive members of an array that you can iterate over without needing to hold the entire data set in memory. At the end of the yielded list of values, the generator can optionally return a final value.

In PHP 7, we can specify what type of variable we expect to return. We discuss this in the next section.

Return Type Declarations

We previously looked at how you can declare what variable type your function arguments will be. You can also specify what variable type the function will return.

To do so, you place a colon and the type name after the parameters braces. The same types are available for return types as can be specified for the arguments.

Let's look at an example:

```php
<?php
function getFullName(string $firstName, string $lastName): string {
    return 123;
}
$name = getFullName('Mary', 'Moon');
echo gettype($name);  // string
```

Because PHP is in coercive mode by default, it converts the integer 123 to a string when it returns from the function. If we declared `strict` mode, then PHP would generate a `TypeError`, just as it did when we were looking at argument type declarations.

■ **Note**   You can't specify `strict` mode for just one of the return or argument type declarations. If you specify `strict` mode, it will affect both.

Return Void

If the function is going to return null, you can specify that it will return "void" (PHP 7.1+), as in this example:

```php
<?php
function sayHello(): void {
    echo "Hello World";
}
// Hello World
sayWorld();
```

■ **Caution**   Trying to specify that it will return `null` will result in a fatal error.

Return by Reference

It is possible to declare a function so that it returns a reference to a variable, rather than a copy of the variable. The PHP Manual notes that you should not do this as a performance optimization, but rather only when you have a valid technical reason to do so.

To declare a function as return by reference, you place an & operator in front of its name:

```php
<?php
function &getValue() {...}
```

Then, when calling the function, you also place the & operator in front of the call:

```php
<?php
$myValue = &getValue();
```

After this call, the $myValue variable will contain a reference to the variable that the getValue() function returns.

■ **Note**   Notice the difference between returning by reference (which is allowed) and passing an argument by reference at runtime (which is not).

The function itself must return a variable. If you try to return, for example, a numeric literal like 1, a runtime error will be generated.

Two use cases for this are the Factory pattern and for obtaining a resource like a file handle or database connection.

Variable Scope in Functions

As in other languages, the scope of a PHP variable is the context in which it was defined. PHP has three levels of scope—global, function, and class. Every time a function is called, a new function scope is created.

You can include global scope variables into your function in one of two ways:

```php
<?php
$glob = "Global variable";
function myFunction() {
    global $glob; // first method
    $glob = $GLOBALS['glob']; // second method
    $glob = "Changed";
}
myFunction();
echo $glob;  // Changed
```

Note that the two methods have an identical effect of allowing you to use the $glob variable in myFunction() and have it refer to the $glob variable declared in the global scope.

■ **Caution**   Most coding standards strongly discourage global variables because they introduce problems when writing tests, can introduce weird context problems, and make debugging more difficult.

Lambda and Closure

A lambda in PHP is an anonymous function that can be stored as a variable.

```php
<?php
$lambda = function($a, $b) {
    echo $a + $b;
};
echo gettype($lambda); // true
echo (int)is_callable($lambda); // 1
echo get_class($lambda); // Closure
```

We can see that in PHP lambdas and closures are implemented as objects instantiated from the Closure[3] class.

Lambda variables and closures can both be used in functions that accept a callable.

---

[3]https://php.net/manual/en/class.closure.php

■ **Note** You can use the is_callable() function to check if a variable is a callable.

A closure in PHP is an anonymous function that encapsulates variables so they can be used once their original references are out of scope. Another way of putting this is to say that the anonymous function "closes over" variables that are in the scope it was defined in.

In practical syntax in PHP, we define a closure like this:

```php
<?php
$string = "Hello World!";
$closure = function() use ($string) {
  echo $string;
};
$closure();
```

That looks nearly identical to a lambda, but notice the use ($string) syntax that occurs just before the code block begins.

The effect of this is to take the $string variable that exists in the same scope of the closure and make it available within the closure.

■ **Note** You can call lambdas and closures using the syntax you use for variable functions.

In this lambda example, the function only had access to the parameters it was passed, and nothing from the containing scope would be passed in. Calling echo $string would result in a warning because the variable doesn't exist.

Early and Late Binding

There are two ways in which a variable can be bound: early and late.

In early binding, we know the value and type of the variable before we use it at runtime. This is usually done in some static declarative manner. The value of the variable that is used inside the parameter will be the value that it was when the closure was defined.

By contrast, when we use late binding we do not know what the variable type or value is until we call the closure. PHP will coerce the variable to a specific type and value when it needs to operate on it.

When it binds a variable to a closure, PHP will use early binding by default. If you want to use late binding, you should use a reference when importing.

This will all be a lot clearer when you walk through a simple example:

```php
<?php
$a = "some string";
// early binding (default)
$b = function() use ($a) {
    echo $a;
};
$a = "Hello World";
// some string
$b();
```

Here we are using the default (early) binding method to bind the value of $a to the lambda $b.

The value of $a is "some string" when we define the lambda. Therefore, when we call the lambda, the value "some string" is output, even though we have changed the value of $a after declaring the lambda.

If we were to specify that $a is to be used as a reference, then the output would be "Hello World", like this:

```php
<?php
$a = "some string";
// late binding (reference)
$b = function() use (&$a) {
    echo $a;
};
$a = "Hello World";
// Hello World
$b();
```

Binding Closures to Scopes

When you create a closure, it "closes over" the current scope and so can be thought of as being bound to a particular scope. The Closure class has two methods—bind and bindTo—and they allow you to change the scope to which the variable is bound:

```php
<?php
class Animal {
    public function getClosure() {
        $boundVariable = 'Animal';
        return function() use ($boundVariable) {
            return $this->nature . ' ' . $boundVariable;
        };
    }
}
class Cat extends Animal {
    protected $nature = 'Awesome';
}
```

```php
class Dog extends Animal {
    protected $nature = 'Friendly';
}
$cat = new Cat;
$closure = $cat->getClosure();
echo $closure(); // Awesome Animal
$closure = $closure->bindTo(new Dog);
echo $closure(); // Friendly Animal
```

There are two important things to notice in this code.

First, binding the closure to a different object returns a duplicate of the original, so you have to assign the result of calling bindTo() to a variable.

Second, the new closure will have the same bound variables and body, but a different bound object and scope. In the previous example, the $boundVariable is duplicated into the new closure when we bind to the new object.

Self-Executing Closures

You can create self-executing anonymous functions in PHP 7 using syntax very similar to JavaScript:

```php
<?php
(function() {
    echo 'Self-executing anonymous function';
    echo $definedInClosure = 'Variable set';
})();
var_dump(isset($definedInClosure));  // bool(false)
```

Note in this example that the variable we define inside the closure is not defined outside the scope of the closure. You can use this sort of structure to avoid polluting your global scope.

Callables

Callables were introduced as a type hint for functions in PHP 5.4

They are callbacks that some functions, for example usort(), accept.

A callable for a function such as usort() can be one of the following:

- An inline anonymous function

- A lambda or closure variable

- A string denoting a PHP function (but not language constructs)

- A string denoting a user-defined function

- An array containing an instance of an object in the first element, and the string name of the function to call in the second element

- A string containing the name of a static method in a class (PHP 5.2.3+)

■ **Note** You can't use a language construct as a callable.

There are examples of all of these in the PHP manual page on callables.[4]

CHAPTER 2 QUIZ

Q1: What is the output of the following code?

```php
<?php
declare(strict_types=1);
function multiply(float $a, float $b): int {
    return $a * $b;
}
$six = multiply(2, 3);
echo gettype($six);
```

Int

Float

Fatal error: Uncaught TypeError

Q2: Some PHP functions, like echo, do not need you to use brackets when calling them. Is this true?

Yes, because you can call it like this: echo "hello";

Yes, because echo is a special case.

No, because echo is a language construct and not a function. All PHP functions require you to use brackets when calling them.

No, because all PHP functions require you to use brackets when calling them, except echo, which only requires brackets when you use more than one argument.

---

[4]https://php.net/manual/en/language.types.callable.php

Q3: You cannot use `empty()` as a callback for the `usort()` function.

————————

True

False

————————

Q4: What is the output of the following code?

```php
<?php
(function Hello() {
    echo "Hello World!";
})();
```

Nothing

Hello World

An error message and "Hello World"

Just an error message

Q5: What is the output of the following code?

```php
<?php
declare(strict_types=1);
function multiply(float $a, float $b): float {
    return (double)$a * (double)$b;
}
$six = multiply(2, 3);
echo gettype($six);
```

int

double

float

This generates a `TypeError`

Q6: What is the output of the following code?

```php
<?php
function complicated($compulsory, ...$extras) {
    echo "I have " . func_get_args() . " arguments";
}
complicated(1,2,3,4);
```

1

2

4

This produces a notice error

Q7: How would you refer to the parameter with the value cat in the following function?

```php
<?php
function complicated($compulsory, ...$extras, $animal) {
    // I want to reference the variable with the value "cat"
}
complicated(1,2,3,"cat");
```

$animal

$extras[1]

$extras[2]

This produces an error

Q8: What will this code output?

```php
<?php
if (!is_callable(function(){echo "Hello";})) {
    function sayHello() {
        echo "World!";
    }
}
sayHello();
```

Hello

World!

Hello World!

This produces an error

Q9: What will this code output?

```php
<?php
namespace A;
function Hello() { echo __NAMESPACE__; }
namespace B;
```

```
function Hello() { echo __NAMESPACE__; }
namespace C;
\B\Hello();
```

A

B

C

This produces an error; functions cannot be namespaced

Q10: What will this code output?

```
<?php
namespace A;
$closure = function() { echo __NAMESPACE__; };
namespace B;
$closure = function() { echo __NAMESPACE__; };
namespace C;
$closure();
```

A

B

C

This produces an error; the closure is not defined in namespace C

This produces an error; functions and closures cannot be namespaced

CHAPTER 3

■ ■ ■

Strings and Patterns

PHP strings are a series of bytes and do not contain any information about how those bytes should be translated to characters.

PHP stores the length of the string along with its contents and does not rely on a terminating character to denote the end of the string. This helps to make strings binary safe, as null characters in the string will not cause confusion.

On 32-bit systems a string can be as large as 2 GB. There is no particular limit on how long a string may be on a 64-bit PHP system.

Declaring Strings

In PHP, strings may be declared either as simple type or complex type. The difference is that complex strings will be evaluated with respect to control characters and variables.

Simple strings are declared in 'single quote marks' while complex strings are declared in "double quote marks".

In this example, the newline character is output after Hello Bob, but in the simple string, the literal characters are output.

```php
<?php
$name = 'Bob';
$a = 'Hello $name\n';
$b = "Hello $name\n";
echo $a;        // Hello $name\n
echo $b;        // Hello Bob
```

Notice also that the variable $name is evaluated as the string "Bob" and is inserted into the complex variable $b when it is output. We'll look at this in more detail in the following section.

Embedding Variables

One of the chief advantages of complex strings is the fact that PHP will parse them and automatically evaluate variable names contained in them.

When using simple strings that are not evaluated, you need to terminate the string and concatenate the variable to it.

© Andrew Beak 2017
A. Beak, *PHP 7 Zend Certification Study Guide*,
https://doi.org/10.1007/978-1-4842-3246-0_3

Variables names are marked by a $ in PHP. When the parser encounters one in a string, it will try to form a variable name by adding as many alphanumeric characters as it can to make a valid variable name.

The following example illustrates the difference between concatenating variables to strings and embedding them in complex strings.

```php
<?php
$catfood = "Cheeseburgers";
echo 'I can haz $catfood';           // I can haz $catfood
echo 'I can haz ' . $catfood;        // I can haz Cheeseburgers?
echo "I can haz $catfood?";          // I can haz Cheeseburgers?
```

Note that the first string is marked with single quotes and so $catfood is not evaluated to a variable. It is rather output as literal characters. To include variables in simple strings you need to concatenate them, as the second example shows.

The third echo statement shows an example of the variable name being evaluated in a complex string. The parser encounters the $ symbol and then grabs all the characters following it that are legal for a variable name. The question mark symbol is not permitted in variable names so PHP inserts the literal value of the variable $catfood into the string.

It is possible to include array and object syntax with double quotes too:

```php
<?php
$dogfood = ['Pellets'];
$catfood = new stdClass();
$catfood->favorite = "Cheeseburger";
echo "$dogfood[0]";              // Pellets
echo "$catfood->favorite";       // Cheeseburger
```

PHP allows the use of curly braces for you to explicitly tell the parser that part of a string must be evaluated.

This is necessary, for example, when outputting an element from an array where it might not be immediately clear that the square brackets are intended as punctuation in the string or as syntax to reference an element in the array.

Let's look at some examples of its usage:

```php
<?php
$burger = "Cheeseburger";
echo "I can haz {$burger}";      // I can haz Cheeseburger
echo "I can haz ${burger}";      // I can haz Cheeseburger
echo "I can haz $burgers";       // no variable $burgers
echo "I can haz {$burger}s";     // I can haz Cheeseburgers
echo "I can haz { $burger }";    // I can haz { Cheeseburger }
```

Note that you cannot use spaces between the braces and the variable that you want to evaluate. Because the braces explicitly denote the end of the variable in the string, it is possible to include characters immediately following them. In an earlier example, we saw that "{$burger}s" is rendered as Cheeseburgers.

Let's look at an example where we mix array and object property syntax to demonstrate how curly braces can help:

```php
<?php
$catfood = new stdClass();
$catfood->name = "Cheeseburgers";
$cat = new stdClass();
$cat->canhaz = [$catfood];
echo "$cat->canhaz[0]->name";        // array to string conversion
echo "{$cat->canhaz[0]->name}";      // Cheeseburgers
```

Control Characters

When PHP encounters a complex string, one that it declared in double quotes, it will evaluate it for variables and control characters.

The control characters are marked by a backslash followed by the code. Using a backslash followed by anything other than a control character will result in the backslash being displayed.

```php
<?php
echo "Hello \World"; // Hello \World
```

The PHP Manual page on escape sequences[1]has a list of control characters that may be used, but here they are in table form:

Sequence	Meaning
\n	Line feed
\r	Carriage return
\t	Tab
\v	Vertical tab
\e	Escape
\f	Form feed
\\	Backslash
\$	Dollar symbol
[0-7]{1,3}	Sequences matching this regular expression are in octal notation
\x[0-9A-Fa-f]{1,2}	Matching sequences are in hexadecimal notation
\u{{0-9a-f}{1,6}}	Matching sequences are a Unicode codepoint, which will be output to the string as that codepoints UTF-8 representation

---

[1]https://php.net/manual/en/regexp.reference.escape.php

Emojis have Unicode endpoints, so we can output the elePHPant like this:

```php
<?php
echo "\u{1F418}"; // 🐘
```

Of course, a more formal use-case for Unicode is internationalization (i18n). We'll find out more about it in just a moment.

Heredoc and Nowdoc

A heredoc is a convenient way to declare a string that spans multiple lines. Instead of having to add multiple newline characters, you can declare the string in one easy format.

Heredoc strings are evaluated for control characters and variables, just like double quoted strings are.

Common uses for heredoc include creating SQL queries, or for creating formatted snippets of HTML for e-mails or web pages. You can also use them to initialize variables, or anywhere else that you want to use a string that spans multiple lines.

Nowdoc was introduced in PHP 5.3.0 and is to heredoc what single quoted strings are to double quoted strings. In other words, nowdocs are not evaluated for special characters and variables.

Heredocs use the syntax like this:

```php
<?php
echo <<<HEREDOC
  This is a heredoc string, note:
  1) the capitalization of the tag
  2) the tag name follows variable naming rules
  3) where the closing tag is
HEREDOC;
```

■ **Note**   The closing tag must start on the first character of a newline.

You specify that a string is a nowdoc and not a heredoc by wrapping the label in single quotes, like this:

```php
<?php
echo <<<'NOWDOC'
This is a nowdoc string, note:
  1) Single quotes around the label
  2) Variables will not be evaluated
  3) Control characters will not be evaluated
NOWDOC;
```

60

Referencing Characters in Strings

You can reference a position in a string by using either square brackets or curly braces to denote the zero-based integer position you want to reference.

```php
<?php
$hello = "world";
echo $hello[0]; // w
echo $hello{1}; // o
```

■ **Caution** Remember that strings are a series of bytes, and you are referencing the byte position. If your character set uses more than one byte per character, you won't have the result you expect.

In its current version, PHP will issue a range warning if you attempt to write to a negative position of a string, or if you do not specify an integer position.

Writing to a position that is out of range will result in the string being padded with spaces to accommodate the missing section.

```php
<?php
$hello = "world";
$hello[10] = "*";
echo $hello; //  world    *
```

Notice the trailing asterisk in the preceding example.

PHP and Multibyte Strings

PHP implements strings as an array of bytes with an integer indicating the length of the buffer (not null terminated). PHP does not store information about how the string is encoded.

A variable-width encoding scheme uses codes of differing lengths to encode a character set. Multibyte encodings use varying number of bytes to encode characters.

Multibyte encoding allows a larger number of characters to be encoded and so represented on a computer. One of the encoding schemes that you will commonly encounter in PHP is UTF-8.[2] It is the default scheme that PHP will try to use for multibyte encoding.

The native string functions in PHP assume strings are an array of single bytes, so functions like substr(), strpos(), strlen(), and strcmp() will not work on multibyte strings.

You should use the multibyte equivalents of those functions, such as mb_substr(), for example.

---

[2]https://en.wikipedia.org/wiki/UTF-8

Unicode

Unicode was an attempt to unify all the code sets that represented characters. Unicode defines codepoints that are abstract concepts of a character. A Unicode codepoint represents a character and is written like this: U+0041. That number is assigned to capital "A".

There is no limit on the characters that Unicode can store. There was some confusion originally about Unicode being two bytes, but that related to the encoding scheme and not to Unicode itself.

▪ **Note** Unicode is not itself an encoding system. Encoding is the way in which a Unicode character is represented.

UTF-8 stores all the codepoints from 0-127 in a single byte. This covers the entire range of the English alphabet, numbers, and some symbols. Codepoints above 127 are stored in multiple bytes (up to 6 bytes).

Because the Unicode codepoints from 0-127 match the ASCII table from 0-127, English text encoded in UTF-8 looks exactly the same as if it were encoded in ASCII.

Only people who wrote characters with accents would ever end up with a file that was encoded differently from ASCII. There are hundreds of encoding schemes that can store some of the Unicode codepoints, but not all.

If you use one of these encodings and encounter a Unicode character that cannot be represented, you'll be presented with a question mark or an empty box.

For example, if your encoding scheme is geared toward storing Hebrew characters and you try to store Russian characters in it, you'll get a bunch of question marks instead of your Russian characters because the encoding scheme doesn't support them.

Telling Clients How a String Is Encoded

You can't detect with certainty how a string was encoded (unless you encoded it yourself) and neither can the clients consuming your output. Unless a client knows how a string is encoded, it won't be able to display it with confidence. It's your job as a PHP programmer to tell the clients reading your HTML output how it is encoded.

You should specify the character-encoding scheme being used in the Content-Type HTTP header. This lets the client know how your output is encoded and therefore how to display it correctly.

Putting the content type in the HTML as a meta tag is slightly less satisfactory because unless the client knows the encoding type, it won't be able to read the HTML to determine the encoding. You can get away with doing it this way, but it's better not to.

Changing Between Encoding Schemes

The mbstring extension provides a number of functions that can be used to help detect and convert between encoding schemes.

The mb_detect_encoding() function will go through a list of possible encodings and attempt to determine how the string is encoded.

You can change the order of the detection with the mb_detect_order() function or by providing a list of encodings as a CSV or array.

You can use mb_convert_encoding() to convert a string between encoding formats.

Practical Example

This example shows some aspects of how strings behave in PHP. It declares an array with three different ways to say "hello" and then runs some string commands on each of them to illustrate some points.

```php
<?php
$waysToSayHello = [
        'emoji' => "\u{1F44B}",
        'latinchars' => "Hello",
        'accentedChars' => "ça va?"
    ];
foreach ($waysToSayHello as $method => $string) {
    echo "$method : encoding [" . mb_detect_encoding($string,
    'ISO-8859-1') . '] ' .
        'encoding [' . mb_detect_encoding($string, ['ASCII','UTF-8']) . '] ' .
        'strlen [' . strlen($string) . '] ' .
        'mb_strlen [' . mb_strlen($string) . '] ' .
        'first character[' . $string[0] . ']';
    echo "\r\n";
}
/*

emoji : encoding [ISO-8859-1] encoding [UTF-8] strlen [4] mb_strlen [1]
first character[◆]

latinchars : encoding [ISO-8859-1] encoding [ASCII] strlen [5] mb_strlen [5]
first character[H]

accentedChars : encoding [ISO-8859-1] encoding [UTF-8] strlen [7] mb_strlen
[6] first character[◆]

*/
```

Remember that PHP doesn't store encoding information in the string so it can only guess at how the string is encoded. The mb_detect_encoding function will examine the string and try to determine what it is.

It does so by comparing the string to a list of encoding schemes and selecting the first scheme under which the string is validly encoded. You can specify encodings (in order) for PHP to try or rely on the default encoding. This explains why the output from mb_detect_encoding is different for the same string—we're giving PHP different hints about what it could be.

Notice that the output from strlen() function differs from mb_strlen. The PHP function strlen returns how many bytes are in the string, not how many characters.

Lastly, notice that if we use the array notation method to access a position in the string, we only get a meaningful result if the string is encoded in single byte format.

63

Matching Strings

Comparing strings in PHP should be done with an appropriate level of care when you're trying to match different variable types. In chapter 1, the section on "Casting Variables," we examined the manual pages relating to casting. Make sure that you're familiar with how PHP casts various variable types to string.

Using comparison operators like > and < might not always work as expected. It's common to expect that PHP would use alphabetical order to evaluate strings against these operators.

Instead of using alphabetical sorting, PHP uses the ASCII value of the character to make the comparison. Lowercase letters have a higher ASCII value than capitals, so you can have the situation where lowercase letters are placed after capitals, like this:

```php
<?php
$a = "PHP";
$b = "developer";
if ($a > $b) {
    echo "$a > $b";
} else {
    echo "$a < $b";
}
// developer comes before PHP in the alphabet
// but this script outputs
// PHP < developer
```

Recall the rules for converting strings to integers discussed in the section on "Casting Variables". In the following example, the string is cast to an integer value of 12, which equals the float value of 12.00 and so the message is echoed.

```php
<?php
$a = "12 o'clock";
$b = 12.00;
if ($a == $b) {
    echo "The mouse ran up the clock";
}
```

Unless you are confident about the strings you're comparing, you should consider using the identity operator === to make this sort of comparison.

In addition to using operators, PHP also provides a number of string comparison functions.

strcmp() is a function to perform binary safe string comparisons. It takes two strings as arguments and returns < 0 if str1 is less than str2; > 0 if str1 is greater than str2, and 0 if they are equal.

■ **Tip**   Remember the spaceship operator? The operator can be used on any variable types, but strcmp is exclusively for strings.

There is also a case-insensitive version named strcasecmp() that first converts strings to lowercase and then compares them.

This example shows the difference:

```php
<?php
$a = "PHP";
$b = "developer";
$comparison = strcmp($a, $b);
echo $comparison . PHP_EOL; // -20
$caseInsensitive = strcasecmp($a, $b);
echo $caseInsensitive . PHP_EOL; // 12
```

The functions strncmp() and strcasencmp() can be used to only compare the first "n" characters of two strings.

PHP has a very powerful function called similar_text() that calculates the similarity between two strings. This can be a very computationally expensive procedure for long sections of text, so be careful before you use it. Also be aware that the order that you pass the arguments in is significant, so similar_text($a, $b) != similar_text($b, $a).

Another function, levenshtein(), can be used to calculate the Levenshtein distance between two strings. The Levenshtein distance is defined as the minimal number of characters you have to replace, insert, or delete to transform str1 into str2.

To compare substrings, you can use the binary-safe substr_compare() function.

PHP has two functions that let you work with the way a string sounds. The soundex() function calculates a key based on how the string sounds. Strings that sound the same will have the same soundex key.

The metaphone() function similarly creates the same key for similar sounding strings. It is more accurate than soundex(), as it is aware of the basic rules of English pronunciation. Of course, this is likely to be of little help in other languages!

There are two other ways to compare strings, but they are discussed in Chapter 6 on security. The hash_equals() function is a timing-attack safe way of comparing strings and password_verify() is a safe way to check that a password matches a hash. You'll learn about them in more detail later, but remember them as string functions.

Extracting Strings

An individual position in a string can be referenced with the same syntax as an array element. All positions in the string are always zero-based—the first character in the string is position 0.

```php
<?php
$string = 'abcdef';
echo $string[0];    // a
```

You can use the substr() function to return a portion, or slice, of a string. The PHP Manual for substr() shows the syntax for the command like this:

```
`string substr ( string $string , int $start [, int $length ] )`
```

You can see that it takes two compulsory parameters and one optional parameter. Both the start and the length parameters can be positive or negative. If the start value is greater than the length of the string, substr() will return false. If the start value is positive (or 0), the slice of the string returned starts at the start'th position of the string counting from the beginning.

Otherwise, if it is negative, the slice starts at the start'th position from the ending of the string.

```php
<?php
echo substr("abcdef", 2) . PHP_EOL;    // cdef
echo substr("abcdef", -2) . PHP_EOL;   // ef
```

If length is omitted, as in the previous example, then the slice will continue from the slice starting point to the end of the string. If length is given as a positive number, then at most length characters will be returned. If length is given as a negative number, then that many characters will be omitted from the end of the string:

```php
<?php
echo substr("abcdef", 0, 2) . PHP_EOL;    // ab
echo substr("abcdef", 0, -2) . PHP_EOL;   // abcd
```

If length is given and is 0, FALSE, or NULL, then an empty string is returned. The same happens when the start parameter is bigger or equal to the string.

The PHP Manual[3] gives some more examples:

```php
<?php
echo substr('abcdef', 1);       // bcdef
echo substr('abcdef', 1, 3);    // bcd
echo substr('abcdef', 0, 4);    // abcd
echo substr('abcdef', 0, 8);    // abcdef
echo substr('abcdef', -1, 1);   // f
```

Searching Strings

Because PHP was written for the web, it is particularly strong at processing strings. You'll be expected to know the ins and outs of the string-manipulation functions. This section introduces the functions that are used to search strings. It is strongly recommended that you experiment with the functions and read up on their manual pages. The Zend exam is very much geared to reward experience rather than an encyclopedic knowledge of the manual.

---

[3]https://php.net/manual/en/function.substr.php

Useful Tips

A common complaint about PHP is that it is difficult to tell the order of parameters for searching strings and arrays.

PHP search parameters have a $haystack and we are searching for a $needle. Compare the order of parameters used for strpos() and array_search():

```php
<?php
$arr = ['a', 'b', 'c', 'd', 'e', 'f' ];
$str = 'abcdef';
echo strpos($str, 'c') . PHP_EOL;
echo array_search('c', $arr) . PHP_EOL;
```

It seems at first that sometimes the $needle parameter comes first and sometimes the $haystack parameter comes first.

However, it's a lot simpler when you remember that PHP is using underlying C libraries and the consistent rule is:

- For string search functions, the order is always $haystack then $needle

- For array search functions, the order is always $needle then $haystack

The next useful tip is to remember the difference between 0 and false. Although Boolean false evaluates to 0, if you cast it to integer, the number 0 is not identical to a Boolean false. Here's an example where we seemingly don't find the letter "a" in the string "abcdef":

```php
<?php
$string = 'abcdef';
if (strpos($string, 'a') == false) {
  echo "False negative!" . PHP_EOL;
}
```

Remember that strings are zero-based, so the first position is position 0. strpos() is returning the integer 0 because it found "a" in the first position. We are using the equality operator == to check the result of strpos() and so we are falsely reporting that the letter "a" does not appear in this string.

■ **Tip** To handle the case where the substring is genuinely not found, you should use the identity === operator.

Quick Overview of Search Functions

PHP has several functions used to search strings. As a general rule, the case-insensitive functions have an "i" after the prefix. The following table lists the PHP Manual definitions for the string search functions.

Function	Used For
substr_count()	Returns the number of substring occurrences in a string.
strstr()	Searches for a substring in a string and returns the portion of the haystack that occurs after the first found occurrence. It returns false if no occurrence is found. Note that using strpos() is preferable because it is faster.
stristr()	A case-insensitive version of strstr().
strchr()	Returns the portion of the string before the first occurrence of the needle.
strpos()	Returns the position of the first occurrence of the needle.[4]
stripos()	A case-insensitive version of strpos().
strspn()	Finds the length of the initial segment of a string consisting entirely of characters contained within a given mask.[5]
strcspn()	Returns the length of the initial segment of subject that does not contain any of the characters in the mask. In other words, it searches for the first occurrence of any of the mask letters in the string and returns the number of characters that exist before it is found.[6]

Replacing Strings

PHP has three functions for replacing strings.

str_replace() and its case-insensitive version str_ireplace() can be used for basic replacements.

```php
<?php
echo str_replace('foo', 'bar', 'Delicious food'); // Delicious bard
```

They both take three compulsory parameters—the search string, replacement string, and the string to operate on. If you pass the optional fourth variable (it is a reference argument), it will be set to the number of replacements that PHP performed.

---

[4]https://secure.php.net/manual/en/function.strpos.php
[5]https://secure.php.net/manual/en/function.strspn.php
[6]https://secure.php.net/manual/en/function.strcspn.php

Both the search and replacement parameters can be arrays. This lets you replace multiple values in one call, as in this example:

```php
<?php
$string = "I like black hot coffee";
$search = ['black', 'coffee'];
$replace = ['green', 'tea'];
echo str_replace($search, $replace, $string); // I like green hot tea
```

You can use the substr_replace() function to replace substrings. substr_replace() replaces a copy of the string delimited by the start and (optionally) length parameters with the string given in replacement.

strtr() is another function to replace substrings and characters. If only two parameters are supplied, the second parameter should be an array of replacement pairs. It otherwise takes three parameters, as in this example from the PHP Manual, it is being used to convert characters with accent marks to English format characters:

```php
<?php
$address = "09479 Huopainenkylä, Pöhjois-Karjala";
$address = strtr($address, "äåö", "aao");
echo $address; // 09479 Huopainenkyloa, Pohjois-Karjala
```

The most flexible and powerful way to replace strings is by using the preg_match() function, which allows you to use regular expressions to find slices of the string to replace. You'll learn more about regular expressions in the "String Patterns: Regular Expressions" section later in this chapter.

Formatting Strings

The printf() function is used to output a formatted string. You should read carefully though the PHP Manual[7] and make sure that you've practiced using it. The general usage is to specify a formatting string and the values that need to be placed into it.

```php
<?php
$minutes = 60;
$timeUnit = "an hour";
printf("There are %u minutes in %s.", $minutes, $timeUnit);
```

In the example, you'll notice that the first parameter to printf() has two placeholders marked by percentage symbols. The following parameters are values that must be typecast and inserted into those placeholders.

---

[7]https://php.net/manual/en/function.printf.php

There are a number of symbols that can be used to format parameters. You'll find this list on the PHP web site,[8] but for your convenience I'm including it here:

Symbol	Format
%%	A literal percent character. No argument is required.
%b	The argument is treated as an integer and presented as a binary number.
%c	The argument is treated as an integer and presented as the character with that ASCII value.
%d	The argument is treated as an integer and presented as a (signed) decimal number.
%e	The argument is treated as scientific notation (e.g., 1.2e+2). The precision specifier stands for the number of digits after the decimal point since PHP 5.2.1. In earlier versions, it was taken as the number of significant digits (one less).
%E	Like %e but uses an uppercase letter (e.g., 1.2E+2).
%f	The argument is treated as a float and presented as a floating-point number (locale-aware).
%F	The argument is treated as a float and presented as a floating-point number (non-locale-aware). Available since PHP 4.3.10 and PHP 5.0.3.
%g	Shorter of %e and %f.
%G	Shorter of %E and %f.
%o	The argument is treated as an integer and presented as an octal number.
%s	The argument is treated as and presented as a string.
%u	The argument is treated as an integer and presented as an unsigned decimal number.
%x	The argument is treated as an integer and presented as a hexadecimal number (with lowercase letters).
%X	The argument is treated as an integer and presented as a hexadecimal number (with uppercase letters).

PHP formats are locale-aware, which affects how they represent numbers and dates. For example, if you set the locale to Dutch then the date would be output in Dutch. This is shown in an example on the PHP Manual:

```php
<?php
// Set locale to Dutch
setlocale(LC_ALL, 'nl_NL');
// Output: vrijdag 22 december 1978
echo strftime("%A %e %B %Y", mktime(0, 0, 0, 12, 22, 1978));
```

---

[8]https://secure.php.net/manual/en/function.sprintf.php

■ **Caution**   Locale information is maintained per process, not per thread.

If you are running PHP on a multithreaded server API like IIS, HHVM, or Apache on Windows, you may experience sudden changes in locale settings while a script is running, although the script itself never called setlocale().

This happens due to other scripts running in different threads of the same process at the same time, changing the process-wide locale using setlocale().

On a POSIX system, you can use the shell command locale -a to list all of the locales it supports. On Windows machines, there are pages on the MSDN listing the regions and you can view them in your control panel.

Formatting Numbers

The number_format() function is a simple way to format numbers.

number_format() is not locale-aware and so won't automatically choose the separator characters for you. By default, the thousands separator is a comma and no decimal places are displayed.

The function takes parameters for the number to be formatted, how many decimal places to display, the character for the decimal point, and the thousands separator character.

You can pass one, two, or four parameters to the function. Here is an example:

```php
<?php
$number = 1234.5678;
// 1,235
echo number_format($number) . PHP_EOL;
// 1,234.568
echo number_format($number, 3) . PHP_EOL;
// 1.234,57
echo number_format($number, 2, ',', '.') . PHP_EOL;
```

To format currency, you can use the money_format() function. It is locale-aware and uses the information set by the host system.

```php
<?php
// Locale is British English
setlocale(LC_MONETARY, 'en_GB');
echo money_format('%.2n', "5000000.123");
// Locale is Denmark
setlocale(LC_MONETARY, 'da_DK');
echo money_format('%.2n', "5000000.123");
```

The output looks like this:

```
£5,000,000.12
kr 5.000.000,12
```

String Patterns: Regular Expressions

Regular expressions are a set of rules against which you match strings. The rules are written as a string using a format that describes the pattern you are searching for. There are several flavors of regex; PHP uses Perl Compatible Regular Expressions (PCRE).

When learning regular expressions, you should find an online regex tester that you like. There are several to choose from and they make it a lot quicker to play with expressions and see how they match strings.[9]

Delimiters

Regular expressions are delimited by characters that appear at the beginning and end of each pattern in your expression. Usually the forward slash is used, but # and ! are also common.

Any character can be used, but the delimiter will need to be escaped inside your expressions, so it is standard to choose a delimiter that is not likely to occur in your search expression. For example, if you're going to be searching directories to find those which match a pattern, the forward slash character might not be the best choice of delimiter.

Meta-Characters

Meta-characters are interpreted to have a meaning in the search pattern. They need to be escaped if you intend to have them as a literal part of the expression. They are listed in the following table.

Character	Meaning
\	General escape character
^	Start of subject or line
$	End of subject or line
.	Match any character except newline
[	Start defining a character class
]	End defining a character class
|	Start of an alternate branch (like an "or")

(continued)

---

[9]For example, the site https://regex101.com/ is a great place to play with regex.

Character	Meaning
(	Start of a sub-pattern
)	End of a sub-pattern
?	Zero or one quantifier
*	Zero or more quantifier
+	One or more quantifier
{	Start min/max quantifier
}	End min/max quantifier

We'll be building on this as we work through this section, but for now just be aware that these symbols convey a certain meaning in a regular expression or pattern. You will need to be familiar with them before sitting for your exam.

Generic Character Types

Regex offers a way for you to specify that a character in your search string may be any of a particular type. You specify them using the backslash (Escape) meta-character and then providing the letter for the type.

The following table lists the character types that are available in PCRE.

Symbol	Character Type
\d	Any decimal digit
\h	Any horizontal whitespace character
\s	Any whitespace character
\v	Any vertical whitespace character
\w	Any "word" character
\D	Any character that is not a decimal digit
\H	Any character that is not horizontal whitespace
\S	Any character that is not whitespace
\V	Any character that is not a vertical whitespace character
\W	Any "non-word" character

You should immediately spot that the capital symbol is the inverse of the lowercase symbol.

A "word" character is any letter, digit, or the underscore character. The actual characters that are included in this are locale-aware.

Boundaries

A word boundary is a position in the string where the current character and previous character do not both match \w or W.

In other words, it is a position in the string where a word starts or finishes, or a position where one of the characters matches \w and the other matches W.

Symbol	Boundary
\b	Word boundary
\B	Not a word boundary
\A	Start of a subject
\Z	End of subject or newline at end
\z	End of subject
\G	First matching position in subject

■ **Tip** PHP uses PCRE expressions. You can find this table in the original specification document at http://www.pcre.org/original/doc/html/pcrepattern.html.

Character Classes

Character classes are very flexible ways to define what set of characters in your search string can be matched. By specifying a small sequence of characters in your pattern, you can match a much larger set of characters in your search string.

You saw in the meta-characters table that you create a character class by putting it inside square brackets. An example of a character class is [A-Z], which stands for all of the letters in the uppercase alphabet.

You can also use all of the generic types in character classes, so [A-Z\d] would match all of the uppercase letters as well as digits.

Matching More Than Once

The expression /[A-Z\d]/ applied against the string "abc123ABCabc" will match the "1" character. In other words, it matches the first occurrence in the search string of a character that matches the expression.

If you refer back to the table on meta-characters, you can see that the + symbol can be used to specify that you want one, or more, of the pattern. So the expression /[A-Z\d]+/ applied against the string "abc123ABCabc" will match the "123ABC" characters.[10]

---

[10]https://regex101.com/r/EXsPkY/2

You can use braces to limit the number of matches. The syntax is best displayed in a table, where you match the expression against the string "abc123ABCabc":

Expression	Limit	Output
/[A-Z\d]+/	One or unlimited	123ABC
[A-Z\d]{3}	Exactly three	123
[A-Z\d]{3,}	Three or more	123ABC
[A-Z\d]{3,5}	Between three and five	123AB
[A-Z\d]{50}	Exactly 50	No match

Capturing Groups

Capturing groups are delineated by brackets and allow you to apply a quantifier to the group. They also produce numbered groups that store the value that was matched, and they can be referenced elsewhere in your expression.

In this example, we create a capturing group around the word "cheeseburger" and use the group to specify that zero or one of them will be matched.

```php
<?php
$subject = "I can haz Cheeseburgers";
$pattern = "/I can haz (Cheeseburger)?/";
$matches = [];
preg_match($pattern, $subject, $matches);
var_dump($matches[0]);
```

This outputs string(22) "I can haz Cheeseburger". Note that the "s" at the end of the string is not matched.

■ **Tip** As an exercise, play with the regex in your favorite editor and see what happens if you use a subject "I can haz" (without a space at the end of the string).

You can use non-capturing groups to optimize your query. You should use these when you don't need to capture the match.

They're marked by placing a ?: mark at the start of your group. The previous example would be written as /I can haz (?:Cheeseburger)?/. Note that this expression will still return the string to PHP as before, but it just won't store the string Cheeseburger as a group for the expression to reference.

It may seem confusing that the ? is a quantifier and also denotes a non-capturing group. Just remember that a quantifier cannot occur at the start of a group because there is nothing to quantify.

Greed and Laziness

By default, matching is "greedy" and will match as much as possible of the string. Consider an example that you'll work with. Imagine that you want to match HTML tags, so you try the following:

```php
<?php
$subject = "Some <strong>html</strong> text";
$pattern = "/<.*>/";
$matches = [];
preg_match($pattern, $subject, $matches);
var_dump($matches[0]);  // string(21) "<strong>html</strong>"
```

This outputs `string(21) "<strong>html</strong>"`, which is clearly more than the HTML tag you were wanting.

It is greed that is to blame for this; the * quantifier is greedy and attempts to find the longest possible match. It returns the characters between the opening < of the strong tag and the last > of the closing tag, which is the longest possible match.

By contrast, a lazy search returns the shortest possible match. You can modify a quantifier to make it lazy by adding a question mark (?) to it.

```php
<?php
$subject = "Some <strong>html</strong> text";
$pattern = "/<.*?>/";  // note the pattern has changed
$matches = [];
preg_match($pattern, $subject, $matches);
var_dump($matches[0]);  // string(8) "<strong>"
```

There are a lot more options to modify quantifiers, but they are outside of the scope of this book.

Getting All Matches

So far your expressions are returning just the first occurrence of the matching portion of a search string. Let's say that you want to find all of the matches in the string.

PCRE has a global modifier (more on those later), but PHP uses a separate function called `preg_match_all()` to return all matches.

```php
<?php
$subject = "Some <strong>html</strong> text";
$pattern = "/<.*?>/";
$matches = [];
preg_match_all($pattern, $subject, $matches);
var_dump($matches);
```

```
/*
  array(1) {
                    [0] =>
                      array(2) {
                        [0] => string(8) "<strong>"
                        [1] => string(9) "</strong>"
                    }
            }
*/
```

Naming Groups

You can name capturing groups by adding ?<name> to the beginning of the bracket that opens the group. For example:

```php
<?php
$subject = "test@example.com";
$pattern = "/^(?<username>\w+)@(?<domain>\w+).(?<tld>\w+)/";
$matches = [];
if (preg_match($pattern, $subject, $matches)) {
  var_dump($matches);
}
```

In this example, we're naming the first part of the matching pattern as username, the next as domain, and the next as tld. This is a somewhat naïve example because it won't work for e-mail addresses like test@example.co.uk, but it does serve to show the syntax. The previous example outputs this:

```
array(7) {
                  [0] => string(16) "test@example.com"
                  'username' => string(4) "test"
                  [1] => string(4) "test"
                  'domain' => string(7) "example"
                  [2] => string(7) "example"
                  'tld' => string(3) "com"
                  [3] => string(3) "com"
      }
```

So you are able to reference $matches['username'] and receive "test" in response, which is convenient.

Pattern Modifiers

You can add a modifier after the closing delimiter of an expression. The following table lists the modifiers.

Modifier	Function
i	The expression is case-insensitive.
m	Multiline mode. Strings can span multiple lines and newline characters are ignored. Instead of matching the beginning and end of the string, the ^ and $ symbols will match the beginning and end of the line.
s	The . meta-character will also match newlines.
x	Ignore whitespace unless you escape it.
e	This causes PHP code to be evaluated and is highly discouraged. It is deprecated as of PHP 5.5 and in PHP 7 will generate a warning, as it is no longer supported.
U	This makes the quantifiers lazy by default and using the ? after them instead marks them as greedy.
u	This tells PHP to treat the pattern and string as being UTF-8 encoded. This means that characters instead of bytes are matched.

CHAPTER 3 QUIZ

Q1: You cannot compare a string variable to an integer variable using the greater than or less than operators. You can only compare string and integer values with the equivalence operator.

_____

True

False

_____

Q2: You can use the _____ function to make binary safe case-insensitive comparisons between strings.

_____

<=>

strcmp

strcasecmp

stricmp

_____

Q3: PHP functions that search strings ALWAYS have the parameters in which order.

`$haystack, $needle`

`$needle, $haystack`

It depends on the function

Q4: What does the `strspn($subject, $mask)` function do?

Searches a string `$subject` for a substring `$mask`

Returns the maximum length of a string in `$subject` that contains only letters contained in `$mask`

Returns the minimum length of a string in `$subject` that contains all of the letters contained in `$mask`

It's a binary-safe way to splice a string specified by `$mask` out of the `$subject` string

---

Q5: What does the `strstr($haystack, $needle)` function do?

It's a faster alternative to `strpos()`

It's a binary safe alternative to `strpos()`

It returns the portion of the `$haystack` that occurs after the first instance of `$needle`

It returns the position in the `$haystack` where the string `$needle` first occurs

---

Q6: What is the output of this code?

```php
<?php
$fact = "Dogs do nothing but sleep";
$fact = strtr($fact, "Dog", "Cat");
echo $fact;
```

0

Cats do nothing but sleep

Cats da nathint but sleep

This generates an error

Q7: Which of these regex expressions will identify both e-mail addresses (and only the e-mail addresses) in the following text. Pick as many as apply.

" Knock over christmas tree stare at kittens@catsaregreat.com the wall, play with food and get confused by dust or going to catch `siamese@catsaregreat.com` the red dot today going to catch the red dot today.".

[a-z]*.[a-z.]+

\b[a-z]+@[a-z]+.com\b

\b[a-z]+@[a-z.]+\b

(\b[a-z]*@\b)([a-zA-Z\d]+)

(\S*)@(\w*).(\S*)

Q8: What is the output of this code?

```php
<?php
echo substr("abcdefgh12345678");
```

abcdefgh12345678

Nothing

A warning

A fatal error

Q9: How would you retrieve the first e-mail address if you run this code?

```php
<?php
$subject = "purr for no reason or eat prawns daintily with a claw then
lick paws mycat@catsaregreat.com clean wash down prawns with a lap of
carnation milk then retire to the warmest spot on the couch to claw";
$pattern = "#(\S*)@(\w*).(\S*)#";
$matches = [];
preg_match($pattern, $subject, $matches);
// how do I echo the full email address?
```

echo $matches[0];

echo $matches[0] . $matches[1] . $matches[2]

You can't; there is a syntax error

You can't; this won't match anything in the string

You can't; this produces an error because the pattern is invalid

Q10: The `preg_replace_callback()` function is used to do which of the following?

Use a callback function to supply the replacement string instead of a static string

Use a callback that returns a list of matches for you to replace

Specify a function to call once `preg_replace()` has finished running

There is no such function

CHAPTER 4

Arrays

In this chapter, we're going to be looking at PHP arrays. PHP arrays are implemented as an ordered map that associates values to keys. There are three types of array in PHP: indexed, associative, and multidimensional.

PHP has a lot of array functions that cover a great many common uses for functions. Before you write a function to operate on an array, you should first check if there is already one. They are implemented in C and so are going to be a lot faster than any function you could write in PHP to achieve the same result. The array manual page[1] lists them in one place, and you should make sure that you study this page and each function's manual page.

This book would be too long to exhaustively list every function. Rather than duplicating this information, this chapter focuses on grouping and explaining some of these functions.

Declaring and Referencing Arrays

We will not dwell on what arrays are and will rather move straight onto the syntax used to declare arrays in PHP.

Arrays are created as a set of value-pairs that are separated by commas.

```php
<?php
// numeric index, auto assigned key
$arr = array(10, 'abc', 30);
// numeric index, key explicitly set
$arr = array(0 => 10, 1 => 'abc', 2 => 30 );
// associative
$arr = array('name' => 'foo', 'age' => 20);
// short syntax
$arr = ['name' => 'foo', 'age' => 20];
```

If you do not specify a key then PHP will assign an auto-incrementing numeric key. In the example, the first two assignments are identical because PHP automatically assigns the key.

A key may be numeric or a string. An array may contain a mixture of numeric and string keys.

---

[1]https://php.net/manual/en/ref.array.php

© Andrew Beak 2017
A. Beak, *PHP 7 Zend Certification Study Guide*,
https://doi.org/10.1007/978-1-4842-3246-0_4

Arrays keyed on numbers are called *enumerative*. The first two examples are enumerative. Arrays that have strings for keys are called associative arrays. The last two examples are associative arrays.

There are two syntax forms to declare an array; choosing one is a question of coding style.

```php
<?php
$shortForm = ['this', 'is', 'short'];
$longForm = array('this', 'is', 'short');
```

Arrays may be nested. In other words, an array value can itself be an array. These are called multi-dimensional arrays.

An individual array element may be referenced using the [ ] operator like this:

```php
<?php
$arr = ['name' => 'foo', 'age' => 20];
echo $arr['age']; // 20
```

If you do not specify a key in the brackets, PHP assumes that you are trying to reference a new element. You can use this to add an element to the end of an array:

```php
<?php
$arr = [0 => 'id', 'name' => 'foo', 'age' => 20];
$arr[] = 'example';
print_r($arr);
```

This will output the following:

```
Array
(
[0] => id
[name] => foo
[age] => 20
[1] => example
)
```

Note that PHP chose the key by incrementing the highest numeric key in the array.

Functions That Create an Array

There are lots of PHP functions that return an array, but I'm going to introduce a few that are directly related to arrays.

The function explode() is used to split up a string into an array. It's easiest to explain by example:

```php
<?php
// The delimiter is a string of any length
$delimiter = ',';
```

```
// This string is broken up by the delimiter
$source = '1, abc, 2, def, 3, ghi';
// The limit determines how many elements explode will return
$limit = -2;
// create an array by splitting the source
$arr = explode($delimiter, $source, $limit);
print_r($arr);
```

The function takes three parameters. The first is a string to be used as a delimiter. Typically, this is just a single character (like a comma when working with CSV), but it could be of any length.

The second parameter is a string containing a list of elements that are separated by the delimiter.

The third parameter limits the number of items that PHP will return. By default, it is set to PHP_INT_MAX and so PHP will return as many items as it can. If it is negative then PHP returns all the elements except the last $limit amount. A zero limit is treated the same as 1.

This example specifies -2 as the limit so PHP returns all the elements except the last two.

The output of this example is:

```
Array
(
    [0] => 1
    [1] => abc
    [2] => 2
    [3] => def
)
```

The implode() function[2] operates in the reverse manner. It joins the elements of an array together into a string delimited by a string you supply.

preg_split() is another function that splits a string into an array. It is similar to explode(), but it uses a regular expression to delimit the field instead of using a literal string. It is documented in the PHP Manual.[3]

You can use the str_split() function[4] to break a string into an array of chunks. It takes two parameters: the string you want to split, and the length of the chunk to use for each element of the array.

```
<?php
$input = '12345678';
$arr = str_split($input, 3);
print_r($arr);
```

[2]https://php.net/manual/en/function.implode.php
[3]https://php.net/manual/en/function.preg-split.php
[4]https://php.net/manual/en/function.str-split.php

This example breaks the string up into an array containing elements of length 3, like this:

```
Array
(
    [0] => 123
    [1] => 456
    [2] => 78
)
```

Notice that the string is not evenly divisible by the chunk size and so the final element is only two characters long. If the chunk size is greater than the length of the string, the entire string is returned as the only element of the array. The function returns FALSE if you try to use a negative chunk length.

Array Operators

PHP arrays can be tested for equivalence and identity. We saw in the section on comparison operators that arrays are equivalent if they have the same key and value pairs. They are identical if they have the same key and value pairs, are in the same order, and the key-value are of the same type.

The + operator will produce the union of two arrays.

When using the + union operator, PHP appends the array on the right of the operator to the left. If a key exists in both arrays, then the left array value is used for the key.

```php
<?php
$a = ['a' => 'hello', 'b' => 'world'];
$b = ['a' => 'goodbye', 'c' => 'cruel'];
echo implode(' ', $a + $b);  // hello world cruel
```

In the previous example, both arrays have the key a. The union of the arrays will therefore have the value from $a for this key, because $a was on the left of the union operator.

Example	Name	Result
$a + $b	Union	$b is appended to $a. If a key exists in both arrays, then the value from $a is placed into the union.
$a == $b	Equality	TRUE if $a and $b have the same key-value pairs
$a === $b	Identity	TRUE if $a and $b have the same key-value pairs, of the same types, and in the same order.
$a != $b	Inequality	TRUE if $a is not equal to $b.
$a <> $b	Inequality	TRUE if $a is not equal to $b.
$a !== $b	Non-identity	TRUE if $a is not identical to $b.

Let's run through a quick example:

```php
<?php
$a = ['a', 'b', '1'];
$b = ['a', 'b', 1];
$c = ['1', 'b', 'a'];
$d = [2 => 1, 0 => 'a', 1 => 'b'];

var_dump($a == $b);      // true
var_dump($a === $b);     // false
var_dump($a == $c);      // false
var_dump($a == $d);      // true
var_dump($a === $d);     // false
```

We can see that $a is equal to $b because the key-value pairs are the same. They are not equivalent, however, because the type of the third element is a string in $a and an integer in $b.

$a and $c are not equal even though they have the same values. Arrays are considered equal if they have the same key-value pairs. In this case, we didn't specify a key so PHP assigned an auto-incrementing key for each value. Therefore, they key-value pairs don't match, even though the values are the same.

$a and $d are equal because the key-value pairs are the same, but are not identical because they are not in the same order.

Properties of PHP Array Keys

PHP arrays are zero-based.

PHP array keys are case sensitive: $arr['A'] and $arr['a'] are different elements.

Keys may only be a string or an integer. Other variable types are cast into one of these types before being stored.

Strings containing decimal valid integers will be cast to the integer type.

```php
<?php
$a = [
"2" =>"hello",
    0x03 =>"world",
    0b100 => ' this is ',
"04" =>"PHP",
    8.7 =>"!!!!"
];
var_dump($a);
/*
array(5) {
  [2]=>
  string(5) "hello"
```

```
    [3]=>
    string(5) "world"
    [4]=>
    string(9) " this is "
    ["04"]=>
    string(3) "PHP"
    [8]=>
    string(4) "!!!!"
}
*/
```

In the preceding example, we see that the string "2" is converted to integer 2. The hexadecimal and binary formats are both converted to decimal. The string "04" is not converted to an integer because it contains an octal representation and not a decimal.

PHP rounds floats toward zero when it casts floats to integers. Another way of putting this is to say that the fractional portion of the number is truncated. For example, the float 133.7 will cast to the integer value 133 (and not rounded up to 134).

Booleans can also be cast to integers. The Boolean value true evaluates to integer 1 and false becomes integer 0.

Null is treated as an empty string. So the null key will be stored under the key ' '.

Composite variables (objects and arrays) and resources cannot be used as key. If you try to do so, PHP will issue a warning "illegal offset type".

Keys are unique; if multiple elements in an array use the same key (after it has been converted as above), then PHP will use the last one for the value and overwrite all the preceding values.

■ **Tip**   This is a good time to review your type juggling!

Filling Up Arrays

You can use the range() function to add values to an array based on a range of values you specify. You specify the beginning, end, and step size for the range.

The PHP Manual has many useful examples, but here is one based on one of the comments:

```
<?php
print_r(array_combine(range(1, 10, 2),range(1,5)));
```

This will output the following:

```
/*
  Array
  (
    [1] => 1
    [3] => 2
```

```
    [5] => 3
    [7] => 4
    [9] => 5
)
*/
```

Another command called `array_fill()` will let you fill up an array with a single value. It takes parameters for the starting index, how many values to fill, and the value to insert.

```php
<?php
print_r(array_fill(10, 5, 'five'));
```

This script outputs:

```
Array
(
[10] => five
[11] => five
[12] => five
[13] => five
[14] => five
)
```

Related to this is the function `array_fill_keys()`. This function will fill up an array with a specific value and lets you specify what keys to use.

```php
<?php
$keys = range(1, 10, 2);
$value = "PHP";
print_r(array_fill_keys($keys, $value));
/*
Array
(
    [1] => PHP
    [3] => PHP
    [5] => PHP
    [7] => PHP
    [9] => PHP
)
*/
```

Push, Pop, Shift, and Unshift (Oh My!)

These four commands are used to add or remove elements from arrays.

Function	Effect
array_shift()	Shifts an element off the beginning of array[5]
array_unshift()	Prepends one or more elements to the beginning of an array[6]
array_pop()	Pops the element off the end of array[7]
array_push()	Pushes one or more elements onto the end of array[8]

You'll probably notice that you can easily implement queues and stacks with these functions.

The commands that remove an element from the array return it to you and shift all the elements down. Numeric keys are reduced until they start counting from 0 and literal keys are left untouched.

```php
<?php
$stack = array("one", "two", "three", "four");
$fruit = array_shift($stack);
print_r($stack);
```

In the output, you will notice that "two" now has the key of 0, where before it was 1:

```
/*
  Array
  (
    [0] => two
    [1] => three
    [2] => four
  )
*/
```

Comparing Arrays

You saw earlier in the chapter that it is possible to use the equality == and identity === operators to compare arrays. When applied to arrays, the equality operator returns true if the arrays have the same keys and values, regardless of their type. The identity operator will only return true if the arrays have the same keys and values, they are in the same order, and they are of the same variable types.

---

[5]https://secure.php.net/manual/en/function.array-shift.php
[6]https://secure.php.net/manual/en/function.array-unshift.php
[7]https://secure.php.net/manual/en/function.array-pop.php
[8]https://secure.php.net/manual/en/function.array-push.php

```php
<?php
$arr = ['1', '2', '3'];
$brr = [1, 2, 3];
var_dump($arr === $brr); // false
var_dump($arr == $brr);  // true
```

There are PHP functions devoted to array comparisons that make more sophisticated comparisons possible.

array_diff()

The array_diff() function takes a list of arrays as arguments. It will return an array containing the values from the first array that were not present in any of the other arrays.

This example uses array_diff() to compare input parameters supplied in the $_POST superglobal against a predefined list of required parameters.

```php
<?php
$requiredKeys = ['username', 'password', 'csrf_token'];
$missingKeys = array_diff($requiredKeys, array_keys($_POST));
if (count($missingKeys)) {
    throw new UnexpectedValueException('You need to provide
    [' . print_r($missingKeys, true) . ']');
}
```

This code finds any keys that are in the required list but not in the post array and creates an array called $missingKeys, which contains them. This lets you validate that a form has been completely filled in.

array_diff_assoc() is an associative version of array_diff() and takes into account the array keys as well as their values. To see the difference, we can use a very simple example:

```php
<?php
$a = ['a' => 'apple', 'b' => 'banana'];
$b = ['a' => 'apple', 'd' => 'banana'];
print_r(array_diff($a, $b));
print_r(array_diff_assoc($a, $b));
/*
Array
(
)
Array
(
    [b] => banana
)
*/
```

The result of array_diff() is an empty array, but array_diff_assoc() returns an array consisting of [b] => banana because the key for the value banana is b in the first array and d in the second.

array_intersect()

The function array_intersect() also takes a list of arrays as parameters. It calculates which values from the first array are also present in all the other arrays.

```php
<?php
$birds = ['duck', 'chicken', 'goose'];
$net = ['dog', 'cat', 'chicken', 'goose', 'hamster'];
print_r(array_intersect($net, $birds));
```

This will output the elements that are in $net as well as in $birds:

```
Array
(
  [2] => chicken
  [3] => goose
)
```

Note that the keys are preserved.

array_intersect_assoc() includes an index check when matching elements. If you apply it to the arrays in the example, it will return an empty array. The return value is empty because, although the values in the arrays match, their indexes do not.

User-Defined Matching Functions

PHP provides functions that allow you to specify your own comparison function.

Consider array_udiff() as an example. It takes a list of array parameters followed by a callable as the last parameter.

Let's consider a trivial example, where we want to compare the lowercase value of the arrays to each other. More realistic use-cases could involve more complicated operations, such as on objects for example.

```php
<?php
$birds = ['duck', 'chicken', 'goose'];
$net = ['Dog', 'Cat', 'Chicken', 'Goose', 'Hamster'];
$diff = array_udiff($net, $birds, function($a, $b){
    $a = strtolower($a);
    $b = strtolower($b);
    if ($a < $b) {
        return -1;
    } elseif ($a > $b) {
        return 1;
    } else {
        return 0;
    }
});
print_r($diff);
```

This code outputs elements in the $net that don't have a matching animal in the list of $birds. We're using a custom function to do the comparison, which first converts both strings to lowercase.

```
Array
(
    [0] => Dog
    [1] => Cat
    [4] => Hamster
)
```

Note the following:

- From the manual[9]: "The comparison function must return an integer less than, equal to, or greater than zero if the first argument is considered to be respectively less than, equal to, or greater than the second."

- You can use closures as callables for any function that takes a callable as a parameter.

- You can use lambdas as callables, also for any function that takes a callable as a parameter. In the example, we're using a lambda.

- The comparison function takes two arguments that will be the values to compare.

There are PHP functions to allow you to specify your own callable to compare keys, values, or both.

---

[9]https://php.net/manual/en/function.array-udiff.php

Quick List of Comparison Functions

This table shows the arrays for performing the difference between functions.

There are similar functions to perform the intersection. They have the same naming convention and parameters, so I'm not listing them here.

Function	Used For
array_diff	Computes the difference of arrays[10]
array_diff_assoc	Computes the difference of arrays with additional index check
array_udiff	Computes the difference of arrays by using a callback function for data comparison[11]
array_udiff_assoc	Computes the difference of arrays with additional index check and compares data by a callback function[12]
array_udiff_uassoc	Computes the difference of arrays with additional index check and compares data and indexes by a callback function

Note that array_udiff_uassoc() takes two callable functions as parameters, one for the values and the last parameter for the indexes. Look at the manual page[13] and make sure you have studied all its related functions.

Combining Arrays

PHP offers some useful functions to help combine arrays.

The combine_array($keys, $values) function creates an array by using one array for keys and another for its values. It will return FALSE if the number of elements in the arrays do not match, and otherwise will return an associative array.

You can use array_replace($array1, $array2, ...) to sequentially replace values in an array with values from other arrays. It takes two or more arrays as parameters and processes them from left to right.

It follows these rules to determine the final result:

- If the first array has a key that is not in the second array, then the key-value pair is left untouched.

- If the second array has a key that is not in the first array, then the key-value pair from the second array is inserted into the first array.

- If the second value has a key that is also in the first array, then the value from the second array replaces the value in the first array.

---

[10]https://php.net/manual/en/function.array-diff.php
[11]https://php.net/manual/en/function.array-udiff.php
[12]https://php.net/manual/en/function.array-udiff-assoc.php
[13]https://php.net/manual/en/function.array-diff-uassoc.php

Let's step through an example of using array_replace():

```php
<?php
$input = ['a', 'b', 'c'];
$replace = [3 => 'd', '1' => 'q'];
$replaceTwo = [2 => 1, 1.3 => 'Z'];
$output = array_replace($input, $replace, $replaceTwo);
echo implode(", ", $output); // a, Z, 1, d
```

I've placed this information into a table so that you can see how the rules are applied. The function works from left to right, replacing each subsequent parameter with the previous array.

Key	$input	$replace	$replaceTwo	$output
0	a			a
1	b	q	Z	Z
2	c		1	1
3		d		d

■ **Note** The string key 1 is cast to an integer and the float key 1.3 is also cast to integer. Both evaluate to 1 and so will replace the value in that position.

The array_merge() function will merge one or more arrays. One might expect that it follows the same rules when merging as the + operator, but there are some situations where it behaves quite differently. Consider this example:

```php
<?php
$arrOne = [
  // integer
  0 => 'One 0',
  // string
  'a' => 'One a',
  // non-empty in One, but empty in Two
  'Overwrite' => 'Not empty',
];

$arrTwo = [
  0 => 'Two 0',
  1 => 'Two 1',
  'b' => 'Two b',
  'Overwrite' => '',
];
```

```
print_r($arrOne + $arrTwo);

print_r(array_merge($arrOne, $arrTwo));
```

I'll show you the output of this code in just a moment. There are two things that you should pay attention to in the code output:

- The array_merge() function reindexes numeric keys, but the operator does not.

- The array_merge() function will not overwrite a non-empty value with an empty value, but the operator will.

As promised, here is the output showing the differences:

```
Array
(
    [0] => One 0
    [a] => One a
    [1] => Two 1
    [b] => Two b
)
Array
(
    [0] => One 0
    [a] => One a
    [1] => Two 0
    [2] => Two 1
    [b] => Two b
)
```

Splitting Arrays

There are several functions that can be used to split up an array. The following table lists them. We'll look at some in detail in the book, but you should make sure that you go through the manual too.

Function	Used To
array_chunk	Split an array into chunks.[14]
array_column	Return a single column from an input array, for example, an array of database query results.
array_slice	Extract an array of the array.

(continued)

---

[14]https://php.net/manual/en/function.array-chunk.php

CHAPTER 4 ■ ARRAYS

Function	Used To
array_splice	Return a slice of the array and replace it with something else in the original array (the argument is called by reference).[15]
extract	Create variables named for the keys of an array that contain the values from the array. Using this function can lead to murky code because it's not immediately clear where a variable is defined.
array_rand	Pick random keys of an array.

Of these functions, the only potentially tricky one is array_splice(). Not only does it return a value (the slice that was extracted), but because the input array is passed by reference, it also affects the array you call it on.

To add further complication, you are optionally able to replace the slice that you extract from the input array with a replacement array.

Let's look at an example:

```php
<?php
$input = [1,2,3];
$replacement = ['hello', 'world'];
// $slice contains the piece we extract
$slice = array_splice($input, 1, 1, $replacement);
// $input is passed by reference and so is amended
print_r($input);
```

This script looks for a slice of the input array that starts at position 1 and is of length 1. We know that arrays are zero based, so position 1 has the value 2. The array_splice() function returns an array of the piece that was found. Therefore, $slice will be an array with a single element containing the value 2.

The input array argument to array_splice() is passed by reference and so will be modified by the function. We replace the slice that we extract with the replacement array.

The output of the script is therefore:

```
Array
(
    [0] => 1
    [1] => hello
    [2] => world
    [3] => 3
)
```

---

[15]https://php.net/manual/en/function.array-slice.php

Destructuring Arrays

The list() language construct is used to assign variables from an array based on their indexes. Here is a basic example of its usage:

```php
<?php
$array = ['one', 'two', 'three'];
list($a, $b, $c) = $array;
echo $a; // one
echo $b; // two
echo $c; //three
```

PHP 7 introduced a syntax change for list() that makes it behave more consistently when you're creating an indexed array. In PHP 7, the variables are assigned in the order you write them, whereas in PHP 5, they're assigned in reverse order. That will make more sense if you see an example:

```php
<?php
$array = ['one', 'two', 'three'];
list($indexedArray[0], $indexedArray[1], $indexedArray[2]) = $array;
var_dump($indexedArray);
```

In PHP 7, this will output:

```
array(3) {
  [0]=>
  string(3) "one"
  [1]=>
  string(3) "two"
  [2]=>
  string(5) "three"
}
```

In PHP 5, the order is reversed and this outputs:

```
array(3) {
  [2]=>
  string(5) "three"
  [1]=>
  string(3) "two"
  [0]=>
  string(3) "one"
}
```

Calculating with Arrays

PHP offers several convenience functions that let you perform mathematical calculations on arrays without needing to iterate through them manually.

Function	Returns
array_count_values	How many times each unique value in the array appears
array_product	The product of all the values in the array
array_sum	The sum of all the values in the array
count	How many elements there are in the array
sizeof	This is an alias of count()

■ **Note** The product of an empty array is 1, not 0.[16]

Iterating Through Arrays

There are two ways to iterate through an array—by using a cursor and by looping through the array.

Looping Through Arrays

An enumerative PHP array can be looped through by incrementing an index counter, but this won't work for associative arrays. A better and more robust approach is to use the foreach() construct.

It lets you quickly look at two possible syntaxes that foreach() uses and then move on. You should already be familiar with its usage if you're considering sitting for your exam, so this is for the benefit of programmers from other languages.

```php
<?php
$arr = [
    'a' => 'apple',
    'b' => 'banana',
    'c' => 'cherry'
];
foreach($arr as $value) {
    echo $value . PHP_EOL;
}
foreach($arr as $key => $value) {
    echo $key . ' = ' . $value . PHP_EOL;
}
```

---

[16]https://en.wikipedia.org/wiki/Empty_product

The first foreach() loop will traverse the array and pass the array values into the code block. The second foreach() loop traverses it and passes the key and value.

By default, PHP the value passed into the code block of a foreach() loop is passed by value. If you change the value in the code block it will not have an effect outside of the code block. You can, however, mark the value to be passed by reference by prefixing it with an ampersand symbol.

■ **Caution**   Generally people will frown at you for using a reference in a foreach() loop.

We'll look at this in the following code example, which also demonstrates that the variable being declared in the foreach block becomes defined in the containing scope. After the loop finishes, it will hold the last value that it had in the loop. Relying on this feature makes your code harder to read, though.

```php
<?php
$arr = [1,2,3];
foreach ($arr as $value) {
    $value += 1;
}
echo implode(', ', $arr) . PHP_EOL;    // 1, 2, 3
echo $value . PHP_EOL;                  // 4
foreach ($arr as &$value) {
  $value += 1;
}
echo implode(', ', $arr) . PHP_EOL;    // 2, 3, 4
echo $value;
```

Since PHP 5.5, the list() construct can be used in foreach() loops to unpack nested arrays. This is particularly useful when dealing with database results.

Here's an example of using a list:

```php
<?php
// assigning to scalars
list($animal, $food, $mood) = ['cat', 'cheeseburgers', 'grumpy'];
echo "{$animal}s eat $food except when they're $mood." . PHP_EOL;

// assigning to an array
$info = [];
list($info[0], $info[1], $info[2]) = ['cat', 'cheeseburgers', 'grumpy'];
var_dump($info);

/*
cats eat cheeseburgers except when they're grumpy.
array(3) {
  [0]=>
```

```
    string(3) "cat"
    [1]=>
    string(13) "cheeseburgers"
    [2]=>
    string(6) "grumpy"
}
*/
```

> ■ **Note**   The each keyword, which could also be used to loop through an array, is
> deprecated in PHP 7.2.0 (so don't use it in PHP 7.1 either)

Using Array Cursors

Every array has a cursor, or pointer, that points at the current element. A number of PHP
functions use the cursor to determine which element to operate on.

Here are the basic cursor functions:

Functions	Performs
reset	Moves the cursor to the beginning of the array[17]
end	Moves the cursor to the end of the array
next	Advances the cursor[18]
prev	Advances the cursor
current	Returns the value of the element the cursor points at
key	Returns the key of the element the cursor points at

Objects can be iterated over using the same syntax, but it's important to know that
they implement an interface iterator.

A less commonly seen use of a cursor is one such as this:

```php
<?php
$arr = [
  'a' => 'apple',
  'b' => 'banana',
  'c' => 'cherry'
];
while (list($var, $val) = each($arr)) {
  echo "$var is $val" . PHP_EOL;
}
```

---

[17]https://secure.php.net/manual/en/function.reset.php
[18]https://secure.php.net/manual/en/function.next.php

list() is a language construct that assigns variables from a supplied array. The each() function returns the current key and value pair from an array and advances the array cursor.

Walking Through Arrays

The array_walk() function applies a user callable to every element in an array. It takes two parameters—a reference to the array and the callable.

The callable function will be passed two parameters. The first is the value of the element from the array and the second is its index.

Some internal functions, such as strtolower() for example, will throw a warning if they receive too many parameters and so are not suitable as a callback for array_walk().

■ **Note**   If you need your callback function to alter the value of the array, you should make sure to pass the first parameter by reference.

Here is an example that will convert all the elements of an array to uppercase:

```php
<?php
$arr = [
  'a' => 'apple',
  'b' => 'banana',
  'c' => 'cherry'
];
array_walk($arr, function(&$value, $key) {
  $value = strtoupper($value);
});
print_r($arr);
```

Note that I pass the value by reference into my lambda function, so changing it in the lambda will affect the $arr variable.

If we had used strtoupper() as a callback, PHP would generate warnings. As an exercise try to work out why this is so.

Sorting Arrays

PHP offers several sort functions.

They follow a naming convention whereby the base sort function is prefixed with r for reverse and a for associative.

All sort functions take a reference to the array as their parameter and return a Boolean value indicating success or failure.

Function	Used For
sort	Sorting arrays alphabetically
rsort	Reverse alphabetical sort
asort	Associative sort
arsort	Reversed associative sort
ksort	Key sort
krsort	Reverse key sort
usort	User-defined comparison function for sorting
shuffle	Pseudo-random sort

The associative sorts will sort by value and maintain the index association. Look at one of their manual pages[19] for an example.

All of the functions (except usort()) accept an optional parameter to indicate the sort flag. These flags are predefined constants:

Flag	Meaning
SORT_REGULAR	Compare items normally; don't change types.
SORT_NUMERIC	Cast items to numeric values and then compare.
SORT_STRING	Cast items to strings and then compare.
SORT_LOCALE_STRING	Use locale settings to cast items to strings.
SORT_NATURAL	Use natural order sorting, like the function natsort().
SORT_FLAG_CASE	Can be combined with SORT_STRING and SORT_NATURAL to sort strings case-insensitively.

Natural Order Sorting

Natural ordering is a sort order that makes sense to human beings. It is an alphabetic sort order, but multiple digits are treated as a single character.

The function natsort() does not take flags and is the same as sort() with the SORT_NATURAL flag set.

As an example, let's start with a string that looks sorted to our human eyes, shuffle it, and then use both forms of sorting to see how it comes out:

```php
<?php
$a = $b = explode(' ', 'a1 a2 a10 a11 a12 a20 a21');
shuffle($a);
shuffle($b);
```

---

[19]https://php.net/manual/en/function.asort.php

```
natsort($a);
sort($b);
print_r($a);
print_r($b);
```

Note that I've used the explode function to break up a string into an array. This outputs:

```
Array
(
    [5] => a1
    [2] => a2
    [0] => a10
    [4] => a11
    [6] => a12
    [3] => a20
    [1] => a21
)
Array
(
    [0] => a1
    [1] => a10
    [2] => a11
    [3] => a12
    [4] => a2
    [5] => a20
    [6] => a21
)
```

Standard PHP Library (SPL): ArrayObject Class

The SPL library includes the ArrayObject class that allows you to create objects from arrays. These objects can use the methods of the ArrayObject class, which are listed on the manual page.

This lets you work with arrays as objects, as in this example from the PHP Manual[20]:

```
<?php
$fruits = array("d" =>"lemon", "a" =>"orange", "b" =>"banana", "c"
=>"apple");
$fruitArrayObject = new ArrayObject($fruits);
$fruitArrayObject->ksort();
foreach ($fruitArrayObject as $key => $val) {
  echo "$key = $val\n";
}
```

---

[20]http://php.net/manual/en/class.arrayobject.php

When constructing an ArrayObject, you pass in an input that can be either an array or an object.

You can also optionally specify flags:

Flag	Effect
ArrayObject::STD_PROP_LIST	Properties of the object have their normal functionality when accessed as a list (var_dump, foreach, etc.).
ArrayObject::ARRAY_AS_PROPS	Entries can be accessed as properties (read and write).[21]

These flags can be set with the setFlags() method, as in this example from the manual:

```php
<?php
// Array of available fruits
$fruits = array("lemons" => 1, "oranges" => 4, "bananas" => 5, "apples" =>
10);

$fruitsArrayObject = new ArrayObject($fruits);

// Try to use array key as property
var_dump($fruitsArrayObject->lemons);
// Set the flag so that the array keys can be used as properties of the
ArrayObject
$fruitsArrayObject->setFlags(ArrayObject::ARRAY_AS_PROPS);
// Try it again
var_dump($fruitsArrayObject->lemons);
```

This example will output:

```
NULL
int(1)
```

CHAPTER 4 QUIZ

Q1: Are PHP keys case-sensitive? What will the output of this script be?

```php
<?php
$arr1 = ["A" => "apple", "B" => "banana"];
$arr2 = ["a" => "aardvark", "b" => "baboon"];
echo count($arr1 + $arr2);
```

---

[21]https://secure.php.net/manual/en/class.arrayobject.php

This produces an error

2

4

None of the above

Q2: What will this script output?

```php
<?php
$arr = [
  'a' => 'apple',
  'b' => 'banana',
  'c' => 'cherry'
];
$keys = array_keys($arr);
if (in_array($keys, 'a')) {
  echo "Found";
}
```

Found

Nothing

Warning: in_array() expects parameter 2 to be array

None of the above

Q3: What will this script output?

```php
<?php
$birds = ['duck', 'chicken', 'goose'];
$net = ['dog', 'cat', 'chicken', 'goose', 'hamster'];
echo count(array_intersect_assoc($net, $birds));
```

0

1

2

3

None of the above

Q4: What will this script output?

```php
<?php
// Array of available fruits
$fruits = array("lemons" => 1, "oranges" => 4, "bananas" => 5,
"apples" => 10);
$fruitsArrayObject = new ArrayObject($fruits);
$fruitsArrayObject->setFlags(ArrayObject::ARRAY_AS_PROPS);
// Try to use array key as property
var_dump($fruitsArrayObject->lemons);
```

This produces an error

int(1)

string(6) "lemons"

None of the above

Q5: What will this script output?

```php
<?php
$a = array('one','two');
$b = array('three','four','five');
echo count($a + $b);
```

This produces an error

2

3

5

Q6: What will this script output?

```php
<?php
$a = array('three','four','five');
$b = array('one','two');
echo count($a - $b);
```

This produces an error

3

2

1

Q7: What is the output of the following code?

```php
<?php
$source = '12,23,34';
$arr = str_split($source, 2);
echo count($arr);
```

This produces an error

2

3

4

Q8: What will this code output?

```php
<?php
$keys = range(1, 6, 2);
$arr = array_fill_keys($keys, 'PHP');
krsort($arr);
$arr = array_flip($arr);
echo $arr['PHP'];
```

There is an error in calling krsort()

There is an error in calling array_flip()

You cannot reference the key 'PHP' because there is more than one of them in the array

1

5

6

Q9: What will this code output?

```php
<?php
$array = [
  [1, 2],
  [3, 4],
];
foreach ($array as list($a, $b)) {
  echo "A: $a; B: $b" . PHP_EOL;
}
```

A: 1; B: 2
A: 3; B: 4
Notice: Undefined offset: 1
Undefined variable $a
None of the above

Q10: What will this code output?

```php
<?php
$arr = [1,2,3,4,5];
$spliced = array_splice($arr, 2, 1);
$number = array_shift($arr);
echo $number;
```

This produces an error

1

3

5

CHAPTER 5

Object-Oriented PHP

Object-oriented code runs slower than procedural code but makes it easier to model and manipulate complex data structures. PHP has supported object-oriented programming since version 3.0 and since then it's object model has been extended and reformed extensively.

This book is not going to try to teach object-oriented programming but will rather focus on the PHP implementation. It's expected that you have at least some experience coding in PHP.

■ **Tip** This is one of the three most important sections of your certification examination.

Declaring Classes and Instantiating Objects

Classes are declared using the class keyword.

```php
<?php
class ExampleClass
{
    // class code
}
```

Classes can be named using the same rules as variables. Your coding standards will determine the case convention you use.

To instantiate an object from a class, you use the new keyword:

```php
<?php
$exampleObject = new ExampleClass();
// If you are not passing constructor parameters you can omit the brackets
if you choose
$anotherObject = new ExampleClass;
```

© Andrew Beak 2017
A. Beak, *PHP 7 Zend Certification Study Guide*,
https://doi.org/10.1007/978-1-4842-3246-0_5

We'll deal with the details later, but the following summary reference table shows the syntax and limitations for inheritance and traits.

Concept	Syntax	Limitation
Inherit from a class	`class A extends A_Parent`	Class may have only one parent
Interface inheritance	`Interface A extends B, C`	Interface can inherit multiple interfaces
Inherit from an abstract class	`Interface A extends B, C`	Interface can inherit multiple interfaces
Implement interface	`class A implements A_Interface`	Class can implement multiple interfaces
Trait	`class Foo { use A_trait; }`	Class can use multiple traits

Object assignment is always by reference.

Notice in the following example how when we change the property in the copied object, the original object also changes. In fact, the two variables occupy the same space in memory because a reference is a pointer to the original data. We don't make an entire new copy of the object.

```php
<?php
$a = new stdClass();
$a->property = "Hello World";
// object assignment is by reference
$b = $a;
$b->property = "Assigned by reference";
// $a has also changed because $b is a pointer to $a
var_dump($a);
/*
object(stdClass)#1 (1) {
  ["property"]=>
  string(21) "Assigned by reference"
}
*/
```

We'll look at this in more detail later when we learn about the clone keyword in the section on "Working with Objects".

Autoloading Classes

Classes should be defined before they are used, but you can use autoloading to load classes when they are required. Together with coding standards like PSR4 that govern where PHP will look for a class, this can be an indispensable feature.

■ **Tip**   You won't be asked questions about PSR4 in the Zend examination, but the standards put forward by the FIG group are very important in the PHP world.

Autoloading in PHP is accomplished the the the `spl_autoload_register()` function. A PSR4 compliant implementation is given on the PHP FIG group web page,[1] but let's look at a simpler demonstration from the PHP manual[2] for an example:

```php
<?php
function my_autoloader($class) {
  include 'classes/' . $class . '.class.php';
}

spl_autoload_register('my_autoloader');

// Or, using an anonymous function as of PHP 5.3.0
spl_autoload_register(function ($class) {
  include 'classes/' . $class . '.class.php';
});
```

Using `spl_autoload_register()` lets you specify what function PHP will call if it is unable to load a class. You can include files in this function and so declare the class. If PHP is unable to find the class after this function has run, then it will throw a fatal error.

Visibility or Access Modifiers

The visibility of a method or property can be set by prefixing the declaration with `public`, `protected`, or `private`.

- Public class members can be accessed from anywhere.

- Protected class members can be accessed from within the class and by its children.

- Private class members can only be accessed from within the class itself.

If you don't explicitly specify a visibility then it will default to `public`.

Interfaces can only include `public` methods. Any class that implements the interface must match the visibility of the method and so these methods will be public in it too.

Methods in `abstract` classes may have any visibility. A method in a class that extends an abstract class must have the same or less restrictive visibility.

---

[1]http://www.php-fig.org/psr/psr-4/examples/
[2]https://php.net/manual/en/function.spl-autoload-register.php

Instance Properties and Methods

Concrete objects that you create from classes are also known as *instances*. When you create an object from a class, you are said to *instantiate* the object. This section focuses on properties and methods, which belong to objects. We'll be looking at what these are, how PHP syntax works, the naming rules, and how to use them.

Properties

Class properties are declared by using one of the visibility modifiers followed by the name of the property. Property names follow the same naming rules as variables.

```php
<?php
class Properties
{
    // You do not have to specify a default value
    public $email;
    // A scalar value is an expression
    protected $name = 'Alice';
    // An array is an expression
    protected $accounts = ['cheque', 'savings'];
    // You can use a constant expression as a default value
    private $balance = 60 * 5;
}
```

Properties can be initialized to default values. They can be initialized with expressions, but not functions.

```php
<?php
class BrokenPropertyInit
{
    private $lastLogin = time();  // won't run
}
```

This example won't run because you cannot initialize the class property using a function.

Methods

Methods are functions within a scope construct. They are declared in a function by using a visibility modifier followed by the function declaration. If you omit a visibility modifier, the method will have public visibility.

```php
<?php
class MethodExample
{
  private $name;

  // explicitly specified visibility
  public function setName($name) {
      $this->name = $name;
  }

  // public visibility by default
  function getName($name) {
      return $this->name;
  }
}
```

Methods can access non-static object properties using the $this pseudo-variable. The $this pseudo-variable is defined in objects and refers to the object itself.

Static methods are declared without an object having been instantiated and so $this is not available.

Static Methods and Properties

Declaring a method or property as static makes it available without needing a concrete implementation of the class.

Because a static method can be called without an instantiated object, the pseudo-variable $this is not accessible in these methods. Static methods and properties may have any visibility modifier applied to them.

You should not call a non-static method statically. This will generate a deprecation warning:

```php
<?php
class A
{
  // this is not a static method
  public function sayHello()
  {
    echo "Hello World";
  }
}
// Deprecated: Non-static method A::sayHello() should not be called
statically
A::sayHello();
```

Referencing a static property or method is done using the scope resolution operator, which is a double-colon.

```php
<?php
class MyClass
{
    // Static functions are declared with the static keyword
    public static function sayHello() {
        echo "Hello World" . PHP_EOL;
    }

    public function someFunction() {
        // self refers to "this class", like $this refers to an object
        self::sayHello();
    }
}
// Static functions can be accessed with the scope resolution operator.
MyClass::sayHello(); // Hello World
$object = new MyClass();
$object->someFunction(); // Hello World
```

When we reference a static property from within the class, we can use self, parent, or static to refer to it. We'll deal with the static keyword in the section on "Late Static Binding" in this chapter.

When referencing the static class member from outside the class, you prefix the scope resolution operator with the name of the class. In the previous example, we referenced the static function with MyClass::sayHello().

Static Properties

Static properties are also declared with the static keyword and can be accessed with the scope resolution operator.

For example:

```php
<?php
class Foo
{
  // Static properties are declared with the static keyword
  private static $message = 'Hello World';

  public function __construct() {
    // Static properties can be accessed with the scope resolution operator.
    echo self::$message;
  }
}
$foo = new Foo;      // Hello World
echo Foo::$message; // PHP Fatal error: Cannot access private property
        Foo::$message
```

In this example, we access the static property in the constructor using the self keyword. As a demonstration that static properties can have any visibility applied to them, we attempt to access it from outside the class and receive a fatal error.

Working with Objects

This is a very important section of this chapter and you should pay close attention to the details. We'll be introducing the difference between a "shallow" and a "deep" copy and looking at how array variables are cast into other variable types. We'll see how to store an object for later use (or to pass it to another program) and also look at some tricks that you can play by aliasing class names.

Copying Objects

Just like with assignment, PHP always passes objects by reference. Instead of making a whole copy of the object, we rather just say "the data can be found at this location". We deal more with PHP memory allocation in the "Memory Management" section of this book.

If you want to create a copy of the object, you must use the clone() keyword.

```php
<?php
// creating a shallow copy of an object
$objectCopy = clone $originalObject;
```

PHP will create a shallow copy of the object. In a shallow copy, if the source contains references to variables or other objects, then those references are copied into the new object. This means that the original and cloned object share a reference to the same target object.

By contrast, a deep copy creates new versions of referenced objects and inserts references to these into the cloned object. This is slower and more expensive because it involves creating a lot more objects. The cloned object will contain references to new copies of objects that the original references.

When cloning an object, PHP will try to execute the __clone() method in the object. You can override this method to include your own behavior for cloning an object. This method cannot be called directly.

■ **Tip** If you want a deep clone of an object, you can implement this logic in the magic method __clone().

Serializing Objects

Object serialization is accomplished with the serialize() and unserialize() functions. These functions support any type of PHP variable, except for resources.

When an object is serialized, PHP will try to call the __sleep() method on it, and when it is unserialized the __wakeup() function is called. These are magic methods and you can implement them in your class to alter how PHP handles these events.

Serializing an object gives a byte-stream representation of any value that can be stored in PHP. Resources cannot be serialized. Strings in PHP can contain byte streams, so you can place serialized objects into them.

The string will refer to the class of the object serialized and will contain all the variables associated with it. References to anything outside of the object cannot be stored and will be lost, but circular references to anything inside the object will be retained.

When you unserialize the object, PHP must have the class declared. If it does not have the class defined, it will be unable to make an object of the correct type and will instead create one of type __PHP_Incomplete_Class_Name, which has no methods.

Here is a simple example where we serialize and unserialize an object.

```php
<?php
$objectOriginal = new A;
$string = serialize($objectOriginal);
file_put_contents('serialize.txt', $string);
// in another PHP file
$string = file_get_contents('serialize.txt');
$objectCopy = unserialize($string);
```

There are a lot of potential security problems around serializing objects. We deal with them in Chapter 6 on security, but it's worth keeping this in mind when you look at the second (optional) argument for unserialize. This argument helps to mitigate an attack where an opponent can change the value of the parameter that is passed to unserialize().[3]

The second argument for unserialize lets you specify what PHP should be willing to unserialize. It is security best practice to always use it.

Value	Meaning
Omitted	PHP can instantiate objects of any class
FALSE	Do not accept any classes
TRUE	Accept all classes
Array of class name	Accept only the classes specified
Any other value	Unserialize() will return false and issue an E_WARNING

---

[3]https://www.owasp.org/index.php/PHP_Object_Injection

Here's a more comprehensive example of how to unserialize an object in PHP:

```php
<?php
class A {
    public function __wakeup() {
        echo "Good morning";
    }
};
class B {}
$a = new A();
$stored = serialize($a);
unset($a);
// this works because the class name is allowed
$a = unserialize($stored, ['allowed_classes' => [A::class]]);
// this creates __PHP_Incomplete_Class because the class doesn't match
$b = unserialize($stored, ['allowed_classes' => [B::class]]);
// this creates __PHP_Incomplete_Class because no classes are allowed
$c = unserialize($stored, ['allowed_classes' => false]);
// this works because all classes are allowed
$d = unserialize($stored, ['allowed_classes' => true]);
// this generates a warning because the parameter type is incorrect
$e = unserialize($stored, ['allowed_classes' => 'Not boolean or array']);
```

■ **Caution**   Do not use serialize() to pass data to the user. Rather use json_encode! Why not? Because of the mantra "all user input is potentially evil". You don't want to give users the chance to run their code through unserialize().

Casting Between Arrays and Objects

We covered casting variables in the chapter on PHP basics. We should note that it is also possible to use the same syntax to cast between an array and an object. Let's look:

```php
<?php
$array = [
    'key' => 'value',
    'nested_array' => [
        'another_key' => 'different_value'
    ]
];
$object = (object)$array;
var_dump($object);
```

In this example, I used the (object) casting syntax to force the array to become an object. PHP will produce an object of StdClass that has properties corresponding to the keys of the array. This code outputs:

```
object(stdClass)#1 (2) {
  ["key"]=>
  string(5) "value"
  ["nested_array"]=>
  array(1) {
    ["another_key"]=>
    string(15) "different_value"
  }
}
```

■ **Note**   The nested array is not converted to a nested object.

It is possible to cast an object to an array using the (array) casting syntax. If we were to run the command assert((array)$object === $array); at the end of that code listing, the code would complete without errors because the assertion passes.

Casting Objects to String

You can define how your object will be cast to string by declaring the __toString() method. PHP will call this method and return its result when it tries to cast your object to a string.

```php
<?php
class User
{
    private $firstName = 'Example';
    private $lastName = 'User';
    function __toString() {
        return $this->firstName;
    }
}
$user = new User;
// 'echo' expects a string type so PHP will implicitly cast the object to string
echo $user; // Example
```

This lets you build and format a string that is meaningful for your object. If you do not declare this method on your object, then PHP will generate a catchable fatal error telling you that it cannot convert an object to a string.

Class Aliases

PHP allows you to create aliases for classes using the class_alias() function. This function accepts three parameters—the original class name, the alias to create for it, and an optional Boolean value to indicate if the autoloader must be called if the class is not found.

At first blush, it may not be immediately apparent what the use-case for aliasing a class might be. Their chief use-case is for conditionally importing namespaces.

The use keyword is processed at compile time and not run time. This means that it is impossible to use conditional logic to change which namespaces to import. The class_alias() function lets you conditionally import namespaces.

For example, you may want to swap which class to use to cache your database depending on whether the memcached extension is available. In the following code, we would not be able to import alternative classes with the use keyword, but by using class aliasing, we can change the class that cache refers to.

```php
<?php
if (extension_loaded('memcached')) {
    class_alias('Memcached', 'Cache');
} else {
    class_alias('InternalCacheProvider', 'Cache');
}
class Database
{
    // The cache class is aliased to either Memcached or the
    InternalCacheProvider
    public function __construct(Cache $cache) {}
}
```

Constructors and Destructors

A *constructor* is a method that is run when an object is instantiated from a class. Similarly, a *destructor* is made when the object is being unloaded.

They are declared as in this example:

```php
<?php
class constructorExample
{
  // called when instantiated
  public function __construct() {

  }
  // called when unloaded
  public function __destruct() {

  }
```

121

```
// PHP4 style constructor - deprecated in PHP7

public function constructorExample() {

}

}
```

Constructor Precedence

In PHP 4, constructor methods were identified by having the same name as the class they were defined in. This form of constructor is deprecated in PHP 7.

```php
<?php
class constructorExample
{
  // PHP4 style constructor - deprecated in PHP7
  public function constructorExample() {
    echo "Constructed!";
  }
}
$test = new constructorExample;
```

For backward compatibility, PHP 7 will search for a function with the same name as the class if it cannot find a __construct() function. This functionality is deprecated in PHP 7 and will be removed in future PHP versions.

If we construct an object from this class, we don't receive a deprecation warning. Why not? PHP 7.1 looks for a modern style constructor first, and if it is present, it will call it. If there is no modern constructor, PHP 7.1 will look for a deprecated constructor and if it is present it will generate a warning and call it.

Constructor Parameters

If a class constructor takes a parameter, you need to pass it in when instantiating an instance of the class.

```php
<?php
class User {
  public function __construct($name) {
      $this->name = $name;
      }
}
$user = new User('Alice');
```

Here we are passing string "Alice" to the constructor function. A practical example of this would be for dependency injection.[4]

Inheritance

PHP supports inheritance in its object model. If you extend a class then the child class will inherit all of the non-private properties and methods of the parent class. In other words, the child will have the public and protected elements of the parent class. You can override them in the child class, but they will otherwise have the same functionality.

PHP does not support inheriting from more than one class at a time.

The syntax to cause a class to inherit is very simple. When declaring the class, we simply indicate the name of the class it is extending, as in this example:

```php
<?php

class ParentClass
{
    public function sayHello() {
        echo __CLASS__;
    }
}

class ChildClass extends ParentClass
{
    // nothing in this class
}

$kid = new ChildClass;
$kid->sayHello(); // ParentClass
```

In this example, the ChildClass is declared as extending the ParentClass. It inherits the sayHello() method.

If we were to define a GrandChildClass that inherits from the ChildClass then it too would inherit all the ParentClass methods. In fact, any class in an inheritance chain will inherit all the methods and properties of its ancestors.

■ **Note** The magic constant __CLASS__ gives the name of the class that is currently being executed. We're calling the inherited method in the child class, but it is executing the function in the parent class and so reporting that the class name is ParentClass.

---

[4]https://en.wikipedia.org/wiki/Dependency_injection

The final Keyword

PHP 5 introduced the final keyword. You can apply it either to a whole class, or to specific methods within a class. The effect of the final keyword is to prevent classes from being extended or methods from being overridden. The visibility of all final properties and methods is public.

Marking classes or functions as final helps you avoid mistakenly changing behavior when you extend a class.

PHP will issue a fatal error if you try to override a final method in a child class or if you try to declare a class that extends a class that is marked final.

You mark a class or method as final by using the final keyword in front of its definition, like this example where I'm marking the function as final:

```php
class Employee
{
    final public function calculateWage(float $hourlyRate, int
    $numHoursWorked)
    {
        return $hourlyRate * $numHoursWorked;
    }
}
```

Let's look at another example that shows the error produced and highlights the usefulness of the keyword.

The code listing in the following example does not have any uses of the final keyword and so will run without error and calculate a rather generous wage packet for the employee. I've commented two lines to show the error that will be thrown if we mark the class or method as final, respectively.

```php
<?php
// Fatal error: Class Oops may not inherit from final class (Employee)
final class Employee
{
    \final public function calculateWage(float $hourlyRate, int
    $numHoursWorked)
    {
        return $hourlyRate * $numHoursWorked;
    }
}
// Fatal error: Class CannotExtendFinalClass may not inherit from final
class (Employee)
class Oops extends Employee {
    // Fatal error: Cannot override final method Employee::calculateWage()
    in /in/afkAJ on line 17
    public function calculateWage(float $hourlyRate, int $numHoursWorked) {
        if ($this->employeeName === 'Andrew') {
            return 1000000;
        }
```

```
        return $hourlyRate * $numHoursWorked;
    }
}
$oops = new Oops;
$oops->employeeName = 'Andrew';
echo $oops->calculateWage(10.00, 50);
```

■ **Note**　This is somewhat different from the use of final in Java, the PHP equivalent of the Java final keyword is const.

Overriding

A child class may declare a method with the same name as the parent class, providing that the method is not marked final in the parent.

The method parameter signature in the child must be like the parent; for example, the following code will generate a warning that the child declaration needs to be compatible with the parent:

```php
<?php
class Employee
{
    public function calculateWage(float $hourlyRate, int $numHoursWorked)
    {
        return $hourlyRate * $numHoursWorked;
    }
}

class Oops extends Employee {

    public function calculateWage(int $hourlyRate, int $numHoursWorked) {
        return $hourlyRate * $numHoursWorked;
    }
}
```

If a function is overridden like this and called on the child, then the parent's class will not be called.

This applies to constructors and destructors, but in these cases, this is quite often worked around like this:

```php
<?php
class ChildClass extends ParentClass
{
    public function __construct() {
        parent::__construct();
```

```
        // more constructor functions here
    }
}
```

The call to parent::__construct() will call the constructor method of the parent class. When control flow returns to the child, the remaining functions in its constructor will be called.

If a child overrides a method from a parent class then the child's class cannot have a lower visibility than the parent class.

In other words, if the parent's method is public then the child cannot override the method as being protected or private.

Interfaces

Interfaces allow you to specify what methods a class must implement without specifying the details of the implementation.

They are commonly used to define a contract in the service-oriented architecture paradigm, but can also be used whenever you want to stipulate how future classes are expected to interact with your code.

All methods in an interface must be declared as public and may not have any implementation themselves.

Interfaces cannot have properties, but they can have constants.

Interfaces are declared as in this example:

```php
<?php
interface PaymentProvider
{
    public function showPaymentPage();
    public function contactGateway(array $messageParameters);
    public function notify(string $email);
}
```

A class would be declared as implementing it like this:

```php
<?php
class CreditCard implements PaymentProvider
{
    public function showPaymentPage() {
        // implementation
    }

    public function contactGateway() {
        // implementation
    }
```

```php
    public function notify(string $email) {
        // implementation
    }
}
```

Classes may implement more than one interface at a time by listing the names of the interfaces separated by commas.

Classes may inherit from only one class but may implement many interfaces.

Abstract Classes

PHP supports abstract classes, which are classes that contain one or more abstract methods. An abstract method is a method that has been declared but not implemented.

In the following example of an abstract class, the function girlDescendingStairs() is an abstract method. It is defined using the abstract keyword and does not have any implementation. Notice that there is no code block for the abstract method.

```php
<?php
abstract class Paintings
{
    abstract protected function girlDescendingStairs();
    protected function persistenceOfMemory() {
        echo " I have an implementation so this is not an abstract method ";
    }
    public function __construct() {
        echo "I cannot be constructed!";
    }
}
```

An abstract class cannot be constructed; we cannot create a new object from the class Paintings.

Abstract classes are intended to be extended. A class that extends an abstract class must define all the methods that are marked abstract in the parent class. If the child class does not implement the methods, they must also be marked as abstract, and so the child class will also be abstract.

When a child class extends an abstract class, it must define the abstract methods with either the same or a less restrictive visibility.

The signature of the methods declared in the child class must match the abstract method's signature. This means that the number and type of required (not optional) arguments to the method must be the same.

Private methods cannot be marked as abstract. Let's look at how we can extend the abstract class:

```php
<?php
abstract class Paintings
{
    abstract protected function girlDescendingStairs();
    protected function persistenceOfMemory() {
        echo "I have an implementation so this is not an abstract method";
    }
    public function __construct() {
        echo "I am being constructed!";
    }
}
class Foo extends Paintings {
    public function girlDescendingStairs() { echo "Whee!"; }
}
$foo = new Foo;  // I cannot be constructed!
$foo->girlDescendingStairs();  // Whee!
```

I define a new class which I've imaginatively called Foo that extends the abstract class. I've implemented the abstract method girlDescendingStairs" and I've changed the visibility from protected to the less restricted scope, public. I haven't overwritten the non-abstract methods that the abstract class defined.

The Foo class has no abstract methods and so I can construct an object from it. Notice that when I do so, the parent's constructor is called and so Foo wrongly reports that it cannot be constructed.

Anonymous Classes

PHP 7 introduced anonymous classes, which allow you to define a class on the fly and instantiate an object from it. Here's a simple example of using an anonymous class:

```php
<?php
$object = new class('argument') {
    public function __construct(string $message) {
        echo $message;
    }
};
```

Notice how we define the class inline and that it's possible to pass in arguments using similar syntax as when creating an object from a named class. This code will output the string "argument" because the constructor is called and the string "argument" is passed to it.

One use-case for anonymous objects is to extend a named class; for example, if you want to override a method or property. Rather than having to declare a class in a separate file, you can create a once-off implementation inline.

Reflection

The PHP reflection API allows you the ability to inspect PHP elements at runtime and retrieve information about them.

The Reflection API was introduced with PHP 5.0 and since PHP 5.3 has been enabled by default.

One of the common places that reflection is used is in unit testing. One example of where reflection is useful is in testing the value of a private property in a class. You can use reflection to make the private property accessible and then make assertions.

There are several reflection classes that allow you to inspect specific types of variables. Each of these classes is named for the type of variable you can use it to inspect.

Class	Used to Inspect
ReflectionClass	Classes
ReflectionObject	Objects
ReflectionMethod	Methods of objects
ReflectionFunction	Functions like PHP core functions, or user functions
ReflectionProperty	Properties

The PHP Manual[5] has exhaustive documentation on reflection classes and their methods.

Let's briefly look at an example of using ReflectionClass.

```php
<?php
$reflectionObject = new ReflectionClass('Exception');
print_r($reflectionObject->getMethods());
```

The parameter passed to the constructor of the reflection class is either the string name of the class, or a concrete instantiation (object) of the class.

The ReflectionClass object has a few methods that allow you to retrieve information about the inspected class. In the previous example, we are outputting an array of all the methods that the Exception class has.

Type Hinting

Type hinting allows you to specify the variable type that a parameter to a function is expected to be.

In the following example, we specify that the parameter $arr being passed to the printArray() function must be an array.

---

[5]https://php.net/manual/en/class.reflectionclass.php

```php
<?php
function printArray(array $arr) {
  echo "<pre>" . print_r($arr,true) . "</pre>";
}

// The parameter to the function must be a class that implements the
PaymentProvider interface
function sendNotificationToPaymentProvider(PaymentProvider $paymentProvider)
{
  $paymentProvider->contactGateway($messageParameters);
}

function sayHello(string $name)
{
  echo "Hello " . $name;
}
```

In PHP 5, if you pass a parameter of the wrong type, then a recoverable fatal error will be generated. In PHP 7, a TypeError exception is thrown.

As of PHP 7 type hinting is being referred to as "type declarations". I'm going to use this new nomenclature but the terms are interchangeable within the context of PHP.

You can specify composite types, callables, and scalar variable types as type hints. Additionally, the NULL type hint can be used if NULL is used as the default parameter for a function.

```php
<?php
function nullExample(null $msg = null) {
    echo $msg;
}
```

If you specify a class as a type hint, then all its children and implementations will be valid parameters.

```php
<?php
class A {}
class B extends A {}
class C extends B {}

function foo(A $object) {}
$testObj = new C;
foo($testObj);  // no error produced
```

In this example, our function expects an object of class A. We're passing through an object of class B. Because B inherits from A our code will run.

If the name of the class you supply is an interface, then PHP will allow any object that implements the interface (or is an ancestor of a class that does) to be passed.

Class Constants

A constant is a value that is immutable.

Class constants allow you to define such values on a per-class basis; they do not change between instances of the class. All objects created from that class have the same value for the class constant.

Class constants follow the same naming rules as variables but do not have an $ symbol prefixing them. By convention, constant names are declared in uppercase.

Let's consider an example:

```php
<?php
class MathsHelper
{
    const PI = 4;

    public function squareTheCircle($radius) {
        return $radius * (self::PI ** 2);
    }
}

echo MathsHelper::PI; // 4
```

Class constants are public and so are accessible from all scopes. We use the scope resolution operator and the name of the class it is declared in when we access it from outside the class.

The value must be a constant expression, not (for example) a variable, a property, or a function call.

Class constants, like traditional constants, may only contain scalar values.

Late Static Binding

Late static binding was introduced in PHP 5.3.0 and is a method to reference the called class (as opposed to the calling class) in the context of static inheritance.

The idea was to introduce a keyword that would reference the class that was initially called at runtime, rather than the class that the method was defined in.

Rather than introduce a new reserved word, the decision was made to use the static keyword.

Forwarding calls

A "forwarding" call is a static call that is introduced by parent::, static:: or one called by the function forward_static_call().

A call to self:: can also be a forwarding call if the class falls back to an inherited class because it does not have the method defined.

Late static binding works by storing the class in the last "non-forwarding call". In other words, late static binding resolution will stop at a fully resolved static call.

I am going to take a detailed walk through a modified example of the PHP Manual example.

```php
<?php
class A {
    public static function foo() {
        echo static::who();
    }

    public static function who() {
        return 'A';
    }
}

class B extends A {
    public static function test() {
        A::foo();
        parent::foo();
        self::foo();
    }
}

class C extends B {
    public static function who() {
        echo 'C';
    }
}

C::test(); // ACC
```

The output of ACC might be counter-intuitive at first, but let's step through it slowly.

The call to C::test() is fully resolved and so class C is initially stored as the last non-forwarding call.

There is no test() method in the function C, so the call is forwarded implicitly to its parent. So the test() method in class B is being called.

The Call to A::foo()

The first call in test() specifically names class A as the scope. This means that the call is fully resolved. The class being stored as the last non-forwarding call is changed to be A.

The foo() method in A is called and the static keyword is resolved to find which class to call the who() method on.

The last non-forwarding call was to a class in A and consequently the who() method in class A is called.

The Call to parent::foo()

The next call in test() refers to the parent of B so the call is being explicitly forwarded to the parent of B, which is A.

This is a forwarded call so the value stored as the last fully resolved static call (which is C) is left unaltered.

The foo() method in A is called and the static keyword is resolved to find which class to call the who() method on.

The last non-forwarding call was to a class in C and consequently the who() method in class C is called.

The Call to self::foo()

Class B does not have the foo() method defined and so the call is implicitly passed to the parent, class A.

This is a forwarded call so the stored value stored as the last fully resolved static call (which is C) is left unaltered.

This results in the who() method of class C being called when the static keyword is resolved in class A.

Magic (__*) Methods

PHP treats any method with a name prefixed by two underscores as magical. PHP calls these methods "magically" (without you needing to call them) at certain times of the object's lifecycle. I like to think of them as being similar to hooks that are called on events. PHP calls the magic method when an associated event happens to the object.

PHP does not provide an implementation for the class, and it is up to you as the programmer to override the method in your class.

Magic methods only pertain to classes; they do not exist as stand-alone functions.

There are 15 predefined magical functions and it is recommended to avoid naming other functions with the double underscore prefix.

__get and __set

These magic methods are called when PHP tries to read (get) or write (set) inaccessible properties.

```php
<?php
class BankBalance {
    private $balance;

    public function __get($propertyName) {
        // echo "No property " . $propertyName;
        return "No value";
    }
```

```php
    public function __set($propertyName, $value) {
        echo "Cannot set $propertyName to $value";
    }
}
$myAccount = new BankBalance();
$myAccount->balance = 100;
// Cannot set balance to 100No value
echo $myAccount->nonExistingProperty;
```

The __get() method is passed the name of the property that was being looked for. You can return a value for the missing property in the method, or handle it how you like.

In the example, the commented code can be replaced with logic to handle the missing property, and properties that don't exist will appear to be set to No value.

An additional parameter, the $value, is passed to __set().

__isset and __unset

The __isset() method is triggered by calling the isset() function or empty() on an inaccessible property.

The __unset() method is triggered by calling the unset() function on an inaccessible property.

Both methods accept a string parameter that contains the name of the property that was being passed as a parameter to the function.

You can use these magic methods to allow the isset(), empty(), and unset() functions to work on private and protected properties.

__call and __callStatic

These magic methods are called if you try to call a non-existing method on an object. The only difference is that __callStatic() responds to static calls while __call() responds to non-static calls.

```php
<?php
class Politician {
    public function __call($method, $arguments) {
        echo __CLASS__ . ' has no ' . $method . ' method';
    }
}

$jacob = new Politician();
$jacob->honesty();  // Politician has no honesty method
```

In both cases, the magic method is passed a string containing the name of the method that the call is trying to find, and an array of the arguments that were passed.

__invoke

The magic method __invoke() is called when you try to execute an object as a function.

```php
<?php
class Square
{
    public function __invoke($var) {
        return $var ** 2;
    }
}
$callableObject = new Square;
echo $callableObject(10); // 100
```

■ **Caution**   This syntax may be confused with variable function names so watch out for that.

__debugInfo

This magic method is called by var_dump() when dumping the object to determine which properties should be output.

By default var_dump() will output all public, protected, and private properties of the object.

```php
<?php
class Dictatorship {
    private $wmd = 'Nuke';
    public $oil = 'Lots';

    // we are going to hide our wmd
    public function __debugInfo() {
        return [
            'oil' => $this->oil
        ];
    }
}

$country = new Dictatorship();
var_dump($country);

/*
object(Dictatorship)#1 (1) {
  ["oil"]=>
  string(4) "Lots"
}
*/
```

This example will prevent the $wmd variable from being included in the var_dump().

135

More Magic Functions

We have dealt with the __construct() and __destruct() functions in the section on "Constructors and Destructors".

We have dealt with __sleep() and __wake() in the section on "Serializing Objects".

We looked at __clone() when discussing "Copying Objects" and __toString() in the section named "Casting Objects to String".

Standard PHP Library (SPL)

The standard PHP library is a collection of classes and interfaces that are recipes for solving common programming problems. It is available and compiled in PHP from version 5.0.0.

The classes fall into categories. For a complete list of the classes, refer to the PHP Manual on SPL.[6]

Category	Used for
Data Structures	Standard data structures, like linked lists, doubly linked lists, queues, stacks, heaps, etc.
Iterators	
Exceptions	
File Handling	
ArrayObject	Accessing object with array functions.
SplObserver and SplSubject	Implementing the observer pattern.

SPL also provides several functions. They mostly fall into broad reflection and autoloading categories.

Data Structures

The first category of functions is data structures. If you're familiar with data structures already, you'll be pleased to know that the SPL implements a variety of them. These include doubly linked lists, heaps, arrays, and maps.

Data structures are widely useful in programming algorithms.

Iterators

Iterators allow you to traverse over objects and collections. Iterators maintain a cursor that points to an element.

---

[6]https://php.net/manual/en/book.spl.php

PHP iterators will allow you to advance or rewind the cursor through all of the elements in the container. They will also let you perform other actions, for example, the ArrayIterator will let you perform sorts on arrays.

Without the classes provided by PHP, you would need to implement these iterators yourself, but luckily all of that hard work has been done by the kind authors of PHP.

There's quite an extensive list of iterators. I shouldn't imagine that you'll need to be able to list them, but you should know that they're part of the SPL. They will at a minimum provide cursor movement abilities and possibly some extra functionality.

Exceptions

The SPL also includes standard Exception classes. It's good practice to throw exceptions that are specific to the type of error that has occurred. This makes it easier to code catch blocks that will properly deal with the exception.

The SPL introduces some exception classes that make it a lot more convenient for you to throw specific exceptions.

SPL exceptions fall under two categories—logic exceptions and runtime exceptions. Each of these categories has a number of exception classes that focus on specific sorts of errors that can occur.

You should at least be able to recognize them if they come up in a question.

Logic Exceptions

- LogicException (extends Exception)
- BadFunctionCallException
- BadMethodCallException
- DomainException
- InvalidArgumentException
- LengthException
- OutOfRangeException
- Runtime exceptions
- RuntimeException (extends Exception)
- OutOfBoundsException
- OverflowException
- RangeException
- UnderflowException
- UnexpectedValueException

File Handling

SPL also offers classes to help with handling files.

The SplFileInfo class offers a high-level object-oriented interface to information for an individual file. It has methods that you can use to find the name, size, permissions, and other attributes for a file. You can also tell if the file is a directory, if it's executable, and a lot of other functions.

The SplFileObject class offers an object-oriented interface for a file. You can use it to open and read from a file. There are methods to advance or rewind through the file, seek to specific positions, and other functions that are useful when you're processing a file.

The SplTempFileObject class offers an object-oriented interface for a temporary file. You can use this file as you would any other output file, but it is deleted after your script finishes. You could use this when image processing or verifying file uploads, for example.

ArrayObject

The SPL also includes miscellaneous classes and interfaces. The first of these, the ArrayObject, allows objects to work as arrays.

When you construct an ArrayObject, you can pass an array as its parameter. The resulting object will have methods on it that mimic the PHP array functions.

There are quite a few limitations to the ArrayObject but one of the strengths is that you're able to define your own way of iterating through it.

Observer Pattern

Finally, let's look at two interfaces included in the SPL—SplObserver and SplSubject. Note that these are interfaces and not classes, so you'll need to implement the actual behavior.

Together these two interfaces implement the observer pattern.

The observer pattern is a software design pattern in which an object, called the *subject*, maintains a list of its dependents, called *observers*, and notifies them automatically of any state changes, usually by calling one of their methods. This pattern is mainly used to implement distributed event handling systems.

Using these interfaces will make your code more portable because other libraries will be able to interact with your subject and observers.

Generators

Generators provide you with an easy way to create iterator objects.

The advantage to using an iterator with a generator is that you can build an object that you can traverse over without needing to calculate the entire data set. This saves processing time and memory.

The use-case could be to replace a function that normally returns an array. The function would calculate all the values, allocating an array variable to store them, and return the array.

A generator only calculates and stores one value and yields it to the iterator. When the iterator requires the next value, it calls the generator. When the generator runs out of values, it can either just exit or return a final value.

Generators can be iterated over as with any iterator, as in this example:

```php
<?php
function generator() {
    for ($i = 0; $i < 99; $i++) {
        yield $i;
    }
}

foreach (generator() as $value) {
    echo $value . " ";
}
```

Yield Keyword

The yield keyword is like a function return, except that it is used to yield a value back to the iterator while pausing execution of the generator.

The scope of the generator is maintained between calls. Variables will not lose their value after the generator yields.

```php
<?php
function exampleGenerator() {
    // some functions
    $data = yield $value;
}
```

Yielding with Keys

It is possible to yield key-value pairs that perform as associative arrays for functions using the generator.

If you don't explicitly yield with keys, then PHP will pair yielded values with increasing sequential keys, just as for an enumerative array.

The syntax to yield a key-value pair is similar to declaring associative arrays:

```php
<?php
function myGenerator() {
    // some functions
    yield $key => $value;
}
```

Yielding NULL

Calling yield without an argument causes it to yield a NULL value with an automatic increasing sequential key.

Yielding by Reference

Generator functions can yield variables by reference and the syntax to do so is to prepend an ampersand to the function name.

```php
<?php
function &referenceGenerator() {
    // some functions
    yield $value;
}
```

Returning from a Generator

After your generator has finished processing, you can return a value from it. This makes it more explicit as to what the final value of the generator was.

```php
<?php
function sowCrops() { return 'wheat'; }
function millWheat() { return 'flour'; }
function bake($flour) { return 'cupcake'; }
function generator() {
    $wheat = yield sowCrops();
    $flour = yield millWheat();
    return bake($flour);
};
$gen = generator();
foreach ($gen as $key => $value) {
    echo $key . ' => ' . $value . PHP_EOL;
}
echo $gen->getReturn();
/*
0 => wheat
1 => flour
cupcake
*/
```

This syntax makes it explicit what the return value of the generator was. Without it, you would need to assume that the last yielded value was the return value.

Generator Delegation

Generator delegation let's you delegate the responsibility for processing values to another traversable object or array.

The syntax to do so is yield from <expression>:

```php
<?php
function generator() {
    $a = [1,2,3];
    yield from $a;
    yield from range(4,6);
    yield from sevenAteNine();
}
function sevenAteNine() {
    for ($i=7; $i<10;$i++) {
        yield $i;
    }
}
$gen = generator();
foreach ($gen as $value) {
    echo $value . PHP_EOL;
}
```

In this example, we're using three ways to delegate generation to another traversable object or array.

The result of running this code is to count from 1 to 9.

Traits

Traits were introduced in PHP 5.4.0 and are designed to alleviate some of the limitations of a single inheritance language.

■ **Note**   Traits do not satisfy the "is-a" relationship of true inheritance. If you're familiar with mixins from other languages, they are more similar to those.

A trait contains a set of methods and properties just like a class, but cannot be instantiated by itself. Instead, the trait is included into a class and the class can then use its methods and properties as if they were declared in the class itself.

In other words, traits are flattened into a class and it doesn't matter if a method is defined in the trait or in the class that uses the trait. You could copy and paste the code from the trait into the class and it would be used in the same manner.

The code that is included in a trait is intended to encapsulate reusable properties and methods that can be applied to multiple classes.

Declaring and Using Traits

We use the trait keyword to declare a trait; to include it in a class, we employ the use keyword. A class may use multiple traits.

```php
<?php
trait Singleton
{
    private static $instance;

    public static function getInstance() {
        if (!(self::$instance instanceof self)) {
            self::$instance = new self;
        }
        return self::$instance;
    }
}

class UsingTraitExample
{
    use Singleton;
}

$object = UsingTraitExample::getInstance();
var_dump($object instanceof UsingTraitExample); // true
```

In this example, we declare a trait that includes the methods and properties needed to implement the singleton pattern.

When we want to make a new class follow the singleton pattern, we can do so just by using the trait. We don't have to implement the pattern within the class, and we don't have to include the pattern in the inheritance hierarchy.

Namespacing Traits

PHP will generate a fatal error if traits have conflicting names, but traits may be defined in namespaces.

If you are trying to use the trait in a class that is not in the same namespace hierarchy, then you will need to specify the fully-qualified name when you include it.

Inheritance and Precedence

Traits may not extend other traits or classes, but you can simply use a trait inside another.

Methods declared in a class using a trait take precedence over methods declared in the trait. However, methods in a trait will override methods inherited by a class.

Expressed more simply, precedence in traits and classes is as follows:

Class members > trait methods > inherited methods

Conflict Resolution

PHP will generate a fatal error if two traits attempt to insert a method with the same name unless you explicitly resolve the conflict.

PHP allows you to use the `insteadof` operator to specify which of the conflicting methods you want it to use.

This lets you exclude one of the trait methods, but if you want to keep both methods, you need to use the as operator. The as operator allows you to include one of the conflicting methods, but use a different name to reference it.

Here is a rather long example that shows this usage:

```php
<?php
 trait Dog {
    public function makeNoise() {
        echo "Woof";
    }

    public function wantWalkies() {
        echo "Yes please!";
    }
}

trait Cat {
    public function makeNoise() {
        echo "Purr";
    }

    public function wantWalkies() {
        echo "No thanks!";
    }
}

class DomesticPet
{
    use Dog, Cat {
        Cat::makeNoise insteadof Dog;
        Cat::wantWalkies as kittyWalk;
        Dog::wantWalkies insteadof Cat;
    }
}

$obj = new DomesticPet();
$obj->makeNoise();   // Purr
$obj->wantWalkies(); // Yes please!
$obj->kittyWalk();   // No thanks!
```

■ **Note** It is not enough to use as by itself. You still need to use insteadof to exclude the method you don't want to use, and you can only then use as to make a new way to reference the old method.

Visibility

You can apply a visibility modifier to functions by extending the use keyword, as in this example:

```php
<?php
trait Example {
    public function myFunction() {
        // do stuff
    }
}

class VisbilityExample {
    use Example {
        myFunction as protected;
    }
}

$obj = new VisbilityExample();
$obj->myFunction(); // PHP Fatal error:  Call to protected method
```

We specify that the method should be made protected in the class, even though it is declared as public in the trait. You can include multiple functions in the block, each of which may have its own visibility.

CHAPTER 5 QUIZ

Q1: Which of these is NOT a valid PHP class name?

exampleClass

Example_Class

Example_1_Class

1_Example_Class

They are all valid class names

Q2: What will the property $name contain after this code is run?

```php
<?php
class SleepyHead {
    protected $name = "Dozy";

    public function __serialize() {
        $this->name = "Asleep";
    }

    public function __unserialize() {
        $this->name = "Rested";
    }
}

$obj = unserialize(serialize(new SleepyHead()));
```

Dozy

Asleep

Rested

This code won't run

Q3: Which of the following statements can we replace the commented line with in order for the script to output "Castor"?

```php
<?php
$star = new StdClass;
// replace this line
$star->name = "Castor";
$twin->name = "Pollux";
echo $star->name; // must be Castor
```

$twin = $star;

$twin = clone($star);

$twin &= $star;

$twin = new clone($star);

Q4: Let's say that object A has a property that is an instance of object B. If we clone object A, then will PHP also clone B, which is one of its properties?

Yes

No

You can't clone objects that contain references to other objects

Q5: You cannot declare two functions with the same name. Choose as many as apply.

True

False; you can declare them in different namespaces

False; you can declare them with different number of parameters in their constructor and PHP will pick the definition that matches your instantiation

False; you can declare them in different scopes

Q6: When you call the `json_encode` function on an object to serialize it, which magic method will PHP call?

__sleep

__wake

__get

__clone

None of these

Q7: True or false: Interfaces can only specify public methods, but your class can implement them however you like.

True

False; interfaces can specify any visibility

False; you cannot change the visibility when you implement at all

False; you can only change the visibility to one that is less visible

Q8: What will the output of this code be?

```php
<?php
class World {
    public static function hello() {
        echo "Hello " . __CLASS__;
    }
}

class Meek extends World {
    public function __call($method, $arguments) {
        echo "I have the world";
    }
}
Meek::hello();
```

Hello World

I have the world

An error

None of the above

Q9: The precedence of functions declared in traits, classes, and inherited methods is which of the following?

Inherited methods ➤ trait methods ➤ class members

Class members ➤ trait methods ➤ inherited methods

Class members ➤ trait methods ➤ inherited methods

Trait methods ➤ class members ➤ inherited methods

Q10: True or False: A protected method cannot call private methods, even if they're in the same class.

True

False

CHAPTER 6

Security

Security is a major concern for web applications. Even major organizations such as the United Nations have been hacked using very simple security flaws.

I'm of the opinion that there is no such thing as a completely secure system. My aim when securing an application is two-fold. First, I aim to make it take as long as possible for an attacker to gain access. My next aim is to minimize the value of any information they can retrieve. In other words, I never assume that my system is impenetrable and I always use defense in depth.

This reduces the feasibility of hacking my application for a hacker—it will take a long time to get in, and when they do, they need to expend considerable effort to get any valuable information.

When you are being chased by a tiger you don't need to run faster than the tiger. You just need to run faster than the chap next to you.

Note One of the major flaws in security is social engineering. A discussion of social engineering is not in scope for your Zend exam, but you must always remember that it is not just your code and servers that are entry points to your data.

Configuration

The best approach when configuring PHP is to make sure that you keep up to date with the releases and use the improvements they bring.

You should have a very strong reason if you are not using the most current stable release of PHP in favor of an older version.

Make sure that you keep your operating system patched. Apply security updates regularly and make sure that you keep abreast of security news.

You should apply other package updates only once you've had a chance to make sure they don't negatively affect your stack or test environments. The odds are that the curators of your distro repository will take care not to bork commonly used stacks, but if you're using an uncommon stack or have installed software from outside your repo, then take care when upgrading.

© Andrew Beak 2017
A. Beak, *PHP 7 Zend Certification Study Guide*,
https://doi.org/10.1007/978-1-4842-3246-0_6

Errors and Warnings

You should configure PHP to hide warnings and errors while in production. Errors and warnings can give a person a clue about the internal workings of your code such as directory names and what libraries you are using. This sort of information can help them exploit vulnerabilities in your stack.

You can set error reporting either in your php.ini file or at runtime with the error_reporting() function. Both take a numeric argument, usually in the form of an expression built from the predefined error constants.

These are the recommended production settings, and the PHP 7.1 default[1] production settings:

Setting	Value
display_errors	Off
log_errors	On
error_reporting	E_ALL & ~E_DEPRECATED & ~E_STRICT

These are also the settings that you can assume to be set in your Zend exam, unless of course the question states otherwise.

In development, your error_reporting setting should be E_ALL and your code must run without warnings—don't use deprecated functions.

How the Flags Work

You might be wondering how the flags are set and why we're using bitwise operators on them. I'll try to explain just to make it easier to understand your config settings.

Picture a number in binary format as a series of 1s and 0s. Each position in the binary number is a flag that is associated with an option. If the number in that position is 1, then the flag is on and the option is set.

Now, E_ALL is a number that is chosen so that all the flags associated. If you var_dump(E_ALL), you get the output int(32767), which is 0b111111111111111.

Each of the options is a number chosen to have one and only one bit set. For example, E_NOTICE is 8, which in binary is 0b1000 and E_DEPRECATED is 8192, which in binary is 0b10000000000000. Note that you can pad 8 on the left with as many 0s as you need to make it the same length.

The bitwise operator ~ flips the bits in a number, so ~E_NOTICE is 0b0111.

The bitwise operator & compares the bit positions of two numbers. If both numbers have a bit in the position set, then the result is true. So, E_ALL & ~E_NOTICE has all the bits set, except for the one that says that E_NOTICE is on.

The result is that you set error_reporting to a number that has the bits set for the options you want to be turned on.

---

[1]https://github.com/php/php-src/blob/master/php.ini-production

Disabling Functions and Classes

You can use the disable_functions and disable_classes directives in your php.ini file to prevent functions and classes from being used. These settings can only be set in your php.ini file and cannot be changed at runtime or in directory ini files.

Common functions to disable include those that allow PHP to execute system commands: exec, passthru, shell_exec, and system.

The DirectoryIterator and Directory classes are also commonly disabled as these can be used by an attacker.

■ **Hint**　Disabling these functions is a "blacklisting" approach. An inventive opponent will see this as a hurdle, but not an insurmountable obstacle.

PHP as an Apache Module

If PHP is running as an Apache module, it will be run using the same user as the Apache server. This means that it will have the same permissions and access as the Apache user.

It is best practice to set up a user for Apache rather than run it as "nobody". The Apache user should have limited access to the file system, and should not be on the sudoers list.

You should use the PHP open_basedir setting to limit what directories PHP can access. You can contrast it to the setting doc_root, which affects which directories PHP will serve files from.

■ **Note**　Setting open_basedir is not affected by safe mode, but doc_root is.

If you keep the directory where you store files that are uploaded by users outside of this directory, you can make it much more difficult for an attacker to be able to upload and execute a file.

PHP as a CGI Binary

I don't know if anybody still runs PHP as a CGI binary but the topic is still in the Zend syllabus. I was trying to understand why Zend felt it was important to understand them.

I think that the value of understanding these problems in a legacy configuration is that there are analogs in modern setups. For example, the "Passing Uncontrolled Requests to PHP" configuration flaw[2] seems to be very much alike the trick to bypass permission checking in CGI (covered shortly).

---

[2]https://www.nginx.com/resources/wiki/start/topics/tutorials/config_pitfalls/#passing-uncontrolled-requests-to-php

PHP-FPM runs using the FastCGI protocol, which is an improvement on CGI. This section is not relevant to PHP-FPM, as requests are passed to it over a socket and cannot be influenced by the URL.

For exam purposes, you'll need to know the three configuration parameters and what they do in the context of CGI attacks. I list them here and then explain them in more detail.

Setting	Function
cgi.force_redirect	Prevents PHP from executing unless the web server calls it. If it's set to on, then PHP will not respond to requests like http://yoursite.com/cgi-bin/php/....
doc_root	Sets the document root. If you have safe_mode set to on, then PHP will not serve files that are outside of this directory.
user_dir	Sets the home directory for the web user.

The doc_root and user_dir settings are not exclusively associated with CGI security and should be set as part of your general security settings.

Malicious CGI Parameters

Usually the query information in a URL after the question mark is passed as command-line arguments to the interpreter by the CGI interface. This applies to any binary file being used as a CGI by the web server.

Because of the convention, the URL http://my.host/cgi-bin/php?/etc/passwd would attempt to pass /etc/passwd to the PHP binary. Usually, CGI interpreters open and execute the file specified as the first argument on the command line.

However, PHP refuses to interpret the command-line arguments when invoked as a CGI binary. This makes it immune to attacks that rely on being able to pass a parameter to the binary.

Bypassing Permission Checking

It is common to use "friendly" URLs that send a search engine friendly human-readable URL to a script. For example, the URL https://yourhost.com/user/nico.php might map to an actual request to https://yourhost.com/cgi-bin/php/user/belieber.php.

Normally, the web server will check the permission and verify that the visitor must access the /user/ directory. If the visitor is allowed, it will create the redirected request.

If the visitor accesses the target of the redirect, that is the full URL including cgi-bin, then the web server checks the permission they have to access the /cgi-bin/ directory and not the actual directory that will be served up.

This means that a visitor can bypass the permission check that protects the user directory by simply requesting the file from PHP in cgi-bin. The malicious visitor can access any file on the web server that PHP can read.

The cgi.force_redirect, doc_root, and user_dir directives are used to prevent access to private documents by PHP.

The cgi.force_redirect setting blocks PHP from being able to be called directly from a URL—it will execute only if it is being called on a redirect from a web server like Apache.

When working with PHP as a CGI binary, you should consider moving the PHP binary outside of the document tree and separating your executable PHP scripts from your static scripts.

Running PHP-FPM

PHP-FPM allows you to easily set up multiple pools, each of which can be run under a different user. If you're hosting multiple clients then you should make sure that each client's web site is running as its own user. The client users should not have any access to files outside of their home directory.

Here are some example settings from a pool file:

```
[pool1]
user = site1
group = site1
listen = /var/run/php5-fpm-site1.sock
listen.owner = www-data
listen.group = www-data
```

We are setting the pool named pool1 up to run as the user site1 in the group site1. We set the listening owner and group to be the web server user so that Nginx/Apache can read and write to the socket.

Once we've set the user that the pool runs, we'll configure file permissions to restrict it to only accessing the directory that the web site is in. This will prevent customers from using file-reading functions to read the contents of another customer's directory.

■ **Tip** Some files, such as wp-config.php in a WordPress site, have predictable names and it's very important to protect user directories from other users.

We configure Nginx to pass PHP requests like this:

```
location ~ \.php$ {
  try_files $uri = 404;
  fastcgi_split_path_info ^(.+\.php)(/.+)$;

  if (!-f $document_root$fastcgi_script_name) {
    return 404;
  }
}
```

```
include         fastcgi_params;
fastcgi_index   index.php;
fastcgi_param   SCRIPT_FILENAME $document_root$fastcgi_script_name;
fastcgi_param   SERVER_NAME $host;
fastcgi_pass unix:/var/run/php5-fpm-pool1.sock;
}
```

Each site passes requests to the socket associated with its own pool. The PHP script runs as the user specified in the pool and is locked into the file permissions that we've set for them.

■ **Note**   In our Nginx config, we're including `try_files $uri = 404;` to prevent the attacks mentioned in the Nginx Manual.[3]

An additional layer of security can be obtained by locking each pool into its own `chroot` jail. Remember that you'll need to make sure that files that PHP needs to access (such as log directories or binaries like ImageMagick) are available inside the jail.

Session Security

The two areas of focus that you need to be aware of are "session hijacking" and "session fixation". You should study the PHP Manual page on session security in addition to this chapter.

Session Hijacking

HTTP is a stateless protocol and a web server can be expected to be serving multiple different visitors at the same time.

The server needs to be able to tell clients apart and does so by assigning each client a session identifier. The session identifier can be retrieved by calling `session_id()`. It is created after the `session_start()` function is called.

When the client makes subsequent requests to the server, they provide the session identifier, which allows the server associate the request with a session.

Clients can provide the session either with cookies or with a URL parameter. Cookies are preferable but are not always available. If PHP cannot use a cookie, it will automatically and transparently use the URL, unless you set the `session.use_only_cookies` setting in your `php.ini` file.

It should be apparent that if you are able to present somebody else's session identifier to the server, you can masquerade as that user.

---

[3]https://www.nginx.com/resources/wiki/start/topics/examples/phpfcgi/

Figure 6-1 shows a scenario where malicious user Bob is able to intercept Alice's message to the server. Bad Bob reads the request and extracts the session identifier (which is contained in the cookie headings of the HTTP request). He is then able to present that session identifier to the server, which is now unable to distinguish him from Alice.

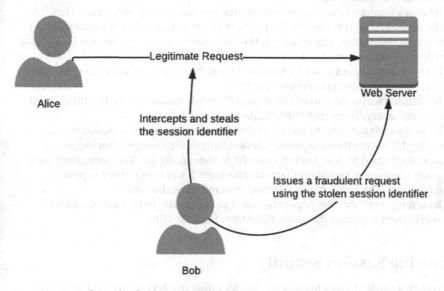

Figure 6-1. Bob steals Alice's session identifier and masquerades as her

Obtaining the session identifier of another user can be accomplished in several ways.

- If the session identifier follows a predictable pattern then the attacker could try to determine what it will be for a user. PHP uses a very random way to generate session identifiers, so you don't need to worry about this.

- By inspecting network traffic between the client and the server, the attacker could read the session identifier. You can set `session.cookie_secure=On` to make session cookies only available over HTTPS to mitigate this. HTTPS will also encrypt the URL being requested, and so if the session identifier is being passed as a parameter in the request, it will be encrypted.

- Attacks made against the client, such as an XSS attack or Trojan program running on their computer, could also reveal the session identifier. This can be partially mitigated by setting the `session. cookie_httponly` directive on.

Forcing PHP to only use cookies will not mitigate an exploit of this attack. The opponent can easily set a cookie value.

155

Session Fixation

Session fixation exploits a weakness in the web application. Some applications do not generate a new session ID for a user when authenticating them. Instead they allow an existing session ID to be used.

The attack occurs when an opponent creates a session on the web server. They know the session ID for this session. They then trick a user into using this session and authenticating themselves. The attacker is then able to use the known session ID and has the privileges of the authenticated user.

There are several ways to set the session ID and the actual method used will depend on how the application accepts the identifier.

The simplest way to do it would be to pass the session identifier in the URL, like this `http://example.org/index.php?PHPSESSID=1234`.

The best way to mitigate the risk of session fixation is to call the function `session_regenerate_id()` every time the privilege level changes, for example after logging in.

You can set `session.use_strict_mode=On` in your config file. This setting will force PHP to only use session identifiers that it creates itself. It will reject a user-supplied session identifier. This will mitigate attempts to manipulate the cookie.

The settings `session.use_cookies=On` and `session.use_only_cookies=On` will prevent PHP from accepting the session identifier from the URL.

Improving Session Security

Don't rely on a single strategy to mitigate attacks, rather use several layers of security. In addition to the mitigation strategies that I have already mentioned, you should also do the following:

- Check that the IP address remains the same between calls. This is not always feasible for mobile phones that move between towers and so change connections, so check your use-cases before you do this.

- Use short session timeout values to reduce the window for fixation.

- Provide a means for users to log out that calls `session_destroy()`.

None of these is particularly effective by itself but each can contribute toward improving your overall security.

Cross-Site Scripting

Cross-site scripting (XSS) attacks are attacks where malicious code is injected onto an otherwise benign site. Usually malicious browser-side code like JavaScript is placed onto the web site to be downloaded and run by clients.

The attack is effective because the client thinks that the code originated from the web site that it trusts. The code can access session identifiers, cookies, HTML storage data, and other information related to the site.

There are a few broad types of XSS attacks: stored, reflected, and DOM.

In a stored XSS attack, the opponent can place input into a stored location on the server. Examples could be In user comments displayed on the site and stored in the database. When the site outputs the list of user comments to another visitor, they would receive the malicious code.

In a reflected XSS attack, the opponent can get the web site to output something directly. The most common form of this attack is a form fill error that prefills the input fields with the previously submitted fields, or outputs the erroneous field value. By sending the visitor to a crafted URL that includes malicious code as an error message (for example), the attacker can trick the client into executing it within the context of the trusted site.

A DOM attack is one that rests entirely within the page. The malicious code is read from an element in the page and the call to the code is made within the page itself.

Furthermore, XSS attacks can be classed either as server-side or client-side attacks. A server-side attack is one where the server delivers the malicious code. Client XSS occurs when untrusted user supplied data is used to update the DOM with an unsafe JavaScript call.

Mitigating XSS Attacks

The most important rule to follow is never allow unescaped data to be output to the client. Always filter data and strip out harmful tags before allowing it to be sent to the client.

■ **Tip**   Remember this mantra "Filter input, escape output".

Three useful functions for this are htmlspecialchars(), htmlentities(), and strip_tags(). Refer to the section entitled "Escape Output" later in this chapter for more details on how to use these functions to help mitigate XSS.

■ **Tip**   The safest method to escape output before displaying it is to use filter_var($string, FILTER_SANITIZE_STRING).

Because of the wide variety of formats that can be used in URLs and HTML to output data, it is not safe to blacklist codes. You should rather whitelist the specific tags that you want to allow. Look at the OWASP filter evasion cheat sheet[4] to see just how many ways there are to evade a blacklist.

You also need to mitigate XSS within your JavaScript on your HTML page, but this is out of scope for this manual.

---

[4]https://www.owasp.org/index.php/XSS_Filter_Evasion_Cheat_Sheet

Cross-Site Request Forgeries

CSRF attacks exploit the trust that a web site has in a client. In these attacks, the opponent tricks the client into executing a command on a web site that trusts that client.

The most common form would be to send a POST request to a form input.

Imagine that Alice is logged onto her bank web site that has a form that allows her to transfer money to another account. Chuck knows the endpoint of that form and what input fields it has. He somehow manages to trick Alice's web browser into sending a POST request to that form instructing the bank to transfer money into his account. The bank trusts Alice's web browser because it has a valid session and performs the request.

There are many ways for Chuck to trick Alice's web browser, including using iframes and JavaScript.

To mitigate these requests, you should generate a unique and very random token that you store in Alice's session. When you output the form, you include this token so that when Alice submits the form, she also submits the token. Before you process the form, you check that the submitted token matches the token stored in her session.

Chuck has no way of knowing what token is in Alice's session and so won't be able to include it in his POST. Your code will reject the request that he tricked Alice into making because it doesn't have a valid token.

Actual banks often require a person to re-authenticate when performing a sensitive operation and will often require two-factor authentication as part of this process.

SQL Injection

SQL injection is the most common form of attack on the web, and one of the easiest to defend against. SQL injection occurs when the attacker can insert malicious commands into a SQL statement for execution by the database.

Many database setups allow the database to write files to disk. This feature allows hackers to create a backdoor by using the database to write PHP scripts to a directory where the web server will serve it.

This means that the effect of SQL injection is not limited to having your database compromised, but could lead to the attacker being able to execute arbitrary code on your database.

At its heart the problem with SQL injection comes from the fact that a SQL statement has a mix of data and syntax. By allowing user-supplied data to be incorporated with function syntax, we create the possibility that malicious data can interfere with the syntax.

Prepared Statements

The most effective way to start to mitigate SQL injection in the PHP language is to exclusively use prepared statements to interact with your database. This will help exclude the majority of SQL injection attacks, but is not sufficient by itself to be foolproof.

Prepared statements are so important that the PDO driver will emulate them if the underlying driver does not support them.

Prepared statements work in three steps:

1. Set up the statement with placeholders for data.

2. Bind actual data to the statement.

3. Execute the prepared statement.

It is possible to bind new data to a statement that you have already executed and then run it again with the new statement. The database engine does not have to parse the SQL again, which gives a performance improvement in addition to the security benefits.

This code gives an example of how to prepare, bind, and execute a statement:

```php
<?php
$stmt = $dbh->prepare("SELECT * FROM REGISTRY where name = ?");
$stmt->bindParam(':name', $_GET['name'], PDO::PARAM_STR, 12);
$stmt->execute();
```

■ **Note** The PDO::prepare() function returns an object of type PDOStatement.

We are using the GET variable directly, so we don't need to escape it because it is being bound as a variable with PDOStatement::bindParam() and cannot alter the syntax of the SQL that is going to be run.

Other database drivers in PHP also support prepared statements. Here is an example from the manual for MySQL[5]:

```php
/* Prepared statement, stage 1: prepare */
if (!($stmt = $mysqli->prepare("INSERT INTO test(id) VALUES (?)"))) {
  echo "Prepare failed: (" . $mysqli->errno . ") " . $mysqli->error;
}

/* Prepared statement, stage 2: bind and execute */
$id = 1;
if (!$stmt->bind_param("i", $id)) {
  echo "Binding parameters failed: (" . $stmt->errno . ") " . $stmt->error;
}

if (!$stmt->execute()) {
  echo "Execute failed: (" . $stmt->errno . ") " . $stmt->error;
}
```

---

[5]https://dev.mysql.com/doc/apis-php/en/apis-php-mysqli.quickstart.prepared-statements.html

Escaping

A less effective way to mitigate SQL injection is to escape special characters before sending them to the database. This is more prone to error than using prepared statements.

If you are going to try escaping special characters, you must use the database specific function (e.g., `mysqli_real_escape_string()`) or `PDO::quote()` and not a generic function like `addslashes()`.

General Principles

You should also always connect to the database with a user who has the least amount of privileges that are required for the application to function. Never allow your web application to connect to the database as its root user.

If you host multiple databases on your server, use a different user for each database on your server and make sure that their passwords are unique. This will help prevent a SQL injection attack on one site from affecting the databases of other sites.

Make sure that you're using an up-to-date version of MySQL and enforce the use of a character set in the client DSN. There is a very subtle way to use mismatching character sets in certain vulnerable encoding schemes to deploy a SQL injection; see the second answer (not the accepted one) on this StackOverflow article[6] for an exposition.

Remote Code Injection

Remote code injection is an attack where an opponent can get the server to include and execute their code.

Functions That Evaluate Strings as Code

Certain functions like `eval()`, `exec()`, and `system()` are susceptible to remote code injection exploits. If you are executing a variable that includes user input, they will be able to inject commands using escape characters.

You can mitigate this by using `escapeshellargs()` to escape the arguments passed to the shell command. The `escapeshellcmd()` function will escape the shell command itself.

■ **Tip** If you're not explicitly using these functions, you should disable them in your `php.ini`. It's not foolproof, but it can help.

---

[6]https://stackoverflow.com/a/12202218/821275

The assert() function is used to make sure that a certain condition is true and take some action if it is not. It's useful for debugging, but you should turn it off for production. You can use the assert_options()[7] function to configure how assert behaves and to turn it off.

If you pass a string value to assert() then PHP will evaluate the string as if it were PHP code. This would let an attacker execute code on your server if they could control what argument you pass into assert().

```php
<?php
function rce(string $a) {
    assert($a);
}
rce('print("hello")'); // hello
```

In PHP 7.2, passing a string to assert is deprecated and this code generates a warning but still evaluates the parameter.

Gaming include and require

Both include() and require() allow the possibility of including files specified by URL if the PHP configuration setting allow_url_include is on.

The most common occurrence of this is when people use a GET variable in the URL to determine some dynamic content to include. This is very much an amateur mistake.

For example, a site could have a URL such as http://example.com/index.php?sidebar=welcome and then dynamically include the welcome.php file into the sidebar.

An opponent could provide an URL instead of the "welcome" string and have their own code executed on the server with the same privilege level as the web server user.

To counter this sort of problem, you can turn allow_url_fopen to OFF, use basename() against the variable you are including so that paths are removed, and only include against a whitelist.

```php
<?php
$page = $_GET['page'];
$allowedPages = array('adverts','contacts','information');
if ( in_array($page, $allowedPages) ) {
    include basename($page . '.html');
}
```

---

[7] https://secure.php.net/manual/en/function.assert-options.php

Email Injection

It is possible for users to supply hexadecimal control characters that allow them to change the message body or recipient list.

For example, if your form allows the person to enter their e-mail address as a "from" field for the e-mail, the following string will cause additional recipients to be included as cc and blind carbon copy recipients of the message:

```
sender@example.com%0ACc:target@email.com%0ABcc:anotherperson@emailexample.
com,stranger@shouldhavefiltered.com
```

It is also possible for the attacker to provide their own body, and even to change the MIME type of the message being sent. This means that your form could be used by spammers to send mail.

You can protect against this in a couple of ways.

Make sure that you properly filter input that you use when sending mails. The filter_var() function provides a number of flags that you can use to make sure that your input data conforms to a desired pattern.

```php
<?php
$from = $_POST["sender"];
$from = filter_var($from, FILTER_SANITIZE_EMAIL);
// send the email
```

You could also install and use the Suhosin PHP extension. It provides the suhosin. mail.protect directive that will guard against this.

You could implement a tarpit to slow bots down or trap them indefinitely. Look at msigley/PHP-HTTP-Tarpit on GitHub[8] as an example of a tarpit.

When setting up your mail server, you must make sure it is not configured as an open relay that allows anybody on the Internet to use it to send mail. You should also consider closing port 25 (SMTP) on your firewall so that outside hosts are unable to reach your server.

Filter Input

When approaching security, it is best to plan for the worst-case scenario and assume that all input is tainted, and that all user behavior is malicious. You should only use input that you've manually confirmed to be safe.

It is possible for input to be in a format that will be ignored by a filter and then parsed by the browser. The XSS evasion cheat sheet that I referred to earlier has a great many examples of where special characters are used to evade detection.

---

[8]https://github.com/msigley/PHP-HTTP-Tarpit

It is possible for input to use a non-standard character set that might not be properly understood by filtering functions. You should use the database native filter functions when working with filtering SQL.

PHP has a very robust filtering function, filter_var(), which can be used to perform a number of different filtering and sanitizing operations. You can find a list of the filters in the PHP Manual.

There are also several functions that can be used to check for individual types of strings. They are locale-aware and so will take language characters into account. The functions will return true if the string contains only characters in the filter and false otherwise.

Function	Filters
ctype_alnum()	Alphanumeric characters only
ctype_alpha()	Alphabetic characters only
ctype_cntrl()	String is control characters only
ctype_digit()	String is digits only
ctype_graph()	Only printable characters and space
ctype_lower()	Only lowercase letters
ctype_print()	Printable characters
ctype_punct()	Any printable that's not whitespace or alphanumeric
ctype_space()	Check for whitespace characters
ctype_upper()	Only uppercase letters
ctype_xdigit()	Hexadecimal digits

It is common to perform filtering on the client side, for example using JavaScript in the browser. This is not sufficient and you must filter and validate on the server side as well.

Escape Output

One of the cardinal rules for writing secure PHP code is to filter input and escape output.

Before you emit data, you must make sure that it is safe for the client. Recall how XSS attacks work as an example of why you need to make sure that what you send to the client is properly sanitized.

If the data you send to a client includes instructions for it to execute code, then it will do so blindly. You must make sure that you send only code you intend for the client to execute, and not code injected by an attacker.

As with filtering input, you must not rely on the client to filter output sent to it. Not all clients will have JavaScript enabled, and it's possible for a hacker to bypass client filtering.

The most secure way to filter output is using filter_var() with the FILTER_SANITIZE_STRING flag. There might be use-cases where this is too restrictive for you, in which case you will need to look at functions like htmlspecialchars(), strip_tags(), and htmlentities().

The htmlspecialchars() and htmlentities() functions have similar effects and you should make sure you understand the difference.

The difference is that htmlentities() will encode anything that has an HTML entity representation, whereas htmlspecialchars() will only encode characters that have special significance in HTML.

```php
<?php
$string = '© 1982 Sinclair Research Ltd.';
echo htmlentities($string); // &copy; 1982 Sinclair Research Ltd.
echo PHP_EOL;
echo htmlspecialchars($string); // © 1982 Sinclair Research Ltd.
```

This table shows the characters that will be converted by htmlspecialchars().

Character	Becomes
& (Ampersand)	&
" (Double quote)	"
' (Single quote)	'
< (Less than)	<
> (Greater than)	>

Both functions take a flag as their second parameter. You should make sure that you know at least these three flags as they are important for escaping JavaScript you're outputting:

Flag	Description
ENT_COMPAT	Converts double quotes, not single quotes
ENT_QUOTES	Converts double quotes and single quotes
ENT_NOQUOTES	Does not convert any quotes

When escaping a JavaScript string, you should use the ENT_QUOTES flag.

The encoding of the string can be specified in the third parameter. In PHP 7.1, the default encoding for both functions is UTF-8.

Avoid Log Poisoning

If you're logging error messages, information messages, and the like, you need to take some precautions with what you log.

Obviously, you must never log sensitive information like user passwords or credit cards. If you're passing this to a logging function, then make sure you obfuscate it. So, a credit card number would be a sequence of asterisks in your log file, rather than the actual number.

Make sure that you filter out executable code and personal information before logging it.

You should also be aware of how a log poisoning attack works. The vulnerability rests on your code improperly including local files. If you allow user input to determine which file is included then an attacker could manipulate that input to include a log file. If the log file contains malicious code then it will be interpreted and run.

All that an attacker needs to do is get their code into your log file, which can be very easy to do. For example, they can poison your web server log by crafting a request that will inject a string containing the commands they want to run into the log. As another example of the attacker can SSH onto your server and use malicious code as their username to poison your authentication log file.

To help you understand the impact, let's run through an example of an exploit. Let's assume that your code is running on your localhost and is vulnerable to local file inclusion and accepts the name of an image that needs to be displayed.

First, we use the command nc localhost 80 to connect to the web server. We then issue the following request to the server:

```
GET /<?php passthru($_GET['cmd']); ?> HTTP/1.1
Host: localhost
```

Apache will write a line in the log file that looks something like this:

```
127.0.0.1 - - [08/Apr/2016:13:57:38 +0000]
"GET /<?php system($_GET['cmd']); ?>
HTTP/1.1" 400 226
"<?php passthru($_GET['cmd2']); ?>"
"<?php passthru($_GET['cmd']); ?>"
```

I'm splitting my log entry over multiple lines but obviously in your log file, it will all be on the same line.

The next step of the exploit is to issue a request to the site that includes the log file (this requires there to be such a vulnerability in your site).

```
http://localhost/?file=/var/log/apache2/access.log&cmd=ls -la
```

Quite a lot needs to go wrong for you to be vulnerable to this:

- The web server user needs read access to the targeted log file

- Your code must allow the attacker to include a targeted file

- You cannot have disabled exec, passthru, and system in your configuration

Encryption and Hashing Algorithms

Encryption and hashing are different concepts and you should make sure you understand the difference. Encryption is a two-way operation; you can encrypt and decrypt. Hashing is a one-way operation and by design it is difficult or time-consuming to take a hash and reverse it to the original string.

You should store passwords in the database as hashes. This way, if attackers get a copy of your database, they are still unable to obtain user passwords unless they can reverse the hash. Typically, reversing the hash will take a significant amount of time, and hopefully you will have enough time to notice the breach of security and alert your users that they need to change their passwords.

The amount of time that it takes to calculate a hash will determine how long a hacker will take to guess passwords by brute force.

Encryption in PHP

Encryption in PHP is provided by the mcrypt module, which needs to be installed and enabled separately. The mcrypt module makes available a wide range of encryption functions and constants.

The algorithms that are available are dependent on the operating system on which PHP is installed. You should not attempt to write your own implementation of an encryption algorithm.

The Zend certification examination does not have a heavy emphasis on encryption.

Hash Functions

Older hashes like MD5 and SHA1 are very quick to calculate and so you must not use them in any place where security is involved. They are still very useful in other areas of programming, but not in any place where you're relying on them being a one-way operation.

PHP 5.5.0 introduces the password_hash() function, which provides a convenient way to generate secure hashes.

For older versions of PHP, you should use the crypt() function.

By default the password_hash() function uses the bcrypt algorithm to hash the password. The bcrypt algorithm has a parameter that includes how many times it should run on the password before returning the hashed result. This is referred to as the "cost" of the algorithm.

By increasing the number of times that the algorithm must run, you can increase the length of time that it takes to calculate a hash. This means that as computers get faster, you can increase the number of iterations in your bcrypt algorithm to keep your passwords secure from brute force attacks.

You can use the password_info() function to retrieve information about how a hash was calculated. This function will tell you the name of algorithm, the cost, and the salt.

The password_needs_rehash() function will compare a hash against the options you specify to see if it needs to be rehashed. This will let you change the algorithm used to hash your passwords, for example increasing the cost over time.

Secure Random Strings and Integers

PHP has two functions that allow you to conveniently generate cryptographically secure integers and strings. These functions will work on any platform where PHP runs.

Function	Parameters	Returns	Description
random_bytes	Int $length	String of bytes	Generates a random string that is $length bytes long
random_int	Int $min, int $max	Random integer	Generates a random integer in the range specified by $min and $max

Here is an example of using random_bytes:

```php
<?php
// get a string that contains 8 random bytes
$randomBytes = random_bytes(8);
$printableVersion = bin2hex($randomBytes);
echo $printableVersion; // d7e263202be1b99b
```

The string that PHP generates will not necessarily be printable, so I'm using the bin2hex() function to convert it to a hexadecimal string. Hexadecimal requires two characters to display a byte so the string that we output at the end is 16 characters long (twice the number of random bytes we generated).

Salting Passwords

A *salt string* is an additional string that is added to the password. It should be randomly generated for every password. It is used to help make dictionary attacks and pre-computed rainbow attacks more difficult.

You can specify a salt for the password_hash() function, but if you omit it then PHP will create one for you. The PHP Manual notes that the intended mode of operation is for you to let it create the random salt for the password.

The crypt() function accepts a salt string as a second parameter, but will not automatically generate a salt if you don't provide your own. PHP 5.6.0+ will issue a notice if you fail to provide a salt.

Checking a Password

If it is possible for an attacker to accurately measure the time it takes to run your password checking routine, they will be able to glean information that can help them in breaking the password. These attacks are referred to as *timing attacks*.

The PHP 5.5.0 password_verify() function is a timing attack[9]-safe way to compare hashes created by password_hash().

---

[9]https://en.wikipedia.org/wiki/Timing_attack

If you're unable to use this function, you will need to calculate the hash for the password supplied by the user and then compare the hash against the one stored. Comparing the hashes is vulnerable to timing attacks.

PHP 5.6.0 introduced the hash_equals() function, which is a timing attack-safe way of comparing strings. You should use this function when comparing crypt() generated hashes.

A Quick Note on Error Messages

You should never confirm to a person that they have entered an incorrect username. Your error message should be that they have entered either an incorrect username or password. The less information you give to an attacker, the longer it will take for them to gain access to your system.

File Uploads

File uploads are a major risk for a web application and need to be secured in several ways.

Recall that the $_FILES[] superglobal contains information about the files that were uploaded by the client. You should treat everything in this array as suspicious and make sure that you manually confirm every piece of information.

The way PHP handles file uploads is to save them to a temporary directory. You can operate on them there and then move them to the location where you want them.

You should check that the file you're working with is a valid uploaded file and that the client has tried to forge its filename and location in the temporary folder.

Use the is_uploaded_file() function to make sure that the file you're referencing was actually uploaded. Use the move_uploaded_file() instead of other methods to move it from the temporary directory to your final location.

When referring to a file, use the basename() function to strip out paths to prevent a person from spoofing the filename.

Don't trust the MIME type specified by the user. Ignore the MIME type supplied by the user and use finfo_file() to determine the MIME type if you need it.

If you're allowing a user to upload an image, you should use a GD image function like getimagesize() on it to confirm that it is a valid image. If this function fails, then the file is not a valid image.

Generate your own filename to store the file as and do not use the one supplied by the user. Using a random hash for the filename and setting the extension manually by inspecting the MIME type is strongly suggested.

Make sure that the folder where you are storing the files only allows access to the web server user.

If you don't need to serve the files that are uploaded, then keep the uploads folder outside of the document root.

Database Storage

In addition to avoiding SQL injection, you should apply some security principles to how you interact with the database.

You should separate your database servers for your different code environments. Your QA, test, development, and production servers should all use different database servers and should not be able to access each other's databases.

You must prevent the Internet from having access to your database server.

This can be accomplished by using a firewall to close the port from outside traffic, using a private subnet that has no route to the Internet, or configuring your database server to listen only to specific hosts.

It's not sufficient to change the port that your database listens on. I'd go as far as to say it's not worth bothering because it's not even a speed bump to an attacker and just makes your server environment harder for your colleagues to use.

If you run several applications on a single database server, make sure that each application has its own username and password on the server. Each application user should have only the least amount of privileges it needs and should never be able to read another applications' databases.

Avoid using predictable usernames and make sure that you use secure passwords. For example, I usually use a randomly generated version 4 UUID as a password.

Encrypt sensitive data with mcrypt() and mhash() before placing it into the database.

You should examine your database logs from time to time. You'll be able to spot attempted injection attacks and other patterns that will let you identify breaches or tighten areas of code.

Avoid Publishing Your Password Online

A good piece of advice is to avoid publishing your database or API credentials online where people can read them. Okay, I'm being facetious, but seriously when would you be likely to publish all your access credentials for the world and his dog to read?

One time you could do this is when committing to a Git repository and pushing it to a service like GitHub or Bitbucket.

Make sure that any configuration files are ignored by your version control system and are never committed or pushed to upstream repositories. There are bots that scrape GitHub for credentials that will punish you for these mistakes.

Just as an aside related to this link, you should not hard-code Amazon credentials into an application. Rather, set an IAM role that allows access to the service you want to use and apply the role to your VM.

CHAPTER 6 QUIZ

Q1: The recommended production setting for the display_error configuration setting is On.

_____

True

False

_____

Q2: Using HTTPS to encrypt your login page will help to prevent session hijacking and session fixation.

_____

True

False   *

_____

Q3: You can force sessions to be contained exclusively in cookies by using the _____ configuration setting.

_____

session.cookie_secure

session.use_cookies

session.use_trans_sid

None of the above

_____

Q4: CSRF involves an attacker tricking the user's browser or device into making a request without them knowing. It exploits the trust that the server has in the browser. You can avoid it by including a CSRF token in your form that increases by one every time a visitor loads the page.

_____

True

False

_____

Q5: Both the crypt() and the password_hash() functions allow you to specify the salt, but will generate a properly random salt for you if you do not.

_____

True

False

_____

Q6: The browser determines the file type by making an OS call and sends this information with the request. You can trust this to determine the extension to use when storing the file.

_____

True

False

_____

Q7: Because PHP deletes the temporary file when it finishes running, you should first make sure that you use the `copy()` function to place the temporary file in a permanent location.

_____

True

False

_____

Q8: By default, PHP is configured to be able to include source code that is stored on a URL.

_____

True

False

_____

Q9: A sufficient counter-measure to prevent XSS is to use the `strip_tags()` function before your content.

_____

True

False

_____

Q10: The `open_basedir` configuration setting has no effect unless PHP safe mode is on. It restricts which directories PHP can access.

_____

True

False

_____

CHAPTER 7

■ ■ ■

Data Formats and Types

This chapter is split into six broad areas:

- XML
- SOAP
- REST web services
- JSON
- Date and time
- PHP SPL data structures

Although this topic is not one of the three high importance areas for the Zend exam, you can expect to be asked a couple of relatively detailed questions from this section.

XML

XML stands for eXtensible Markup Language and is a way to store data in a structured manner. An advantage of using XML is that it is a well recognized data standard and so is a convenient way to exchange data between systems.

In the industry, there has been a shift away from XML and toward JSON as a data exchange process, but XML is still relevant to everyday practice and is part of the Zend examination.

The Basics of XML

This isn't an introductory book on PHP, so I won't introduce all the elements of XML in excruciating detail. This book would be far too long if we went into that level of detail. Make sure that you are at least familiar with all the terms in the following table, because we'll be using them as we examine the XML processing capability of PHP.

Term	Description
SGML	Standardized General Markup Language. XML is a subset of this.
Document Type Declaration	The DTD defines the legal building blocks of an XML document structure with a list of legal elements and attributes.
Entity	An entity can declare names and values that are not permitted in the rest of the XML document. For example, HTML declares < as an entity to represent the less than symbol <. These declarations can also be used as shortcuts and to maintain consistency of spelling and value throughout a document.
Element	Elements are the basic building blocks of an XML document. Elements can be nested and contain elements, or they can contain a value. Elements may have attributes.
Well-formed	A well-formed document in XML is a document that adheres to the syntax rules specified by the XML 1.0 specification in that it must satisfy both physical and logical structures.[1]
Valid	An XML document validated against a DTD is both "Well Formed" and "Valid".

If you're at all shaky about these definitions, then please make sure that you read a comprehensive tutorial on XML and read the linked footnotes from this section.

Well-Formed and Valid

Let me expand on what these terms mean because it's important to know the difference.

A document is well-formed if:

- It has a single root element

- Tags are opened and closed properly

- All its entities are well-formed, according to this list:

  - They contain only properly encoded Unicode characters

  - No syntax marks like < or & appear

  - Tag names must match exactly and may not contain symbols

A document is valid if it is well-formed and conforms to the DTD.

---

[1]https://en.wikipedia.org/wiki/Well-formed_document

■ **Note**   PHP does not require XML documents to be valid but it does require them to be well formed to parse them with standard libraries.

XML Processing Instructions

Processing instructions allow documents to contain instructions for applications. They are enclosed in <? and ?> marks and look like this, for example:

```
<?PITarget PIContent?>
```

One use-case could be to inform an application that an element is to be a particular data type, as in this example:

```
<?var type="string" ?>
```

The most common usage is to include an XSLT or CSS stylesheet, like so:

```
<?xml-stylesheet type="text/xsl" href="style.xsl"?>
<?xml-stylesheet type="text/css" href="style.css"?>
```

XML Transformations with PHP XSL

The PHP XSL extension allows PHP to apply XSLT transformations.

Although this is commonly used to apply stylesheets, it is important to know that many other forms of transformation are possible.

XSL is a language for expressing stylesheets for XML documents. It is like CSS in that it describes how to display an XML document.

XSL defines XSLT that is a transformation language for XML documents that allows XML documents to be processed into other documents.

An XSLT processor takes an input XML file, some XSLT code, and produces a new document. Figure 7-1, taken from Wikipedia Creative Commons, illustrates this.

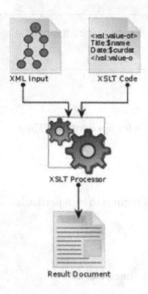

Figure 7-1. *XSLT processor*

A use-case for this could be to create an XHTML document that can be rendered by a browser.

Input XML would be received from a PHP program that includes processing instructions about where to retrieve an XSL stylesheet. The browser would retrieve this stylesheet and apply the XSLT code in it to produce the XHTML.

Acronym	What It Is
XSL	Language to express stylesheets
XSLT	Transformation language to process XML into another XML document

The PHP manual[2] has a simple example of how to use PHP to transform an XML file using an XSL:

```php
<?php

$xslDoc = new DOMDocument();
$xslDoc->load("collection.xsl");
```

```
$xmlDoc = new DOMDocument();
$xmlDoc->load("collection.xml");

$proc = new XSLTProcessor();
$proc->importStylesheet($xslDoc);
echo $proc->transformToXML($xmlDoc);
```

Parsing XML in PHP

There are two types of XML parsers available in PHP. There are several PHP extensions that parse XML, but they all fall under one of these two types.

All the PHP XML extensions use the same underlying library, so it is possible to pass data between them.

All XML routines require both the LibXML extension and the Expat library to be enabled. These are both enabled by default in PHP.

Tree Parsers

Tree parsers attempt to parse the entire document at once and transform it into a tree structure. It should be clear that this could present problems if you're trying to parse a very big document.

There are two tree parsers in PHP:

- SimpleXML

- DOM

Event-Based Parsers

These parsers are quicker and consume less memory than tree parsers. They work by reading the XML document node by node and providing you the opportunity to hook into events associated with this reading process.

Two examples of event-based parsers are:

- XMLReader

- XML Expat parser

The XML Expat parser is a non-validating event based parser that is also built into PHP's core. It does not require a DTD because it does not validate XML and only requires that XML be well-formed.

Error Codes

The PHP manual[3] lists several XML error codes. This list is a subset of the 733 error codes of the underlying libxml library.

Here is a partial list of XML constants that you should be familiar with because they're more common than other codes.

Prefix Code	Description
XML_ERROR_SYNTAX	The XML is not well-formed.
XML_ERROR_INVALID_TOKEN	You are using an invalid character in XML.
XML_ERROR_UNKNOWN_ENCODING	Your XML could not be parsed because the encoding scheme couldn't be determined.
XML_OPTION_CASE_FOLDING	Enabled by default and sets element names to uppercase.
XML_OPTION_SKIP_WHITE	Skips excess whitespace in the source document.

Character Encoding

When PHP parses an XML document, it performs a process called source encoding to read the document.

There are three forms of encoding that are supported:

- UTF-8

- ISO-8859-1 (default)

- US-ASCII

UTF-8 is a multibyte encoding scheme, which means that a single character may be represented by more than one byte. The other two schemes are both single byte.

PHP stores the data internally and then performs target encoding when it passes the data to functions.

The target encoding is set to the same as the source encoding by default, but this can be changed. The source encoding, however, cannot be changed after the parsing object has been created.

If the parser encounters a character that the source encoding cannot represent, it will return an error.

If the target encoding scheme cannot contain a character, then that character will be demoted to fit the encoding scheme. In practice, this means that they are replaced with a question mark.

---

[3]https://php.net/manual/en/xml.error-codes.php

The XML Extension

The XML extension allows you to create XML parsers and define handlers. You should be familiar with the following functions.

Function	Use
xml:parser_create($encoding)	Creates an XML parser with the specified encoding.
xml:parser_create_ns($encoding, $separator=":")	Creates an XML parser with the specified encoding that supports XML namespaces.
xml:parser_free($xmlparser)	Frees up an XML parser.
xml:set_element_handler($xmlparser, $start, $end)	This tells the parser which functions to call at the start and end of each element in the XML document. You can pass FALSE to disable a particular handler. Both $start and $end must be callable and are usually the string names of a function that exists in scope.

The function that handles the start of an element must accept three parameters:

- The XML parser resource
- A string that will contain the name of the element being parsed
- An array of attributes that the element has

The end handler function must accept two parameters:

- The XML parser resource
- A string that will contain the name of the element being parsed

The xml:set_object($xmlparser, $object) function allows the XML parser to be used within the object. This means that you can set the methods of the object as functions for the setting the element handler.

The xml:parse_into_struct($parser, $xml, $valueArr, $indexArr) function parses an XML string into two parallel array structures, one (index) containing pointers to the location of the appropriate values in the values array. These last two parameters must be passed by reference.

DOM

DOM is an acronym of Document Object Model. The DOMDocument class is useful for working with XML and HTML.

It uses UTF-8 encoding and requires the libxml2 extension (Gnome XML library) and expat library. It is a tree parser and reads the entire document into memory before creating an internal tree representation.

Here is a basic example of some DOMDocument syntax:

```php
<?php
$domDoc = new DomDocument();
$domDoc->load("library.xml");
// $domDoc->loadXML($xmlString);
// $domDoc->loadHTMLFile("index.html");
// $domDoc->loadHTML($htmlDocumentString);
$domDoc->save(); // (to a file in XML format)
$xmlString = $domDoc->saveXML();
$htmlDocumentString = $domDoc->saveHTML();
$domDoc->saveHTMLFile(); // (to a file in HTML format)
$xpath = new DomXpath($dom);
$elements = $xpath->query("//*[@id]"); // find all elements with an id
echo "I found {$result->length} elements<br>";
if (!is_null($elements)) {
    foreach ($elements as $element) {
        echo "<br/>[". $element->nodeName. "]";

        $nodes = $element->childNodes;
        foreach ($nodes as $node) {
            echo $node->nodeValue. "\n";
        }
    }
}
```

You should be familiar with the following methods of the DOM class:

Method	Description
createElement	Creates a node element that can be appended with the appendChild method of the node class.
createElementNS	As with createElement, but supports documents with namespaces.
saveXML	Dumps the XML tree back into a string.
save	Dumps the XML tree back into a file.
createTextNode	Creates a new instance of class DOMText.

DOM Nodes

The DOMNode class is used to work with nodes in the DOM tree.

You can retrieve nodes by calling one of these methods of the DOMDocument:

- getElementById
- getElementsByTagName
- getElementsByTagNameNS

These methods return a DOMNodeList object, which can be traversed over using foreach().

The getElementById() function requires that you specify which attribute will be of the type id. You can do this either by including a DTD that defines it, or by calling the setIdAttribute() function. In either case, the document must be validated for the function to be called.

When inserting a node as a sibling using insertBefore(), you need to reference the parent node and also specify the sibling node that you are wanting to insert the new node before. This example shows the syntax:

```php
<?php
$xmlString = <<<XML
<root>
<teams>
<team>Silverbacks</team>
<team foo="winner">Golden Eyes</team>
</teams>
</root>
XML;

$domDoc = new DOMDocument();
$domDoc->loadXML($xmlString);
$xpath = new DomXPath($domDoc);
$team2 = $xpath->query('teams/team[2]');
$parent = $xpath->query('teams');
$textElement = $domDoc->createElement('team', 'Bearhides');
$parent->item(0)->insertBefore($textElement, $team2->item(0));
```

In the example, we want to insert a new team between the two existing teams. To do so, we find the team and the parent.

■ **Note** These variables contain DOMElements. We cannot use the parent() method because it is defined on the DOMNode class.

You should be familiar with these methods of the DOMNode class.

Method	Description
appendChild	Adds a new child node at the end of the children.
insertBefore	Adds a new child before a reference node.
parentNode	The parent of the node, or null if there is no parent.
cloneNode	Clones a node and optionally all of its descendent nodes.
setAttributeNS	Sets an attribute with namespace namespaceURI and name name to the given value. If the attribute does not exist, it will be created.

■ **Note**   You need to pass a node as an argument to these functions.

If you're trying to use appendChild() then you must first use a function like DOMDocument::createElement() to create the node.

SimpleXML

SimpleXML is an extension that sacrifices robust handling of complex requirements in favor of offering a simple interface. It requires the simpleXML extension and only supports version 1.0 of the XML specifications.

■ **Caution**   SimpleXML is a tree parser and loads the entire document into memory when parsing it. This may make it unsuitable for very large documents.

SimpleXML offers an object-oriented approach to accessing XML data. All the objects that it makes are instances of the SimpleXMLElement class. Elements become properties of these objects and attributes can be accessed as associative arrays.

Creating SimpleXML Objects

You can create SimpleXML objects using procedural methods, or through an object-oriented approach:

```php
<?php
// procedural from string variable
$xml = simple_xml:load_string($string_of_xml);
// procedural from file
$xml = simple_xml:load_file('filename.xml');
// object oriented from variable
$xml = new SimpleXMLElement($string_of_xml);
```

Iterating Over SimpleXML Objects

The children() method returns a traversable array of child objects.

You can create an algorithm that inspects the children of a node and then iterates through them recursively. There is such an example on the PHP Manual page.

Retrieving Information

Function	Action
SimpleXMLElement::construct()	Creates a new SimpleXMLElement object.
SimpleXMLElement::attributes()	Identifies an element's attributes.
SimpleXMLElement::getName()	Retrieves an element's name.
SimpleXMLElement::children()	Returns the children of the given node.
SimpleXMLElement::count()	Returns how many children a node has.
SimpleXMLElement::asXML()	Returns the element as a well-formed XML string.
SimpleXMLElement::xpath()	Runs an xpath query on the current node.

xpath

XPath[4] is a language to define parts of an XML document. It models an XML document as a series of nodes and uses path expressions for navigating through and selecting nodes from the document.

SimpleXMLElement::xpath() runs an XPath query on XML data and returns an array of children that match the path specified.

W3Cschools has examples of XPath usage on their web site.[5]

You should note that, unlike PHP structures, XPath results are not zero-based. The XPath /college/student[1]/name will return the first student, not the second, as would be the case if it were zero-based.

PHP arrays containing xpath results are zero-based. In other words, if you store your results in an array variable called $array then $array[0] will correspond to the college/student[1]/ name in the previous example.

You can retrieve text values by using an XPath like this: /college/student/name[text()].

You can specify ranges like this: /college/student[attendance<80]/name.

Exchanging Data Between DOM and SimpleXML

The function simple_xml:import_dom() will convert a DOM node into a SimpleXML object.

You can convert a SimpleXML object to a DOM with dom_import_simplexml().

---

[4]https://en.wikipedia.org/wiki/XPath
[5]https://www.w3schools.com/xml/xml:xpath.asp

SOAP

SOAP[6] was originally an acronym of Simple Object Access Protocol. Versions 1.0 and 1.1 were released by the industry. As of version 1.2, the standard is controlled by the W3C and the acronym has fallen away, making SOAP just a plain name.

The PHP SOAP extension is used to write SOAP servers and clients. It requires that libxml is enabled, which is the case in default PHP installations.

SOAP cache functions are configured in the php.ini file with the soap.wsdl_cache_* settings.

If SOAP is available, then it makes available a set of predefined constants. These constants relate to SOAP versions, encoding, authentication, caching, and persistence.

There are only two SOAP functions:

- is_soap_fault() returns whether a SOAP call has failed.

- use_soap_error_handler() is used for the SOAP server and sets whether PHP should use the SOAP error handler. If it is set to false, the PHP error handler is used instead of sending a SOAP error to the client.

The rest of the SOAP functionality is provided in classes.

What SOAP Does

SOAP allows complex data types to be defined and exchanged and provides a mechanism for various messaging patterns, the most common of which is the Remote Procedure Call (RPC).

This in effect allows a developer to execute a function on a server, pass it complex data as parameters, and receive complex data back.

SOAP web services are defined by a WSDL (Web Service Description Language). Most people pronounce this acronym as "whizz-dill".

The WSDL defines the data types using an XML structure. It also describes the methods that may be called remotely, specifying their names, parameters, and return types.

SOAP messages between a server and client are sent in XML structures called SOAP envelopes.

Using a SOAP Service

The SoapClient class is used to connect to and use a SOAP service.

It is possible to parse a WSDL file to discover what methods are available and then present these to you in an easy-to-use manner.

```php
<?php
$client = new SoapClient("http://example.com/login?wsdl");
$params = array('username'=>'name', 'password'=>'secret');
```

---

[6]https://en.wikipedia.org/wiki/SOAP

```
// call the login method directly
$client->login($params);

// If you want to call __soapCall, you must wrap the arguments in another
array as follows:
$client->__soapCall('login', array($params));
```

In the previous example, we connect to an example WSDL and call the login method using two different methods. Note that using the SoapClient::__soapCall() method requires you to wrap the parameters in an array.

It is not compulsory for a SOAP service to provide a WSDL. If you need to use such a service you may pass null as the WSDL file but then need to provide information about the service endpoint. You must provide the location and URI options and may optionally provide other information about the version of the SOAP service, as in this example:

```
<?php
$client = new SoapClient(null,
    ['location' => 'http://example.com/soap.php',
     'uri' => 'http://test-uri/',
     'style'    => SOAP_DOCUMENT,
     'use'      => SOAP_LITERAL));
]);
```

When you construct the SoapClient class, you can set the trace parameter to true to enable debugging the raw SOAP envelope headers and body.

The following two debugging commands require that the trace be true and allow you to inspect details of the request:

- SoapClient::__getLastRequestHeaders()

- SoapClient::__getLastRequest()

Offering a SOAP Service

The SoapServer class provides a SOAP server. It supports versions 1.1 and 1.2 and can be used with or without a WSDL service description.

Here is an example of setting up a SOAP server:

```
<?php
$options = ['uri'=>'http://localhost/test'];
$server = new SoapServer(NULL, $options);
$server->setClass('MySoapServer');
$server->handle();
```

We can see that we first create the server with an array of options. In this example, we are not supplying a WSDL in the first parameter and so we must supply the URI of the server namespace in the options array.

Once we have an instance of the SoapServer class, we pass in the name of the class that it will use to serve requests. The methods in the class will be callable by a SOAP client connecting to the server.

Instead of setting a class you may also use a concrete object to handle SOAP requests by passing it as a parameter with the `SoapServer::setObject()` function.

REST Web Services

REST is an acronym for Representational State Transfer and is an architectural style rather than a PHP extension or set of commands. REST has several constraints that are intended to improve performance and maintainability of web services.

■ **Tip** Compare "Service Oriented Architecture," which is typically implemented in SOAP to "Microservice Architecture," which is more often implemented in REST.

REST has several verbs that are similar to HTTP request types. This leads to some confusion, but it is important to note that REST does not have to use HTTP as a transport layer to communicate. HTTP just happens to be very convenient for REST because it is stateless and the request types translate well into REST verbs.

REST exposes Uniform Resource Identifiers (URI) that are linked to resources. These links are called REST endpoints. Depending on the HTTP type used to access them, they will perform an action on the resource (change its state). The HTTP type is used to signal the REST verb to be performed.

REST focuses on resources and providing access to those resources. A resource could be something like a "user". Much like a database schema represents the user entity, REST will represent the user in a JSON or XML structure.

A representation should be readable by both the server and the client. REST can be used to transfer JSON, XML, or both. We'll look at this in a bit more detail later.

In PHP, one of the most common uses for REST APIs is to provide services for an AJAX enabled frontend, such as one written in Angular or ReactJS.

Application and Resource States

A REST server should not remember the state of the application and the client should send all the information necessary for execution.

This means that every request to a server is self-contained. If a request to a server failed it will not affect the success or failure of other requests. This improves the reliability of the application.

The server is not responsible for remembering what state the application is in and relies on the client to send all the information it needs to process the request. This means that the client stores and maintains the application state (and not the server).

Application statelessness has important implications for scaling horizontally. Because no individual server is maintaining state, a request can reach any server in a group and be handled correctly.

The resource that REST is providing access to has state that is expected to persist between requests. Resource state is maintained on the server.

REST Verbs

REST has several verbs that are used to alter the state of a resource on the server. Verbs operate either on a single resource or a collection of resources.

Resource	GET	PUT	POST	DELETE
Collection	Lists the URIs where you can retrieve the members	Replace the collection with another collection	Create a new entry in the collection	Deletes the entire collection
Single Entity	Retrieve a representation of the single element	Replace the element, or create it if it doesn't exist	Creates a new member	Deletes the member

PUT and POST look similar, but have an important distinction. POST requires you to specify all the required attributes for an element and will create a fresh element. PUT will replace the attributes you specify for an existing record and you don't need to supply all the attributes unless you're creating a new record.

To explain with an example, let's consider a user who has a name and a title. First, we POST to create a new user with a name "Alice" and the title "Mrs". Then Alice graduates and becomes a doctor, so we PUT to her record and include just the title as "Dr". We don't have to specify her name and, because we don't, her name will not be changed.

HATEOAS

HATEOAS stands for "Hypertext As The Engine Of State". In this concept, the response from the server will include information about what actions the client can take next. These options will be marked up in hypertext.

The aim is for the client not to require prior knowledge of the endpoints of the REST service. Rather, they will be provided with the endpoints they need to proceed through the application when they make a query.

Let's consider an example:

```
GET /account/12345 HTTP/1.1

HTTP/1.1 200 OK
<?xml version="1.0"?>
<account>
<account_number>12345</account_number>
<balance currency="usd">100.00</balance>
<link rel="deposit" href="/account/12345/deposit" />
<link rel="withdraw" href="/account/12345/withdraw" />
<link rel="transfer" href="/account/12345/transfer" />
<link rel="close" href="/account/12345/close" />
</account>
```

In the previous example, from the Wikipedia page on HATEOAS,[7] we are retrieving information about a bank account. The server responds with a list of URIs that can be used for further actions. If the account had a negative balance, for example, the server may not include the link to withdraw money. The server is guiding the client through the API by exposing additional URIs that are relevant to the last operation.

Request Headers

HTTP allows passing headers in its request. REST clients will use these to indicate to the server what they are providing and what they are expecting back.

A REST client should use the accept header to indicate to the server what sort of content (representation) it wants back. For example, if a client sets the accept header to text/xml, it is telling the server that it wants an XML-formatted response.

The client will also set a Content-Type header to inform the server of the MIME type of its payload. See the section in the response header for more detail.

Response Headers and Codes

The Content-Type header is sent by the server and defines the MIME type of the body that is being sent. For example, a server may set the content-type to application/json to indicate that the body of the response contains JSON formatted text.

The server will also set a status code that informs the client of the result of the request. Some of the common codes are listed here, but there are many more.[8]

Code	Meaning
200	The request processed successfully
201	The resource was created
202	The resource was accepted for processing, but has not yet been processed
400	Bad request (client error)
401	Unauthorized; the client must authenticate itself before accessing this resource
403	Forbidden; the client has authenticated itself but does not have permission to access this resource
500	Server or application error

■ **Tip** It is very poor practice to send a message in the response body that contradicts the HTTP response code.

---

[7]Https://en.wikipedia.org/wiki/HATEOAS
[8]https://www.w3.org/Protocols/rfc2616/rfc2616-sec10.html

Within the Zend framework the term "context switching" refers to changing the output of your program depending on whether it is responding to a REST request or some other request.

For example, you may respond with an HTML page for normal requests or respond with JSON if the request originated via XMLHttpRequest (AJAX).

You could also respond with XML or JSON, depending on what content type the client indicates it wants as a response.

Another example could be to respond with different layouts, depending on what sort of browser is being used (mobile device versus desktop for example).

You should be familiar with the concept of the server responding differently to a call to the same URL, depending on how the client sets up its request.

Sending Requests

The curl extension is a common way to send REST requests in PHP. Curl lets you specify headers and request types.

There are libraries that wrap the curl functions. One of the popular ones is Guzzle,[9] which is easy to install and use. It offers a very wide range of features and, at the time of writing, is in my opinion the best choice of request client for PHP.

JSON

JSON is an acronym of JavaScript Object Notation. In PHP, it is used a lot with Ajax, which is an acronym for Asynchronous JavaScript and XML.

JSON lets you serialize an object as a string so that it can be transported between services. Ajax is a means to transport the string.

Together these technologies allow you to communicate between JavaScript applications in the browser and PHP applications on the server.

The JSON extension is loaded in PHP by default and provides methods to handle converting to and from JSON.

It provides a number of constants, including:

Constant	Meaning
JSON_ERROR_NONE	Confirms whether a JSON error occurred or not.
JSON_ERROR_SYNTAX	Confirms if there was a syntax error parsing JSON and helps detect encoding errors.
JSON_FORCE_OBJECT	If an empty PHP array is encoded, this option will force it to be encoded as an object.

There are three functions provided by the extension.

json_decode() takes a string as its first argument and returns an object. If the second parameter is set true, it will return an associative array.

---

[9]http://docs.guzzlephp.org/en/stable/

From PHP 5.3 onward, two additional options are supplied—$depth and $options. Depth refers to the recursion depth and currently the only option is JSON_BIGINT_AS_STRING, which changes casting large integers as floats to be cast as strings.

If the recursion depth is exceeded, json_decode() will return NULL and json_last_error_msg() will return "Maximum stack depth exceeded". This will happen if the array has more levels than the depth you have specified as acceptable.

As an example, consider this code:

```php
<?php
$arr = [
    "fruits" => [
        "apple" => ["taste" => "sweet", "color" => "yellow"],
        "banana" => ["taste" => "sour", "color" => "green"],
        "cherry" => ["taste" => "sweet", "color" => "red"]
    ],
    "vegetables" => "yuck"
];
$str = json_encode($arr);
$decode = json_decode($str, true, 1);
echo json_last_error_msg(); // Maximum stack depth exceeded
```

The array has two levels because each of the fruits contains an array. We specify that we want to decode only one level of depth and so $decode will be NULL and the script will output "Maximum stack depth exceeded".

json_encode() takes a variable of any type (other than a resource) as a parameter and returns the JSON representation. It has two optional parameters—$depth and $options—which are the same as described previously.

json_last_error() returns the last error code that occurred in either of the previous functions and json_last_error_msg() returns a string message.

■ **Tip**   Remember from Chapter 6 that JSON is the preferred way to serialize data that is transported to the client.

Date and Time

PHP supplies several functions that retrieve the date and time from the server. You should set a default time zone in your configuration or set it at runtime in your script. You should set the time zone to match the time zone that your server is in, so that PHP can correctly interpret the server time. This also lets your script be aware of adjustments like daylight savings time.

PHP 5.2 introduced the DateTime class, which deals with a wide range of date and time calculations. It is recommended to use this class instead of working with the functions like date() and time().

To create a new `DateTime` object, you pass it a string that it can parse. It understands a wide range of string formats, such as shown in this example:

```php
<?php
$strings = [
    'Next monday',
    'Yesterday',
    '', // now
    '2016-12-25',
    '25 December 2016',
    '-1 week',
    '+1 days'
];
foreach ($strings as $example) {
    $dateTime = new DateTime($example);
    echo $dateTime->format(DateTime::COOKIE) . PHP_EOL;
}
```

All the strings in the array from this example will be understood.

If a date format is ambiguous, then you can use the `DateTime::createFromFormat()` command to create the object.

For example, the date 3 June 2013 will be written as 06-03-2013 by an American, while the rest of the world would write it as 03-06-2013. If you gave either of these strings to PHP, it would not know whether you mean 3 June 2013 or 6 March 2013.

To resolve the ambiguity, you can specify which format you're using in your string, like this:

```php
<?php
$dateTime = DateTime::createFromFormat('d-m-Y', '06-03-2013');
echo $dateTime->format(DateTime::COOKIE);
```

This script will output something like Wednesday, 06-Mar-2013 12:56:42 CET. Note that if you omit the time when creating a `DateTime` class, the time that the script is running at will be used.

Formatting Dates

In these examples, we've used one of the class constants provided by `DateTime` to format our date.

The manual has a list of these constants, which are common use-cases for date display or storage. They appear in this table:

Constant	Format
ATOM	Y-m-dTH:i:sP
COOKIE	l, d-M-Y H:i:s T

(continued)

Constant	Format
ISO8601	Y-m-dTH:i:sO
RFC822	D, d M y H:i:s O
RFC850	l, d-M-y H:i:s T
RFC1036	D, d M y H:i:s O
RFC1123	D, d M Y H:i:s O
RFC2822	D, d M Y H:i:s O
RFC3339	Y-m-dTH:i:sP
RSS	D, d M Y H:i:s O
W3C	Y-m-dTH:i:sP

These are string constants and contain date and time formatting codes. The formatting codes are replaced with a value by the DateTime class. For example, the symbol "Y" is replaced with the four-digit year of the date being stored.

Obviously, the point of declaring the constant is so that you don't have to memorize the strings, so don't worry about studying the formats. I included the formatting strings because they are a good indication of the commonly used ones.

Date and time formatting codes are case-sensitive. For example, "y" is a two-digit year and "Y" is a four-digit year.

Characters in the formatting string that are not recognized as formatting characters will be placed into the output unchanged. So, the string "Y-m-d" would include the hyphens between the year, month, and day when output—like this "2015-12-25".

You can find a list of the PHP date and time formatting codes on the manual page,[10] but here are the ones that are in the previous table:

Code	Replaced With	Example(s)
Y	A full four-digit year	1999
M	Two-digit month, with leading zeroes	06
d	Day of the month, two digits with leading zeros	14
D	A three letter textual day	Mon, Tue, Wed
H	24-hour format hour with leading zero	00, 09, 12, 23
i	Two-digit minute, with leading zeroes	05,15,25,45
s	Two-digit seconds, with leading zeroes	05,15,25,45
P	Difference to Greenwich time (GMT) with colon between hours and minutes (PHP 5.1.3+)	+02:00
O	Difference to Greenwich time (GMT) in hours	+0200
T	Time zone abbreviation	EST, CET

---

[10]https://php.net/manual/en/function.date.php

Date Calculations

The most simple calculations can be performed using the DateTime class method modify(). For example, to find the date and time that is one month in the future, you can do the following:

```php
<?php
$dateTime = new DateTime();
$dateTime->modify('+1 month');
echo $dateTime->format(DateTime::COOKIE) . PHP_EOL;
```

PHP offers a much more flexible way to work with date calculations, however.

The DateInterval class is used to store either a fixed amount of time (in years, months, days, hours, etc.) or a relative time string in the format that DateTime's constructor supports.

The DateTime class allows you to add() or sub() a DateInterval from a DateTime. It will handle leap years and other time adjustments while doing so.

To specify a fixed amount of time when creating a DateInterval object, we pass its constructor a string. The string always starts with P and then lists the number of each individual date unit in descending order. Optionally, the letter T appears and then the time units are included.

This makes a lot more sense with some examples:

String	Description
P14D	14 days
P2W	Two weeks
P2W5D	This is invalid; you may not specify weeks and days together in one string; the weeks will be ignored
P2WT5H	Two weeks and five hours
P1Y2M3DT4H5M	One year, two months, three days, four hours, five minutes

Note that:

- Every string begins with P
- The number of units precedes the letter indicating the unit
- Time units are split from the date units by the letter T
- Units are sorted in descending order

Here is an example in code:

```php
<?php
$dateTime = DateTime::createFromFormat('d-m-Y H:i:s', '01-12-2016 13:14:15');
$dateInterval = new DateInterval('P1M2DT3H4M5S');
$dateTime->add($dateInterval);
echo $dateTime->format(DateTime::COOKIE) . PHP_EOL;
```

193

This code outputs the date and time that is one month, two days, three hours, four minutes, and five seconds after 1st December 13:14:15.

Manual Date Calculations

Occasionally, you will need to work with a UNIX style timestamp. This timestamp is a number that holds the number of seconds that have passed since the UNIX epoch, 1 January 1970. One advantage of the timestamp is that it is agnostic of time zones.

There are several PHP functions that let you create a timestamp. The strtotime() function is a very flexible way to convert a date-time description into a timestamp. It is intelligent enough to recognize phrases like "next Monday" or "+1 year", as well as more mundane strings like "1 April 2017".

The mktime() function accepts a parameter for each of hour, minute, second, month, day, or year. mktime() returns the UNIX timestamp of the arguments given. If the arguments are invalid, the function returns FALSE.

Note that the order of the parameters does not increase in unit size, but is in the order "h i s m d y".

You can leave out parameters right to left in which case they will default to the current date value. So if the current year is 2016 and you call mktime() without specifying the year, PHP will assume that you mean 2016.

If you pass a parameter to mktime() that is greater than the value that should be allowed, mktime() assumes that you mean that you're referencing the next period.

For example, there are 31 days in December. If you call mktime(0, 0, 0, 12, 32, 2016) then you will be given a timestamp for the first day in the next month; in other words, for 1 January 2017.

Comparing Dates

The DateTime::diff() method allows you to compare the difference between two DateTime objects. It returns a DateInterval that contains the period of time between the two dates being represented.

Note that the DateTime class handles time zone and daylight savings time conversions for you.

Let's try to find out how long it is to Christmas.

```php
<?php
$now = new DateTime();
$christmas = new DateTime('25 december');
if ($now > $christmas) {
    $christmas = new DateTime('25 december next year');
}
$interval = $christmas->diff($now);
// 97 days until Christmas
echo $interval->days . ' days until Christmas' . PHP_EOL;
```

Notice the following in this snippet:

- Passing no parameter to the construct uses the current date and time.

- We can use mathematical operators like >, <, and == to compare DateTime objects.

- We can use fairly flexible language when creating a DateTime, such as "25 december next year" for the case where the current date is between Christmas and New Year.

- The diff() method returns a DateInterval.

- TheDateInterval object has a number of public properties that can be accessed to measure years, months, and in this case days.

PHP SPL Data Structures

The standard PHP library (SPL) is a collection of interfaces and classes that are meant to solve common problems. It includes several classes that help you work with standard data structures.

Interfaces Related to Data Structures

Before we look at the SPL data structure classes, it is worth looking at some of the interfaces that they implement. This makes it considerably easier to remember what functions the classes have.

Iterator

The Iterator interface extends the Traversable interface.

The Iterator interface[11] defines five methods that are used to move through the collection.

Method	Purpose
current	Returns the current element
key	Returns the key of the current element
next	Moves forward to next element
rewind	Rewinds the iterator to the first element
valid	Checks if current position is valid

---

[11]https://php.net/manual/en/class.iterator.php

Traversable

A class that implements the traversable interface[12] can be looped over using foreach().

This interface cannot be implemented by itself, it can only be implemented by implementing an interface that tells the class how to iterate over the collection.

In practical terms, this means that to implement the traversable interface, you must implement either the Iterator or IteratorAggregate interface.

ArrayAccess

This interface provides the ability to access objects as arrays. To do so, you need to implement four methods:

Method	Purpose
offsetExists	Whether an offset exists
offsetGet	Offset to retrieve
offsetSet	Assign a value to the specified offset
offsetUnset	Unset an offset

If your class implements this interface, then you will be able to use array syntax when referencing an object instantiated from it.

Countable

If your class implements the Countable interface, you will be able to use the count() function to find how many elements it has.

The Countable interface has an abstract method called count. This method will be called when you call the PHP function count() on an object instantiated from a class that implements the interface.

```php
<?php
class BadCount implements Countable
{
  public function count()
  {
    return 42;
  }
}
$a = new BadCount;
echo count($a);  // 42
```

---

[12]https://php.net/manual/en/class.traversable.php

In the trivial example, the count() method in this class always returns the number 42. In a more complicated example, we could implement logic here that defines how you want to return the count of your object.

Lists

A *list* is an ordered collection of elements. The same value may appear more than once in a list. A doubly linked list is list where each element contains a link to the previous and next element in the chain.

The SplDoublyLinkedList[13] class implements the Iterator, ArrayAccess, and Countable interfaces. In addition, it implements methods that let you change the iterator behavior as well as add or remove items to the front or back of the list.

The SplStack class[14] extends the SplDoublyLinkedList class. It is essentially a SplDoublyLinkedList where you have called setIteratorMode()[15] and set the list to iterate using IT_MODE_LIFO and to behave in mode IT_MODE_KEEP. This tells the iterator to traverse the list like a stack (last in, first out) and to traverse the elements instead of deleting them.

The SplQueue class[16] also extends the SplDoublyLinkedList class. It implements the methods enqueue and dequeue, which will add an element to the end of the queue or remove the one at the front of the queue, respectively.

■ **Caution**   Both the SplStack and SplQueue classes inherit from the SplDoublyLinkedList class and so you can mistakenly call the wrong methods on them.

Here's an example of using a stack that shows some of the methods that you can use. This table shows the values contained in the stack.

Code	Stack Contains
`<?php`	
`$stack = new SplStack();`	Null
`$stack->push(5);`	5
`// this uses array syntax to add a new element`	
`$stack[] = 4;`	5, 4
`// now we push another number to the end of queue`	
`$stack->push(3);`	5, 4, 3

(*continued*)

---

[13]https://php.net/manual/en/class.spldoublylinkedlist.php
[14]https://php.net/manual/en/class.splstack.php
[15]https://php.net/manual/en/spldoublylinkedlist.setiteratormode.php
[16]https://php.net/manual/en/class.splqueue.php

Code	Stack Contains
`// this inserts the number 100 into position 1`	
`// elements below it are shuffled down`	
`$stack->add(1, 100);`	5, 100, 4, 3
`// this returns the last value in the queue`	
`echo "Pop: " . $stack->pop() . PHP_EOL;`	0, 100, 4
`foreach ($stack as $key => $value) {`	
`echo "$key => $value" . PHP_EOL;`	
`}`	

The output of this code is as follows:

```
Pop: 3
2 => 4
1 => 100
0 => 5
```

■ **Note** The keys are contained in the stack in descending order (2,1,0).

Heaps

Heaps are tree-like structures where parent nodes can have zero, one, or more child nodes. Heaps define a comparison rule that allows you to determine whether one node is greater or less than another node. In a heap, a parent node will always be equal to or greater than its children. The comparison function is used to determine whether a node is greater than or less than another.

■ **Note** The SplHeap class is an abstract class. When you use it, you need to implement the compare function.

The SplHeap class implements the Iterator[17] interface, which means that you can use foreach() to move through it.

The SplMaxHeap class extends from SplHeap and keeps the maximum value at the top. It does this by implementing the compare() function for you. Similarly, the SplMinHeap class keeps the minimum value at the top.

---

[17]https://php.net/manual/en/class.iterator.php

Let's look at an example of a straight-forward heap:

```php
<?php
class MyHeap extends SplHeap
{
  function compare($a, $b)
  {
    return $a <=> $b;
  }
}

$heapExample = new MyHeap;
$heapExample->insert(10);
$heapExample->insert(5);
$heapExample->insert(15);

while ($heapExample->valid()) {
  echo $heapExample->current() . PHP_EOL;
  $heapExample->next();
}
```

This code outputs the numbers in sorted descending order, because when we insert them, it applies the compare() function to determine where to place them.

I can hear you saying with annoyance that SplMinHeap is supposed to keep the lowest value on top, so why is the output showing that 15 is still on top? The answer is because all that the SplMinHeap and SplMaxHeap classes provide is a default implementation of the compare() function, which we are overriding in the class definition.

You can extend SplMinHeap but as long as your compare() function remains the same, as in the previous example, you will always have a max heap. To get a working implementation of a min heap (in our example), you need to either swap the operands for the spaceship operator or avoid implementing the compare() function entirely and use the one declared in SplMinHeap.

Arrays

The SplFixedArray[18] structure stores data in a continuous manner, accessible by indexes. It is faster than normal PHP arrays, but is also less flexible because it is of fixed length and can only use integers as indexes.

The SplFixedArray class implements the Iterator interface and the ArrayAccess interface.

Maps

A map is a structure that holds key-value pairs. A PHP array is a sort of map because it stores values against integer (or string) keys.

The SplObjectStorage provides a map from objects to data, or if you ignore data, it can function as an object set.

SplObjectStorage is not an abstract class and can be instantiated directly. It implements the Countable, Iterator, Serializable, and ArrayAccess interfaces.

Because it implements the ArrayAccess interface, you can use array syntax to reference the data of objects inside the structure, like this:

```php
<?php
$bucket = new SplObjectStorage();
$file = new StdClass;
$metaData = ['name' => 'passwords.xslx', 'size' => '102400'];
$bucket[$file] = $metaData;
```

In the example, we are mapping data (the metadata) against a specific instance of an object (the file).

Summary of SPL Data Structures

SplHeap	A heap is a tree collection where the children of a parent must always have a value lower than their parent. There are different types of heap.
SplMaxHeap	This is a type of heap where the maximum is kept at the top of the heap.
SplMinHeap	In this type of heap, the minimum is kept at the top.
SplPriorityQueue	This is a queue where each element also has a "priority" associated with it. An example of a use-case is bandwidth management wherein traffic of a certain type has a higher precedence over other traffic.
SplFixedArray	This is a faster implementation of an array, but it limits you to using an array of fixed length that only contains integers.
SplObjectStorage	This class provides a convenient way to map objects and their data.

---

[18]https://php.net/manual/en/class.splfixedarray.php

There is also an extension called DS that provides alternative data structures. You can find its documentation on the PHP web site[19] and its source code on GitHub. You won't need to know about it for your Zend exam.

CHAPTER 7 QUIZ

Q1: True or false? Characters that cannot be encoded in the target XML encoding scheme generate an error.

True

False; they generate a warning

False; they are fitted into the encoding scheme (converted to question marks)

None of the above

Q2: True or false? It is not possible for a server to send a REST response with HTTP status code 200 if the request failed.

True

False

Q3: What will this code output?

```php
<?php
$arr = [
  "fruits" => [
    "apple" => ["taste" => "sweet", "color" => "yellow"],
    "banana" => ["taste" => "sour", "color" => "green"],
    "cherry" => ["taste" => "sweet", "color" => "red"]
  ],
  "vegetables" => "yuck"
];
$str = json_encode($arr);
$decode = json_decode($str, true, 1);
echo json_last_error_msg();
```

---

[19]https://docs.php.net/manual/en/book.ds.php

Syntax error; it will not run

Nothing; there is no error msg so the echo statement outputs nothing

Maximum stack depth exceeded

Fatal error, the second parameter to json_decode cannot be "true"

Q4: You should set the default time zone for your PHP application. Which of the following methods can you use to do so? Choose as many as apply.

Using the function set_date_default_timezone()

Editing php.ini

Using the Linux time() command on PHP

Using the PHP ini_set() function, like this:
ini_set('date.timezone', 'Europe/Edinburgh');

Q5: What will this code output?

```php
<?php
$stack = new SplStack();
$stack->push(5);
$stack[1] = 4;
echo $stack->pop();
```

4

5

A fatal error will occur

Q6: What is wrong with the following PHP code?

```php
<?php
$client = new SoapClient("http://example.com/login?wsdl");
$params = array('username'=>'name', 'password'=>'secret');
// call the login method directly
$client->login($params);
```

Syntax error; it won't run at all

The parameters to the login method need to be passed like this: $client->login([$params]);

You can't call a method on the SoapClient directly

Nothing is wrong; this will work

Q7: What will this code output?

```php
<?php
$xmlString = <<<XML
<root>
<teams>
<team>Silverbacks</team>
<team>Golden Eyes</team>
</teams>
</root>
XML;
$xml = new SimpleXMLElement($xmlString);
$result = $xml->xpath('teams/team[1]');
echo $result[0];
```

Syntax error; it won't run

Silverbacks

Golden Eyes

It will generate a warning because the xpath will fail to evaluate

Q8: You can convert a SimpleXML object to DOM with the _____ function.

```
dom_import_simplexml()

simple_xml:import_dom()

simple_xml:export_dom()

None of the above
```

Q9: What is the output of this script?

```php
<?php
$xmlString = <<<XML
<root>
<teams>
<team>Silverbacks</team>
<team foo="winner">Golden Eyes</team>
</teams>
</root>
XML;
$domDoc = new DOMDocument();
$domDoc->loadXML($xmlString);
$textElement = $domDoc->createElement('team', 'Bearhides');
$result = $domDoc->xpath('teams/team[2]');
$result[1]->insertBefore($textElement);
echo $domDoc->saveXML();
```

This will produce a fatal error

An XML document with a new team at the beginning of the list of teams

An XML document with a new team between the two teams

None of the above

Q10: What will the following code output?

```php
<?php
$dateTime = new DateTime();
$interval = new DateInterval('P1Y2M3D4H5M');
$dateTime->add($interval);
echo $dateTime->format(DateTime::COOKIE);
```

This will produce a fatal error

A date one year, two months, three days, four hours, and five minutes in the future

None of the above

CHAPTER 8

Input-Output

In this chapter, we're going to be looking at how PHP manages input-output. We'll be examining how we can read from or write to the file system as well as the network.

Files

There are two main groups of functions to deal with files: those that work with file resources, and those that work with a filename.

Remember that a resource is a type of variable that can't be stored directly in PHP. A file resource is an operating system file handle.

All the functions that deal with file resources begin with a single f letter and then have a verb describing their function. For example, fopen() opens a file resource.

Functions that work with the string name of a file all start with the word file and are followed by a verb descriptive of what they do. For example, file_get_contents() takes a string filename and returns the contents of that file.

Opening Files

The function fopen() is used to open files. It returns a resource variable that is a handle to the file.

You must pass two parameters to fopen():

- The name of the file in your file system
- The file mode that you want to open it with

File Modes

Files can be opened in different modes. File modes describe how we will be interacting with the file.

File modes relate to operating system file privileges. For example, if the PHP user only has read access to a file then an attempt to open it in write mode will be denied by the operating system. If we try with a lesser privilege (such as read only), then the operating system will create a file handle for us.

© Andrew Beak 2017
A. Beak, *PHP 7 Zend Certification Study Guide*,
https://doi.org/10.1007/978-1-4842-3246-0_8

We communicate two pieces of information about how we intend to use a file when we specify a mode:

- Whether we are reading, writing, or both

- Whether we want to place the file pointer at the beginning or ending of the file

The file pointer is like an iterator cursor. It stores the file position that will be returned on the next read.

The following table summarizes the common file modes.

Mode	Read/Write	Pointer	Behavior
r	R	Start	
r+	RW	Start	
w	W	Start	Truncates an existing file or creates a new file if it doesn't exist
w+	RW	Start	
a	W	Start	Creates a new file if it doesn't exist and preserves the current file if it does
a+	RW	Start	
x	W	N/A	Tries to create a new file for write; returns FALSE if the file already exists and generates E_WARNING
x+	RW		
c	W	Start	Tries to create the file if it doesn't exist; if it does exist, places the cursor at the front of the file
c+	RW		

You'll notice that adding a + symbol to a file mode has the effect of indicating that you also want to perform the opposite of the default mode. So, when we're overwriting a file, if we add a + symbol then we indicate that we also want to read the file. The behavior remains the same, however, and so I've omitted it from the table to keep it easier to read.

When using the w modes to overwrite a file, PHP will truncate the file to zero bytes. This is useful if you want to have a file that is overwritten with new data.

The x modes will return FALSE and generate a warning if the file already exists. This is useful if you want to avoid overwriting data that you want to keep.

The c mode will create a file if it exists or open an existing file. The pointer will be set to the start of the file for existing files.

File Mode Flags

There are two flags that you can specify by adding them to the end of the mode string. The default flag is defined by your SAPI and the version of PHP that you're using, so for compatibility purposes you should specify them.

You can specify a b flag to specify that you're working with binary files. This means that no characters will be translated. This is necessary when you're working with images or other binary files.

On a Windows server, you can specify a t flag to translate \n to \r\n.

■ **Tip** To keep your code portable, you should use the b flag and make sure that your code uses the correct line endings.

Reading Files

You can read from a file resource using the fread() function.

```php
<?php
$handle = fopen('info.txt', 'r');
while (!feof($handle)) {
    echo fread($handle,1024);
}
```

In this example, we're using the file function feof(), which is a function that returns TRUE when the file pointer is at the end of the file and FALSE otherwise. Using it in a while loop has the effect of continuing the loop until we reach the end of the file.

The fread() function takes two parameters. The first is the variable holding the file resource, and the second is the number of bytes to read. If it reaches the end of the file, then fread() will stop reading.

Here are four more PHP functions that make it more convenient to read files:

Function	Used To
fgetcsv()	Read a line from file pointer and parse for CSV fields
file_get_contents()	Take a string filename and read the results into a string
readfile()	Read a string filename and write the contents to the output buffer
file()	Read an entire file into an array

Writing to Files

Writing to a file is done with the binary-safe fwrite() function. fputs() is an alias to this function.

The fwrite() function takes two parameters—the file resource to write to and the string to write to the file.

There is a writing counterpart for the fgetcsv() function, namely fputcsv() which formats an array as CSV and writes the line to a file. In addition to parameters for the file resource and array, it takes optional parameters to define the CSV format.

If you want to write formatted strings to a file, you should use fprintf(), which works like the printf() command.

If you want to dump the contents of a file to a connected client, you can use fpassthru(). This function will start at the current file position and write the rest of the file to the output buffer.

Finally, there is a convenient function to quickly write a string to a file. The function file_put_contents() doesn't require you to provide a file resource and just requires the filename and the string you want to write.

Here is a simple example of some of these functions being used:

```php
<?php
$filename = 'test.csv';
$dataString = '1,2,3,4,5';
file_put_contents($filename, $dataString);
$handle = fopen($filename, 'r');
$myData = fgetcsv($handle);
echo gettype($myData); // array
echo count($myData); // 5
```

In the example, we use the shortcut function file_put_contents() to output the string to a file. We don't need to have a file resource available, because file_put_contents() handles this for us. After we've written the string I open a file resource to read from it and use fgetcsv() to read from the file. The string was a valid CSV list and so $myData contains an array of five elements.

File System Functions

PHP has an extensive list of functions that connect you to the file system. We'll deal with a few of them in this chapter, but as I so often do, I'm going to refer you to the PHP manual for the exhaustive list.

Directories

This group of functions let you traverse, create, and delete directories.

Function	Use
chdir()	Changes PHP's current working directory.
chroot()	Changes root directory of the running process to the specified directory and sets PHP's working directory to /.
rmdir()	Deletes a directory.
readdir()	Returns the name of the next entry in the directory handle passed as a parameter. The entries are returned in the order in which they are stored by the file system.
scandir()	Reads the directory specified by the string parameter and returns a list of the files and directories it contains.

The difference between scandir() and readdir() is the parameter that they take. Where readdir() uses a directory handle, scandir() accepts the name of the directory as a string.

■ **Caution** This is possibly confusing because it seems that the naming convention of file functions (f* versus file*) doesn't apply to directories.

File Information

We referred to these functions in the security chapter, but there are other use cases where you need to obtain information about a file.

PHP provides the finfo_open() function, which returns a new instance of a fileinfo resource. You provide it with two parameters—a predefined option constant and the string location to a magic database file.

The magic database file is a format used to describe file types and is also used by the Unix standard command, file.[1] If you don't supply a path to the magic database, then PHP will use the one that it comes bundled with.

Once PHP knows how to identify files you can use the finfo_file() function to obtain information about the file. It takes at least two parameters—the fileinfo resource you just created and a string name of the file you want to check.

Here is an example from the PHP manual[2]:

```php
<?php
$finfo = finfo_open(FILEINFO_MIME_TYPE);
foreach (glob("*") as $filename) {
    echo finfo_file($finfo, $filename) . "\n";
}
finfo_close($finfo);
```

Both functions have object-oriented styles of use, as in this example from the PHP manual:

```php
<?php
// finfo will return the mime type
$finfo = new finfo(FILEINFO_MIME, "/usr/share/misc/magic");

/* get mime-type for a specific file */
$filename = "/usr/local/something.txt";
echo $finfo->file($filename);
```

---

[1]https://en.wikipedia.org/wiki/File_(command)
[2]https://php.net/manual/en/function.finfo-file.php

Managing Files

You can use PHP to manage files. Some of the common functions are listed in this table.

Function	Purpose
copy	Copies a file.
unlink	Deletes a file.
rename	Renames a file. You can use this to move a file between directories.
chmod	Sets file permissions.
chgrp	Changes the group of the file.
chown	Changes the owner of the file (superuser only).
umask	Changes the current umask.

Determining the Type of a File System Object

It is good programming practice to verify that files and directories exist and that you have the proper permissions to use them in the way you intend.

PHP provides functions that return Boolean values if the object matching the string you pass as the parameter meets the test. These functions take a string parameter that is the name of a file or directory.

In the following table, the check is against an object found that matches the name given in the parameter.

Function	Checks
is_dir	Is a directory
is_file	Is a file
is_readable	Is a file or directory and can be read
is_writeable	Is a file or directory and can be written to
is_executable	Is a file or directory and can be executed
is_link	Is a symlink
is_uploaded_file	Was uploaded by a POST request

All the functions will return FALSE if no file system object was found that matched the name given in the parameter.

Magic File Constants

PHP has several magic constants that you can use in relation to the file currently executing.

Constant	Refers To
__LINE__	The line of the file currently executing
__FILE__	The full path and filename of the file
__FUNCTION__	The current function name
__CLASS__	The name of the class in scope
__METHOD__	The name of the method being executed

These constants are very useful when writing debug logs. For example, I typically start all of my log messages with the __METHOD__ tag so that it's immediately clear which class and method the log message is generated in.

Streams

Streams in PHP are a way of generalizing file, network, data compression, and other operations that share a set of common functions and uses.

A stream is almost like a conveyer belt of things that come to you one by one. In PHP, you can also skip along the conveyer belt and seek to a position instead of waiting for it to come to you.

Streams are referenced in a format that you might recognize:

scheme://target

For example, http://www.php.net specifies the http scheme and the target as the URL of the PHP web site.

Stream Wrappers

Wrappers are code objects that translate the stream into a particular encoding or protocol. The PHP manual[3] has a list of the wrappers that are implemented within the language, and the stream_wrapper_register() function lets you define your own.

---

[3]https://php.net/manual/en/wrappers.php

Protocol	Use
`file://`	Accessing the local file system
`http://`	Accessing HTTP(s) URLs
`ftp://`	Accessing FTP(s) URLs
`php://`	Accessing various I/O streams
`compress.zlib://`	Compression streams
`data://`	Data (RFC 2397)
`glob://`	Find pathnames matching a pattern
`phar://`	PHP archive
`ssh2://`	Secure Shell 2
`rar://`	RAR
`ogg://`	Audio streams
`expect://`	Process interaction streams

The PHP streams that you can access are `stdin`, `stdout`, `stderr`, `input`, `output`, `fd`, `memory`, `temp`, and `filter`.

Note that in order to improve readability, I've omitted the protocol for all of these streams. When you use them, they should all be prefixed by the `php://` protocol, for example, `stdin` is `php://stdin`.

As an example of reading a stream, let's look at how to read the body of a PUT request. At some time in your career you will be coding a REST API and will need to read and parse the body of PUT requests that clients are making to your server. There is no superglobal for this request type as there is for GET and POST, so how is it done? The answer is in the `php://input` stream!

```php
<?php
// reads the PUT body
$input = file_get_contents('php://input');
// parses the input into an array
parse_str($input, $params);
print_r($params);
```

Filters

Stream filters can be applied to streams and perform transformation operations on data leaving the stream.

Filter	Function
string.rot13	Encodes the data with ROT13
string.toupper	Converts the string to uppercase
string.tolower	Converts the string to lowercase
string.strip_tags	Strips XML tags from the string
convert.*	Converts data according to an algorithm, for example
mcrypt.*	Provides symmetric encryption using libmcrypt
mdecrypt.*	The decryption filter using libmcrypt
zlib.*	Uses the ZLIB library to compress and uncompress data

These filters are attached to a stream using the stream_filter_append() function. You can apply the filter to the read and write directions of the stream independently.

```
<?php
$handle = fopen("files.php", 'a+');
stream_filter_append($handle, 'string.rot13');
while (!feof($handle)) {
    echo fread($handle,1024);
}
```

You can provide a third parameter to stream_filter_append() to attach it to reading or writing the stream. The parameter is one of the predefined constants STREAM_FILTER_READ, STREAM_FILTER_WRITE, or STREAM_FILTER_ALL. By default, the filter is attached to reads and writes.

This example will output something like this:

```
<?cuc
$unaqyr = sbcra("svyrf.cuc", 'n+');
fgernz_svygre_nccraq($unaqyr, 'fgevat.ebg13');
juvyr (!srbs($unaqyr)) {
    rpub sernq($unaqyr,1024);
}
```

Stream Contexts

Stream contexts are wrappers for a set of options that can modify a stream's behavior.

You create a context with the stream_context_create() function. You pass it two optional parameters, both of which are associative arrays. The first parameter is the options, and the second is an array of context parameters.

Each type of stream has its own set of context options. The PHP manual has the exhaustive list of them.

The only parameter currently available is a callable that will be called when an event occurs on a stream. The events are all predefined STREAM_NOTIFY_* constants.

The prototype for the callback function is in the PHP Manual, along with an example of notify events for the HTTP stream.

As an example, if you are downloading a file, you could set up your callback function to respond to the STREAM_NOTIFY_FILE_SIZE_IS event and abort the download if it is too big. This example prevents us from downloading the home page of www.example.com if it is larger than a kilobyte.

```php
<?php
function callback($notification_code,
    $severity,
    $message,
    $message_code,
    $bytes_transferred,
    $bytes_max)
{
    if ($notification_code == STREAM_NOTIFY_FILE_SIZE_IS) {
        if ($bytes_max > 1024) {
            die("Download too big!");
        }
    }
}

$context = stream_context_create();

stream_context_set_params($context,
    ["notification" => "callback"]);

$handle = fopen('http://www.example.com', 'r', false, $context);

fpassthru($handle);
```

You can change the options and parameters with the stream_context_set_params() function, while the stream_context_get_params() will return the current parameters for the stream.

CHAPTER 8 QUIZ

Q1: Assume that the web server user owns the data.csv file and that it contains the string "Hello World" before this script runs. What will the output of this code be?

```php
<?php
file_put_contents('data.csv', '1,2,3,4,5');
$handle = fopen('data.csv', 'c+');
$data = fgetcsv($handle, 2);
var_dump($data[1]);
```

string(0) ""
string(1) ","
string(1) "1"
string(1) "2"
This will produce an error

Q2: What will this code output?

```php
<?php
file_put_contents('test.csv', '1,2,3,4,5');
$handle = fopen('test.csv', 'c');
fputcsv($handle, ['6', '7', '8']);
fclose($handle);
echo file_get_contents('test.csv');
```

This will produce an error

1,2,3,4,5,6,7,8

6,7,8,1,2,3,4,5

6,7,8
1,2,3,4,5

6,7,8,1,2,3,4,5

1,2,3,4,5
6,7,8

Q3: If you are writing a REST interface and need to read the parameters sent in a PUT request, how can you do this?

Reference the $_REQUEST superglobal
Reference the $_POST superglobal
Read the php://input stream
Read the http://input stream

Q4: I want to write log entries to a file when my PHP program runs. I do not want to lose old log entries and I need my log entries to be in proper date order with the most recent entries following older entries. What file mode should I open my file in?

r

a

x

c

Q5: Assume that the file I retrieve is a valid GIF format image and that I am running PHP in Linux. What will the output of this code be?

```php
<?php
// This is a valid GIF image
$url = ' https://goo.gl/QycgqH';
file_put_contents('earth.gif', file_get_contents($url));
if (!rename('earth.gif', 'earth.jpeg')) {
    throw new RuntimeException('Could not rename the file.');
}
$finfo = new finfo();
echo $finfo->file('earth.jpeg') . PHP_EOL;
```

This produces an error

GIF image data, version 89a, 400x400

JPEG image data, 400x400

image/gif

image/jpeg

Could not rename the file

None of the above

CHAPTER 9

Web Features

PHP is a language created for the web. Its original purpose was to make it easier to make web pages and it remains heavily focused on server-side scripting. This chapter looks at some of the language features that make it one of the world's most popular server-side web programming languages.

Request Types

HTTP has several different request methods[1] that are commonly referred to as HTTP verbs. The HTTP specification[2] lays out in considerable detail what each verb is intended for. Your application should adhere to this specification so that it is compatible with the clients using it.

Verb	Used To
GET	Retrieve a representation of the specified resource
HEAD	Identical to GET but without any response body
POST	Submit an entry to the server, often resulting in a change such as adding a new resource
PUT	Replace the specified resource with the one in the request payload
PATCH	Apply a partial modification to the specified resource
DELETE	Delete the specified resource
CONNECT	Initiate an HTTP tunnel[3]
OPTIONS	Describe the communication options for the target resource
TRACE	Performs a message loop-back test to the target resource

---

[1]https://developer.mozilla.org/en-US/docs/Web/HTTP/Methods
[2]https://www.w3.org/Protocols/rfc2616/rfc2616-sec9.html#sec9
[3]https://developer.mozilla.org/en-US/docs/Web/HTTP/Methods/CONNECT

A. Beak, *PHP 7 Zend Certification Study Guide*,
https://doi.org/10.1007/978-1-4842-3246-0_9

Request Data

In a typical production web environment, PHP accepts requests passed to it by the web server. It runs and processes the request before terminating and waiting for the next request. The web server can pass data along with the request and this data forms part of the context[4] in which PHP runs.

An HTTP request consists of three parts: the URL, the headers, and the body. Data can be included in any of these parts of the request and will be made available to your PHP application as follows:

Source	Passed In	Available In
GET	Parameters in the request URL	$_GET
POST	Body of the request	$_POST
PUT	Body of the request	Read with php://input
PATCH	Body of the request	Read with php://input
Cookie	The "cookie" header	$_COOKIE
Uploaded file	Body of the request	$_FILES

If PHP is processing a request from the command line, then $_SERVER['argv'] contains an array of the arguments passed and $_SERVER['argc'] contains the number of arguments that were passed.

In addition to data contained in the HTTP request, PHP can accept data from the environment in which it runs. For example, you could run PHP in a docker container and set an environment variable that contains the address of the database server. You'd be able to reference this in your PHP script using the $_ENV superglobal.[5]

The Request Superglobal

The $_REQUEST superglobal is an associative array that by default contains the contents of $_GET, $_POST, and $_COOKIE.

The php.ini setting variables_order determines which of the ENV, GET, POST, and COOKIE variables are present in the $_REQUEST array as well as the order.[6]

If the same variable is in multiple request types, it will take on the value of the last one in the sequence of this settings value.

So, for example, imagine the configuration is set to EGPCS, indicating that POST comes after GET. Then if both $_GET['action'] and $_POST['action'] are set, then $_REQUEST['action'] will contain the value of $_POST['action'].

---

[4]https://en.wikipedia.org/wiki/Context_(computing)
[5]https://php.net/manual/en/reserved.variables.environment.php
[6]https://php.net/manual/en/ini.core.php#ini.variables-order

Because you won't be certain of exactly where the data in $_REQUEST is coming from, you should use this array with caution. Introducing uncertainty in your code complicates your testing and could impact security.

POST

By convention, POST requests are used to send data to the web site and instruct it to create a new entity. It is a write operation in the CRUD paradigm.

Receiving POST Data

Variables sent in a POST request are included in the body. Contrast this with GET requests that pass variables in the URL.

If a user submits a form, then the browser will encode the values into the body of the request and send it to you. Similarly, an application POSTing to an API endpoint will need to encode the variables into the request body. PHP will make them available to you in the $_POST variable.

For example, here is an example of a POST to a web site that is sending Ronald as the value of the name variable. This request would be used to add a person called Ron to the fan club.

```
POST   HTTP/1.1
Host: bieberfanclub.com
Content-Type: application/x-www-form-urlencoded
Cache-Control: no-cache

name=Ronald
```

If the application running bieberfanclub.com were running PHP, then the $_POST array would be an array containing an element called name with the value Ronald.

There are three advantages to sending variables with POST:

- POST data can be encoded in a particular character set, which isn't the case with GET.

- Because your variables are being sent in the message body, you're not limited as to how much data you can send by the length of the URL.

- POST allows you to upload files but GET does not.

There is no difference in security between the two methods.

There is no limit in the HTTP protocol on the length of the URL, but there are limits on browsers and other clients. As a general rule, don't create a URL longer than 2000 characters.

Sending POST Data

When you want to make a POST request to another application, you need to take responsibility for encoding the variables into the body. The simplest way to do this is with the curl extension.[7] Curl supports several protocols and makes it easy to set up your request exactly as you want it.

Using curl involves the following process:

1. Initialize a curl session.

2. Set options for the session.

3. Execute the session (make the call).

4. Close the session and release the resource.

Let's look at how you can use curl to set up the request you looked at before, where you POSTed the variable name containing the value Ronald to the Bieber fan club.

```php
<?php
// We specify the url when we initialize the curl resource
$curlResource = curl_init("https://requestb.in/13fkcqj1");
// This array contains the variables we want to POST
$postData = ['name' => 'Ron'];
// Tell curl to do a application/x-www-form-urlencoded POST
curl_setopt($curlResource, CURLOPT_POST, true);
// We specify the values to POST
curl_setopt($curlResource,CURLOPT_POSTFIELDS, $postData);
// Execute the request and store the response
$response = curl_exec($curlResource);
// If there is an error it will be stored in $err
$err = curl_error($curlResource);
// Close the handle
curl_close($curlResource);
```

If you run this code, you will be able to see the result at https://requestb.in/13fkcqj1?inspect.

■ **Tip**   It is possible to pass curl_setopt() an array of all the options you want to set instead of calling it multiple times.

GET

GET requests are typically used to get either a single entity or a collection of entities from a server. You can think of it as reading data from the server.

---

[7]https://php.net/manual/en/book.curl.php

Receiving GET Data

Variables sent in a GET request are encoded into the URL. Here is an example of how variables are encoded into a URL:

http://bieberfanclub.com/topfan.php?name=Ron&rank=cheerleader

The variables begin with a question mark and are delimited by ampersand symbols. Each variable is a key-value pair with the equals sign denoting the value.

PHP will automatically make variables passed in the URL available in the $_GET superglobal.

It is possible to pass arrays through GET using syntax like this:

http://example.com/users.php?sort[col]=name&sort[order]=desc

You would be able to access these variables like this:

```php
<?php
echo $_GET['sort']['col'];
echo $_GET['sort']['order'];
```

Sending GET Data

PHP includes a function that makes it very easy to build the URL string to pass your GET data.

```php
<?php
$getData = ['fans' => ['Ron', 'Jonathan', 'Anne Frank']];
// fans%5B0%5D=Ron&fans%5B1%5D=Jonathan&fans%5B2%5D=Anne+Frank
echo http_build_query($getData);
```

The http_build_query() function converts an array to a properly URL-encoded query string.

The HTTP specification for the URL only allows a very limited set of characters to be used. Any character that is not in this set must be encoded.[8] PHP provides the urlencode() function, which will properly encode a string to be used as part of a URL. The urldecode() function will convert an encoded string back to its original representation.

```php
<?php
$getData = ['fans' => ['Ron', 'Jonathan', 'Anne Frank']];
// fans%5B0%5D=Ron&fans%5B1%5D=Jonathan&fans%5B2%5D=Anne+Frank
$encodedString = http_build_query($getData);
// fans[0]=Ron&fans[1]=Jonathan&fans[2]=Anne Frank
echo urldecode($encodedString);
```

In this example, we're decoding the properly URL-encoded string that http_build_query() generated so that we can see how an array is encoded in a parameter.

---

[8]https://en.wikipedia.org/wiki/Percent-encoding

PUT

PUT requests are used to replace an entire entity or collection. Typically, a PUT request will require you to specify all the mandatory attributes of an entity. It is a write operation because it replaces an entity with the state that you provide.

PATCH requests are similar in that they are used to replace data, but a PATCH request will only replace the part of the entity that you provide. For example, if a user has a name, surname, and e-mail field, you will be able to use a PATCH request to change just one of those fields while leaving the others the same. API servers often don't implement PATCH and rather require you to use PUT.

Receiving PUT Data

PHP does not make a superglobal available for PUT. To get access to it, you need to read the php://input stream. You can use the parse_str() function to convert it into an array:

```php
<?php
$putVariables = [];
parse_str(file_get_contents("php://input"), $putVariables);
```

Sending PUT Data

PUT data is transmitted exactly as with POST, so curl is the simplest way to send it in PHP.

```php
<?php
$data = ["fan" => "Ron"];
$curlResource = curl_init();
$options = [
    CURLOPT_URL => 'https://requestb.in/oxk2utox',
    CURLOPT_CUSTOMREQUEST => 'PUT',
    CURLOPT_POSTFIELDS => $data
];
curl_setopt_array($curlResource, $options);
$response = curl_exec($curlResource);
```

In the previous example, we are telling curl to make a PUT request and we stipulate the values to pass exactly as we did for POST.

Notice that we are using the curl_setopt_array() function to set multiple curl options at once instead of calling curl_setopt() multiple times.

Sessions

HTTP is a stateless protocol, which means that the connection between the client and the server is lost once the transaction ends. Furthermore, PHP terminates when it finishes processing a request and its application state is lost.

A session is a means for the server to persist application state for consecutive requests from a visitor.

Information like whether the user is logged in can be stored in the session. Another example of where a session could be used is with an online shopping site, where the contents of the visitor's shopping cart could be stored in a session.

Session information is stored on the server and is associated with a unique identifier. The client will send the session identifier to the server with every request and this allows the server to associate the request with a particular session.

If you have multiple web servers, then you'll need to find a way to either share the session information between them or ensure that a visitor is always directed to the server that holds her session information.

Web sites that don't need to remember who a user is or keep any preferences don't need to use sessions. An example of such a site would be one that serves static content that is the same for all visitors.

PHP supports sessions by default, but they can be disabled through a configuration setting in php.ini.

Starting a Session

A session in PHP is started when you call the function session_start() or automatically if your php.ini configuration specifies session.auto_start = 1.

If you are using session_start(), then you must make sure that you call this function before any output is sent to the client.

When the session starts, the user is assigned a random unique session identifier called the session id. The session ID is either stored in a cookie on the client or passed through the URL if you enable the session.use_trans_sid configuration setting.

Accepting sessions from the URL can be risky and it is better to configure PHP to only use cookies with the session.use_only_cookies setting. Chapter 6 on security has more information about this.

Session Identifier and Session Variables

The session extension makes available the SID predefined constant that holds the session identifier. You can also use the session_id() function to get or set it.

You can use the function session_regenerate_id() to make a new session identifier for a client. You should call this immediately after calling session_start() to help protect against session fixation.

Once a session has started, the superglobal $_SESSION is available as an associative array containing the session variables.

Ending a Session

To properly end a session, you should do three things:

1. Set the $_SESSION array to an empty array.

2. Set the session cookie expiry time to the past.

3. Call the function session_destroy().

223

The effect of Step 2 is to let the client browser know that it can delete the cookie containing the session identifier. There is no guarantee that the client will do so, however. Of course, if you're not using cookie-based sessions then there is no need to do this.

Session Handlers

PHP supports creating your own session handler, but by default PHP sessions are stored on disk and use the serialize() and unserialize() commands to encode and decode the data.

In addition to disk-based sessions, PHP also ships with a memcached session handler that can be configured in php.ini.

If you want to write your own session handler, you should implement the SessionHandler interface. This will let you use alternative ways of storing your sessions and customize how you encode and decode the session data.

File Uploads

We'll focus on how file uploads work and the PHP syntax associated with them in this section. Make sure that you study the section on file uploads in Chapter 6 in conjunction with this section.

Forms allow files to be uploaded by means of a "multi-part" HTTP POST transaction.

You can specify that you want to encode your POST using multi-part form data in your HTML by declaring a form something like this:

```
<form enctype="multipart/form-data" action="" method="post">
```

Note that I've left the "action" attribute blank. By default, an HTML form will submit to the URI that it is served from.

Limiting the Size of Uploads

You do not want people to be able to upload massive files that fill up your disk. To manage the size of files that people can upload, you can limit the size in the browser and on the server.

To tell the client to limit the size of the upload, you can add an input to your form like this:

```
<input type="hidden" name="MAX_FILE_SIZE" value=" 1000000" />
```

Limiting the size in the browser should be done just to improve user experience. It is very simple for a user to disable or change the limit to bypass the limit.

You should rather configure PHP to limit the size of a POST operation. The post_max_size setting limits the maximum of data any POST may contain. The upload_max_filesize is applied to limit the size of files that can be uploaded.

Temporary Files

PHP stores the uploaded file in a temporary location and makes it available to the script that the form POST'ed to.

You can process the file in the temporary location and then optionally move it to a permanent location. PHP will automatically delete the temporary file when the script finishes running so if you want to keep it you must move it.

In addition to creating the temporary file, PHP will populate the $_FILES superglobal array. Each file that was uploaded in the form will have an entry in the array.

You need to be aware that the information in the $_FILES array can quite easily be spoofed so you should manually validate every piece of information.

Each file be represented by an array in the $_FILES superglobal and will key for the name, type, size, temporary filename, and error code.

Key	Description
name	The original name of the file stored on the client
type	The MIME type provided by the client
size	The size in bytes of the file
tmp_name	The name of the file in its temporary location
error	An error code, or UPLOAD_ERR_OK if the upload was successful

■ **Note**   Chapter 6 has more information on dealing with file uploads.

Forms

Forms allow users to submit data to your PHP script.

When declaring a form in HTML, you specify the method it uses to send information to the server. Although you can choose GET or POST, you should make sure that you choose a request method that matches what you intend to do.

PHP automatically makes form data available to your script in one of two superglobals—$_GET or $_POST—depending on which method the form used to make the request.

Form Elements

These superglobals can easily be edited by the client and so should always be filtered carefully and not trusted.

Dots and space in form field names are converted to underscores. As an example, consider the HTML input tag:

```
<input name="email.address" type="text">
```

The value that it contains will be placed in either $_GET['email_address'] or $_POST['email_address'] depending on the forms method.

Arrays in HTML Forms

Form data can be turned into an array using syntax like this in HTML:

```
<form action="formhandler.php" method="POST">
<input type="text" name="name[first]">
        <input type="text" name="name[last]">
        <input type="submit">
</form>
```

This will result in $_POST or $_GET being an array that looks like this:

```
array(
  'name' => array(
    'first' => '',
    'last' => ''
  )
)
```

One of the most useful ways that arrays help is in grouping inputs together. Consider a checkbox that can have multiple values:

```
<h1>What pets do you want in your home?</h1>
<form action="formhandler.php" method="POST">
<input type="checkbox" name="pets[]" value="cats" id="lotsacats">
<label for="lotsacats">Lots of Cats</label>
<input type="checkbox" name="pets[]" value="dog" id="adog">
<label for="adog">Just a dog</label>
<input type="submit">
</form>
```

If the person checked both boxes before submitting the form, then the $_GET or $_POST array will contain the following:

```
array(
  'pets' => array('cats', 'dog')
)
```

This makes checkboxes a lot neater and easier to use. You can read more about this in the PHP Manual.[9]

---

[9]https://secure.php.net/manual/en/faq.html.php#faq.html.arrays

Selecting Multiple Items from a List

Last, you will need to use an array if you want the user to be able to select multiple items from a select list:

```
<select name="var[]" multiple="yes">
```

Note that the name of the select is an array, so each value that the user selects will be added to the "var" array in your superglobal array.

Cookies

Cookies let you store a small (4 to 6 KB) amount of data on the client device. The client will read them and send them with each request.

You can store any sort of information in a cookie, but they are most commonly associated with sessions. PHP can store its session identifier in the cookie. The session information is stored on the server and matched to the client through the identifier in the cookie. PHP does this for you when you start your session. By default, PHP session cookies are valid until the person closes their browser.

You cannot control cookies on the client device. They can be edited or deleted at any time by the client. This means that you should neither trust the information sent with them nor rely on them to exist. You should also not store sensitive information in cookies.

If you want to delete a cookie, you can set an expiry date that is in the past. This will let the client know that the cookie is no longer needed and can be deleted. You have no guarantee that the client will respect this.

A server will set a cookie using the Set-Cookie response header. The client will include it with future requests using the Cookie request header.

Setting Cookies

The setcookie() function is used to set a cookie. The parameters are explained in the PHP Manual and are given in the order of this table:

Parameter	Used For
value	Storing a scalar value in the cookie.
expire	Unix epoch timestamp when the cookie expires. You can't rely on the cookie existing until it expires, as it is common for people to delete their cookies.
path	The base path on the domain that the cookie will be available on. If you set it to /, then it will be available on all paths; otherwise, it will be available on the path and all sub-paths from it.
domain	The cookie will be available on this and all sub-domains under it. You can only set a cookie that matches the domain the cookie is being served from.

(continued)

227

Parameter	Used For
secure	Tells the client that it should only send the cookie if it is being sent over an HTTPS encrypted connection.
httponly	Tells the client that it should only send the cookie using HTTP and not make it available to scripting languages like JavaScript. To a limited degree, this can help reduce XSS and session fixation attacks on clients that support it.

Cookies can only store scalar values. You can, however, use syntax like the following example:

```php
<?php
setcookie("user[name]", "Alice");
setcookie("user[email]", "alice@example.com");
```

The next time the person makes a request to the site, the $_COOKIE variable will contain something like this:

```
Array
(
        [PHPSESSID] => jlm5od9ngqi3krmu6fkjcebcb4
        [user] => Array
    (

        [name] => Alice
        [email] => alice@example.com
    )

)
```

Note that user is an array and that the cookie value also contains the PHP session identifier.

Retrieving Cookies

You can access the cookie information using the $_COOKIE superglobal.

Remember that this array is populated with information from the cookie sent by the client. This means that if you use setcookie() to create or change a cookie, the $_COOKIE array will only contain the new information when the client makes a new request.

HTTP Headers

HTTP headers are sent with the request from the client and with the response from the server. They are used to convey information about the HTTP message such as what sort of information is being provided and what will be accepted in return.

HTTP headers take the form of a name-value pair in a clear text string. A carriage return and line feed character follows each header. There is no limit in the standard but most servers and clients impose limits on the length of a header and the total number of headers that may be sent in one request/response.

PHP will automatically emit valid headers for you, but there are several cases where you may want to send your own header.

Sending Headers

The PHP function header() lets you send a header to the client. You may only send headers before any normal content has been sent to the client. One of the reasons that it is common to omit the closing ?> tag in included PHP files is to avoid having a newline character occur after the tag. This character would be sent as HTML content and would prevent you from being able to send headers.

The parameters sent to header() are as follows:

Parameter	Description
Header string	String containing the header to set. For example, "Cache-Control: no-cache, must-revalidate".
Replace	Boolean to indicate whether this header must replace a previously sent header with the same name.
Response code	The HTTP response code to send with the header.

There are two special cases for headers. The first is for headers that begin with the string "HTTP/". These can be used to explicitly set the HTTP response code, as in this example from the PHP manual[10]:

```php
<?php
header("HTTP/1.0 404 Not Found");
```

The second special case is for using the "Location" header. This header indicates to the client that the document they are looking for is in the location you specify.

■ **Note**   PHP will automatically set a 302 HTTP status code if you use this header, unless you've already set a 2xx or 3xx header.

Here's an example:

```php
<?php
header("Location: http://www.example.com/");
exit;
```

---

[10]https://php.net/manual/en/function.header.php

In this example, the server will respond with status code 302 and the client will be redirected to the example domain.

Note the usage of the exit language construct after sending the redirect header. Your code continues to run after sending the header unless you stop it. It is up to the client to respect your redirect header. If they decide not to respect it, your code will continue to output and they will see whatever output it generates. Make sure you explicitly terminate your program after sending a redirect header.

Tracking Headers

The headers_list() function will return an array of headers that are ready to be sent or have already been sent to the client. You can determine if the headers have been sent by calling headers_sent().

If you want to prevent a particular header from being sent, you can use the headers_remove() function to unset a header from the list to be sent.

HTTP Authentication

PHP can send a header to the client that causes it to pop up an Authentication Required dialog box. When the user fills in the dialog with a user and password, the URL of the PHP script is called again.

On the second call, PHP will have three predefined variables available in the $_SERVER array. These are PHP_AUTH_USER, PHP_AUTH_PW, and AUTH_TYPE and are set to the username, password, and authentication type respectively.

You should then authenticate the user using whatever method you see fit, such as checking the user and password against a database.

Examples of HTTP authentication are given on the PHP manual page[11]:

```php
<?php
 if (!isset($_SERVER['PHP_AUTH_USER'])) {
     header('WWW-Authenticate: Basic realm="My Realm"');
     header('HTTP/1.0 401 Unauthorized');
     echo 'Text to send if user hits Cancel button';
     exit;
 } else {
     echo "<p>Hello {$_SERVER['PHP_AUTH_USER']}.</p>";
     echo "<p>You entered {$_SERVER['PHP_AUTH_PW']} as your password.</p>";
}
```

In this example, we just output the contents of the variables in the $_SERVER array, but in real life we would perform some form of authentication.

The password sent by the client is base64encoded to standardize the character set, but there is no hashing or encryption performed. This is a very weak form of protecting your site and unless you are using HTTPS, the password will be readable by anybody between your client and server.

---

[11]https://php.net/manual/en/features.http-auth.php

HTTP Status Codes

HTTP status codes are sent with responses and follow standards set by the Internet Engineering Task Force, as well as de facto standards used within the industry.

HTTP status codes are divided into ranges of 100 codes each. All of the status codes in the range will have a similar meaning, as in this following table.

Range	General Meaning
200	The request was successful
300	The request needs to be redirected
400	There was an error on the client side
500	There was an error on the server side

You won't need to know all of the status codes by heart for your exam. When you're writing an API in real life, you'll be able to visit Wikipedia[12] and choose the right code for your response.

For your exam, you just need to know the most important ones:

Code	Status
200	OK; the request was successful.
201	Created; the request resulted in a new resource being created.
301	Moved permanently; the resource will always be found at the location specified.
400	Bad request; there was something in the request that was malformed or otherwise prevented its execution.
401	Unauthorized; the client has not been authenticated as being allowed to make this request.
403	Forbidden; the (authenticated) client is not allowed to make this request.
418	I'm a teapot; the client is attempting to send coffee making protocols to the server, which is in fact a teapot.[13] Okay this isn't an important status code, but it's fun to know about.
500	Internal server error; the server was not able to complete the request and can't respond more appropriately. Commonly associated with a crash or misconfiguration.

---

[12]https://en.wikipedia.org/wiki/List_of_HTTP_status_codes
[13]https://en.wikipedia.org/wiki/Hyper_Text_Coffee_Pot_Control_Protocol

When using APIs the HTTP status code is very important. If you're coding an API, you should make sure that you send the correct status code for the error.

For example, if the request failed and you send an error message in the body, you should make sure that the HTTP status code is 400 and not 200.

As you work with PHP, you'll become more familiar with the status codes, but if in doubt, you should look up a list and make sure that you're sending an appropriate response.

Output Control Functions

Instead of outputting from your script immediately, it is often very useful to store your output in a buffer and then flush the whole buffer at once. This could be useful for escaping output before sending it to the user, or using PHP's built-in compression routines to compress the response you send to compatible browsers.

The ob_start() function is used to start output buffering. Anything that your script would normally output in the body of the response will be stored into the buffer. This function takes an optional parameter, which is a callable and will be called when the buffer is either output or discarded.

Here is an example of setting a callback function. I've included the output of the script as a comment.

```php
<?php
function escapeOutput(string $buffer): string {
    return htmlentities($buffer);
}

ob_start("escapeOutput");

// &lt;script&gt;alert(&quot;xss&quot;);&lt;/script&gt;
echo '<script>alert("xss");</script>';
```

In this example, the buffer was implicitly flushed when the script ended. You can use the ob_flush() function[14] to explicitly flush the buffer and output its contents. One time that this could be useful is when you're writing a CLI script and want to be able to see progress, and another (arguably bad) use case could be to write the server for a long-polling JavaScript client.

```php
<?php
ob_start();
// this is a cli script
for ($i=1; $i<5; $i++) {
    echo $i;
    // each character is output one by one
    ob_flush();
    sleep(1);
}
```

---

[14]https://php.net/manual/en/function.ob-flush.php

The ob_flush function will output the buffer and allow further output to be buffered. Compare this to ob_end_flush,[15] which will output the buffer and disable any further buffering.

■ **Note** The flush() function can be used if your web server is buffering output and you want to try override this behavior and send something directly to the browser. This won't always work, however.

PHP has a built-in way to help you compress data before you send it over the network. If you enable it, then PHP will detect if the browser is able to support compressed data and, if so, use the GZIP algorithm to reduce the size of the response. To set it up, you specify the compression function as the callback for ob_start(). Look at the PHP manual[16] for more examples, but here is a simple example:

```php
<?php
ob_start("ob_gzhandler");
?>
{"string": "my json api output is compressed now"}
```

CHAPTER 9 QUIZ

Q1: Assume that the variables_order is set to the PHP default. What would the value of $_REQUEST['biggestfan'] be for the following HTTP request?

```
POST  HTTP/1.1
Host: thebeebfanclub.com?biggestfan=Ron
Content-Type: application/x-www-form-urlencoded
Cache-Control: no-cache

biggestfan=Ronald
```

Ron

Ronald

Something else

None of the above

---

[15]https://php.net/manual/en/function.ob-end-flush.php
[16]https://secure.php.net/manual/en/function.ob-gzhandler.php

Q2: Each of these inputs is in a properly constructed form that POSTs to your site. Which one is the correct way in which to place the name entered into the input box into a variable that you can access like this $_POST['justin']['numberonefan']?

```
<input type="text" name="justin.numberonefan">
<input type="text" name="justin(numberonefan)">
<input type="text" name="justin[numberonefan]">
<input type="text" name="justin_numberonefan">
```
None of the above

Q3: Cookies are a reliable way to store information without wasting server resources. Choose the most correct option.

Yes, storing information on the client side saves server disk space

No, a copy of the information is still kept in the session data

No, they are not reliable

Yes, it is common to store all of the session data in cookies

Q4: What will this code output? Choose all that apply

```
<?php
echo $a;
session_start();
echo session_id();
```

A notice because $a is undefined

A warning because $a is undefined

A warning because you cannot start the session

A random string containing the session_id

Q5: The domain property of a cookie is used to do which of the following?

Limit which part(s) of your web site the cookie is valid for

Specify the name of your web site

Prevent the browser from sending this cookie to other web sites

None of the above

CHAPTER 10

■ ■ ■

Databases and SQL

Databases are a tool to persist data that you intend to refer to regularly and need to keep for a long time.

PHP uses extensions to interact with a range of databases. For example, to interact with the MySQL database, you can use the functions provided by the `mysqli` extension.

■ **Note** There is an "i" at the end of `mysqli`. This is the replacement for the now deprecated `mysql` extension. Features like "prepared statements" are only available with the new extension.

PHP also offers abstraction layers that provide an application layer between your code and the database. We'll be looking at PDO (PHP Data Objects) in this book.

We'll be focusing on relational databases in this book, but it is worth mentioning in passing an alternative to relational databases. MongoDB is a very popular NoSQL database and it has contributed a driver for PHP that allows you to connect to the database. We'll be focusing on the native relational databases and the MongoDB driver is not likely to be included in your Zend examination.

You will be expected to know basic SQL for your Zend examination. The assumed environment will be MySQL if the question does not specify otherwise.

Database Basics

Let's begin by making sure that some of the concepts of relational databases are clear.

Keys

Keys impose constraints, such as PRIMARY and UNIQUE. A primary key can be defined on either a single or multiple columns. It guarantees that each row in the database will have a unique value combination for the columns in the key. A row may not have a null value for its primary key.

© Andrew Beak 2017
A. Beak, *PHP 7 Zend Certification Study Guide*,
https://doi.org/10.1007/978-1-4842-3246-0_10

A table may have only one primary key. A foreign key can also be defined on either a single or multiple columns. It references the primary key on another table. This is a unique reference, so only one row in the referenced table will be linked to the table containing the foreign key.

Figure 10-1 refers to the category that a product belongs to with the foreign key category_id.

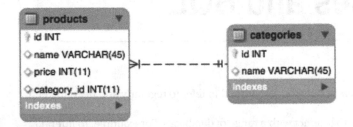

Figure 10-1. *Both tables have primary keys named id*

Indexes

Indexes are data structures that are needed to implement the key constraint. Indexes make retrieving records faster. The database engine will create a structure on disk or in memory that contains the data from the indexed columns. This structure is optimized for lookups and helps the database find the row in the table faster.

Whenever you insert a row into a table, the indexes need to be updated. This adds an overhead to writing.

You cannot have a key without an index, but it is possible to index columns that are not keyed. You would do this in cases where you don't want to enforce uniqueness but do want to speed up SELECT statements that include these columns in their WHERE clauses.

The binding between keys and indexes is very tight and in MySQL they are considered synonymous.

Relationships

Relationships are a core feature of relational databases. By declaring how tables are related, you can enforce referential integrity and minimize dirty data.

There are several types of relationships.

Relationship	Description
One-to-one	One row in the parent table can reference exactly one row in the child table.
One-to-many	One row in the parent table can be referenced by many rows in the child table.
Many-to-many	Any number of rows in the parent table can be referenced by any number of rows in the child table.

By having relationships between tables, you can store data that is logically related together in a table distinct from other data.

For example, you can have a products table that stores information about what you sell. Products belong to categories. A single category can have lots of different products in it. This means that one row in the category table can be referred to by multiple rows in the products table.

SQL Data Types

Columns in a SQL database table have a data type assigned to them. Just as with PHP variable types, SQL types can each store different formats of data.

Each database manager will implement the SQL data types slightly differently and will have different optimizations between its types.

We discuss a few of the common data types and avoid focusing on any particular implementation of SQL.

Numeric Types

The types of integers vary in the amount of bytes that they take to store their value.

The following table illustrates the sizes of integers for the MySQL database:[1]

Integer Type	Bytes	(Signed) Values	(Unsigned) Values
BIGINT	8	-9223372036854775808 to + 9223372036854775807	0 to 18446744073709551615
INTEGER	4	-2147483648 to +2147483647	0 to 4294967295
MEDIUMINT	3	-8388608 to +8388607	0 to 16777215
SMALLINT	2	-32768 to +32767	0 to 65535
TINYINT	1	-128 to +127	0 to 255

■ **Tip** MySQL allows you to specify a parameter for integers, which is actually a display value and doesn't affect the underlying storage. It's a fairly common misconception that the parameter is for precision.

Non-integer types can be stored in either NUMERIC or DECIMAL values. The SQL-92 standard specifies that a NUMERIC type must have the exact precision stipulated, while the DECIMAL type must be at least as precise. The implementation of these data types does differ between vendors.

---

[1]https://dev.mysql.com/doc/refman/5.7/en/integer-types.html

They both take the same parameters:

```
NUMERIC(21,3)
```

The first parameter specifies the total number of digits of precision, and the second parameter specifies how many digits of decimal precision must be stored.

In the example, we are going to store a number that has 21 digits in total, of which three appear after the decimal point.

Character Types

SQL allows for character to be stored either in fixed- or variable-length strings.

A fixed-length string is always allocated the same number of bytes on disk. This can help speed up read performance in some database implementations. The trade-off is that if a string being stored in a fixed length data store is shorter than the number of characters allocated, you are storing more characters than you have to.

Variable-length strings can swell up to the limiting size given to them. The database engine allocates storage according to the length of the string. Database implementations will store the length of the string being stored. This will be at least one character to indicate the end of the string, but in some engines each variable string will incur heavier storage overhead.

In general, when storing a string that you know is always going to be of a particular length, such as a hash for example, you should store it in a fixed-length character field. This will improve performance and you won't incur storage waste.

Working with SQL

We won't focus on any specific implementation of SQL and will rather try to use generic statements. The Zend examination will not be testing your knowledge of a particular database engine, but will be expecting you to know basic SQL syntax.

Creating a Database and Table

The CREATE statement can be used to create databases and tables. Creating a database is simple; you just specify the name of the database:

```
CREATE DATABASE mydatabase;
```

When creating a table, you can specify a list of the columns you want to store in it. For each column, you specify the name, data type, and attributes.

```
CREATE TABLE IF NOT EXISTS users (
  id int unsigned NOT NULL AUTO_INCREMENT,
  name varchar(255) NOT NULL,
  email varchar(255) NOT NULL,
  password varchar(60) NOT NULL,
```

```
  PRIMARY KEY (id),
  UNIQUE KEY users_email_unique (email)
);
```

Dropping Database and Tables

The inverse of CREATE is the DROP statement.

```
DROP TABLE category;
DROP DATABASE mydatabase;
```

If you have specified foreign keys, the database will not let you drop a table if this will violate one of the constraints.

As an example, refer to our example with products and categories. If we try to drop the category table and there are still products referencing it, the database engine should not allow the operation.

Retrieving Data

The SELECT statement is used to retrieve data. The syntax for SELECT can be very complicated and is one of the statements that differs the most between vendors. You will need to understand basic usage and joins for your Zend certification.

In this simple pseudo-code example of a query, we retrieve the names of products from our table that cost more than 100 currency units. We specify that we want the results to be returned in descending order of price.

```
SELECT name
  FROM products
  WHERE price > 100
  ORDER BY price DESC
```

You can specify multiple column names separated by commas or use the wildcard * to receive all columns.

The format of the data that PHP receives is dependent on the driver and function that you use to call the query. You'll generally receive an object or an array that has keys/properties corresponding to the columns.

Inserting New Data

The INSERT statement is used to create new rows in the database. You will need to provide a list of the columns and the values to insert to them. Columns that are marked NOT NULL are mandatory and must have a value specified when you create the row.

```
INSERT INTO products
  (name, price, category_id) VALUES
  ('cheeseburger', 100, 3)
```

If you don't specify the names of the columns, SQL will assume that you're providing values in the order that the columns appear in the table. This can be a drawback if ever you change the structure of your table.

Otherwise, as in the example, you specify the names of the columns, and then the values. The values are assigned to the columns in order. So, in this example the name of the product is set to 'cheeseburger', its price is 100, and it is placed into the category that has an ID value of 3 (whatever that may be).

Updating Data

The UPDATE statement accepts a list of values similar to the INSERT statement, as well as an optional WHERE clause similar to the SELECT statement.

You must specify what values to update the existing data to, and the criteria for the rows that must be updated.

```
UPDATE products
  SET price = price + 100
  WHERE category_id = 3;
```

Aggregating Data

You can use the database to perform calculations and send you the results.

Statement	Returns
AVG	Average value of the data values
SUM	Total of all the data values found
COUNT	How many records were found
DISTINCT COUNT	How many unique records were found
MIN	The lowest value in the data set
MAX	The highest value in the data set

Using these functions looks as follows:

```
SELECT AVG(price) FROM products;
```

Grouping Data

You can tell SQL to group data by a column or combination of columns before returning it to you. This is often useful in conjunction with the aggregating functions.

Let's consider an example where we want to find out the total amount of sales that each of our customers has purchased.

```
SELECT email, SUM( sales_value )
       FROM  `transactions`
       GROUP BY email
```

In this example, we group transactions that have the same e-mail address. The SQL database engine will apply the SUM statement by adding the sales values in each group and then returning that.

I included the e-mail address in the SELECT statement so that the output will have the e-mail address of the customer, and the sum of all the sales values of transactions with their e-mail address.

Joins

Joins are used to connect tables based on supplied criteria. This lets you retrieve information from related tables.

In the products and categories database, you can retrieve the category name of products by joining the categories table to the products table:

```
SELECT *
FROM  products
JOIN categories ON categories.id = products.category_id
```

We are joining the categories table to the products table and giving instructions to SQL on how to match rows. A row from the categories table will be included if its id column matches the category_id column in the products table.

Join Types

There are several ways to join tables.

Join Type	Effect
INNER JOIN	Selects records that have matching values in both tables, as in the previous example
LEFT OUTER JOIN	Selects tables from the left table that have matching right table records
RIGHT OUTER JOIN	Selects records from the right table that have matching left table records
FULL OUTER JOIN	Selects all records that match either left or right table records

These joins can be represented diagrammatically, as shown in Figure 10-2.

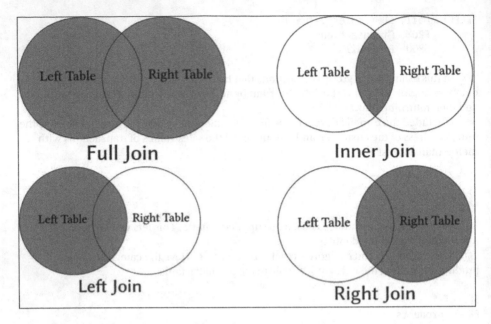

Figure 10-2. *Many ways to join tables*

Prepared Statements

When you issue a command to a SQL engine, it must parse the command in order to execute it. After the statement has been executed, SQL will discard the compiled code with the result that repeated calls with the same SQL command will need to be parsed individually. Obviously, this results in duplicated effort.

You can save SQL from having to repeat its efforts by using prepared statements that become parsed code templates that SQL stores for multiple reuse.

Prepared statements also offer significant security advantages. Parameters are bound to the prepared statement, and are not included as part of the code string. This means that it is not possible for your parameters to intrude on the code, which means that you no longer need to worry about escaping code to prevent SQL injection. Just keep in mind the possibility of stored XSS attacks before you stop worrying about escaping data coming into or out of your database.

```php
<?php
// prepare and bind
$stmt = $conn->prepare("INSERT INTO users (username, password) VALUES
(?, ?)");
$stmt->bind_param("ss", $username, $password);

// set parameters
$username = "bob";
$password = password_hash("password", PASSWORD_BCRYPT);
```

```
// run the statement
$stmt->execute();
```

Transactions

A transaction is a set of SQL statements that will either all succeed or else have no effect.

After a transaction finishes the database must not have any table constraints invalidated and must be in a state where all the changes have been persisted. A database must have some way of ensuring that transactions can run at the same time and not interfere with each other, for example, by incrementing a primary key that another transaction is depending on.

In summary, a transaction is a set of SQL statements that must complete successfully in an "all or nothing" manner. After it runs the database must be in a consistent state and must be recoverable from error.

The syntax for transactions varies between vendors, but there are three important statements.

- One statement will mark the beginning of the transaction block. The SQL statements following this will be part of the transaction.

- There are two statements that can end a transaction. One of them will tell SQL to go ahead and make all the changes that the transaction is making.

- The other end statement will tell SQL that for whatever reason you want to abandon the transaction and rather revert to the state the database was in when the transaction started.

Here are the three most common vendor statements:

MySQL	MS-SQL	ORACLE
START TRANSACTION	BEGIN TRANSACTION	START TRANSACTION
COMMIT	COMMIT TRANSACTION	COMMIT
ROLLBACK	ROLLBACK WORK	ROLLBACK

PHP Data Object (PDO)

The PDO is a data abstraction layer that offers a single interface for you to interact with multiple data sources. While using the PDO, you can use the same functions to interact with your database, no matter the vendor.

It's important to understand that PDO is an access abstraction layer and does not abstract SQL or data types. The SQL that you pass to the PDO::query() or prepared statements must be valid for the vendor you are connecting to.

PDO uses database adapters to connect to the database. These adapter classes implement PDO interfaces and expose vendor-specific functions as regular extension functions.

PDO is configured in the PHP configuration file. At runtime, you can change options with the PDO::setAttribute() function.

The PDO extension makes several predefined constants available. You won't need to remember them all for the Zend examination, but look through the PHP manual and familiarize yourself with them.

The PDO will emulate prepared statements for databases that don't support them, but will otherwise use the native prepared statement functionality of the database.

Connecting to PDO

To connect to the database with PDO, you create an instance of the PDO class. The constructor accepts parameters for the database source (DSN) and the username/password if these are required.

```php
<?php
try {
    $dbh = new PDO('mysql:host=localhost;dbname=test', $user, $pass);
} catch (PDOException $e) {
    echo "Error connecting to database: " . $e->getMessage();
}
```

If there are errors connecting to the database then a PDOException will be thrown. It is very important to note that the stack trace of the exception will probably contain the full database connection details. Make sure that you catch it and don't let it be displayed RAW.

To close a connection when you're done with it, you can set the PDO variable to null.

```
$dbh = null;
```

Database connections are automatically closed at the end of your running script unless you make them persistent. Persistent database connections are not closed but are instead cached for another instance of the script to use. This reduces the overhead of needing to connect to the database every time your web application runs.

Transactions in PDO

PDO offers transaction commands too, but does not emulate proper transaction handling. This means that you can only use the PDO transaction functions on databases that natively support transactions. The functions are PDO::beginTransaction(), PDO::commit(), and PDO::rollBack().

```php
<?php
$dsn = 'mysql:host=localhost;dbname=example';
$pdo = ncw PDO($dsn, 'dbuser', 'dbpass');
$pdo->setAttribute(PDO::ATTR_EMULATE_PREPARES, TRUE);
$pdo->setAttribute(PDO::ATTR_ERRMODE,
    PDO::ERRMODE_EXCEPTION);
$password = password_hash("password", PASSWORD_BCRYPT);
try {
    $pdo->beginTransaction();
    $pdo->exec("
        INSERT INTO users
            (username, password)
        VALUES
            ('bob', '{$password}'");
    // some more update or insert statements
    $pdo->commit();
} catch (PDOException $e) {
    $pdo->rollBack();
    echo 'Rolled back because: ' . $e->getMessage();
}
```

In the example, we make a connection to the database with PDO and start a transaction.

We wrap all the PDO transaction functions in a try...catch block. If a PDO statement fails to run, it will throw a PDOException. We use the catch block to roll back the transaction.

Fetching PDO Results

We use the PDO::fetch() method[2] to retrieve data from a PDO result. PDO will maintain a cursor to traverse the result set and will use this to determine which element to return to you.

PDO will return the data to you in a format that you specify in the first parameter to fetch().

---

[2]https://secure.php.net/manual/en/pdostatement.fetch.php

Fetch Style	Returns
PDO::FETCH_ASSOC	Returns an associative array with your database columns as keys.
PDO::FETCH_NUM	Returns an array indexed by column number as returned by your result set.
PDO::FETCH_BOTH	Returns an array with both the indexes of ASSOC and NUM style fetches.
PDO::FETCH_BOUND	Returns true and assigns the values of the columns in your result set to the PHP variables to which they were bound with the PDOStatement::bindColumn() method.
PDO::FETCH_CLASS	Returns a new instance of the requested class mapping the columns of the result set to named properties in the class.
PDO::FETCH_INTO	Updates an existing instance of the requested class, mapping as for FETCH_CLASS.
PDO::FETCH_OBJ	Returns an anonymous object with property names that correspond to the column names from your result set.
PDO::FETCH_LAZY	Combines PDO::FETCH_BOTH and PDO::FETCH_OBJ and creates the object variable names as they are accessed.
PDO::FETCH_NAMED	As for PDO::FETCH_ASSOC, returns an associative array. If there are multiple columns with the same name, the value referred to by that key will be an array of all the values in the row that had that column name.

Prepared Statements in PDO

Not all database engines support prepared statements and this is the only feature that PDO will emulate for adapters that don't.

The syntax for a prepared statement in PDO is very similar to using a native function.

```php
<?php
$stmt = $dbh->prepare("INSERT INTO users (name, email) VALUES
(:name, :value)");
$stmt->bindParam(':name', $name);
$stmt->bindValue(':email','alice@example.com');

// insert one row
$name = 'one';
$stmt->execute();
```

Walking through the example, we see that the prepare() method is used to create the statement object.

We're using two different forms of binding parameters to demonstrate the difference.

In the first, bindParam(), we're binding a variable to the statement parameter. When the statement executes, the parameter will take the value of the variable at execution time.

The second way to bind variables, bindValue(), binds a literal to the statement parameter. If you used a variable name in bindValue(), then the value of the variable at bind time is used. Changes to the variable before the statement executes will not affect the parameter value.

You can also pass the values to bind as an array in your call to execute, as in this example:

```php
<?php
$stmt = $pdo->prepare('SELECT * FROM users WHERE email = :email AND
status=:status');
$stmt->execute(['email' => $email, 'status' => $status]);
$user = $stmt->fetch();
```

Only values can be bound in a SQL statement, not entities like table names or columns. You can only bind scalar values, not composite variables like arrays or objects.

Repeated Calls to PDO Prepared Statements

You have seen that the bindParam() method inserts the value of a variable at the time the statement is executed into the statement parameter. You can see that using bindParam() allows you to repeatedly call the prepared statement, using different values for the parameters on each call.

The method closeCursor() is used to clear the database cursor and return the statement to a state where it can be executed again. Some databases have problems executing a prepared statement when a previously executed statement still has unfetched rows.

CHAPTER 10 QUIZ

Q1: You can use the _____ function to build an HTTP query string suitable to use for GET or POST out of an array.

```
http_build_query()
http_build_param()
parse_url()
urlencode()
```

Q2: The PHP function `encodeurl()` is used to:

Make sure that an URL is UTF-8 encoded.

Convert reserved characters in a URL to % encoded symbols.

Build a string suitable for GET parameters from an array.

There is no such PHP function.

Q3: What are the advantages of using prepared statements; choose as many that apply?

They can be more secure than using normal queries.

They are faster for repeated queries.

You can use the same query in different database vendors.

None of the above.

Q4: I have information about customers stored in a table. Each row has an `account_id` that is a foreign key to a table called `accounts`. How can you select the `postcode` column from the address table for a customer with ID 123?

SELECT `postcode` FROM `accounts` WHERE customer_id = 123;

SELECT `postcode` FROM `accounts` AS `acc`
JOIN `customers` as `cust` ON `cust.id` = `acc.id` WHERE `c`.id = 123

SELECT `postcode` FROM `accounts` AS `a`
JOIN `customers` as `c` ON `c.account_id` = `a`.`id` WHERE `c`.id = 123

SELECT `postcode` FROM `accounts` AS `a`
FULL OUTER JOIN `customers` as `c` ON `c.id` = `a.id` WHERE `c`.id = 123

CHAPTER 11

Error Handling

Error handling accounts for some of the biggest changes between PHP 5.6 and PHP 7.1 and it makes sense to address this important topic separately even though we have touched on it at relevant places elsewhere in this book.

Throwables

We're going to be looking at the Error and Exception classes in this chapter. For now, all that you need to know is that they both implement the Throwable interface that was introduced in PHP 7.

Tip   The reason that PHP defined a new Error class that does not extend the Exception class was to maintain backward compatibility with PHP5.6 code.

The Throwable Interface

Exceptions and error exceptions both implement the Throwable interface, so you can catch both types in a single block like this:

```php
<?php
try {
    // ...code
} catch (Throwable $e) {
    echo "A class that inherits from either Exception or ErrorException was
    caught";
}
```

In just a moment we'll see the matching rules that PHP uses to compare ErrorExceptions and Exceptions against catch blocks.

You can find the methods defined in the Throwable interface in the PHP manual,[1] but here they are for your convenience:

```
Throwable {
/* Methods */
abstract public string getMessage ( void )
abstract public int getCode ( void )
abstract public string getFile ( void )
abstract public int getLine ( void )
abstract public array getTrace ( void )
abstract public string getTraceAsString ( void )
abstract public Throwable getPrevious ( void )
abstract public string __toString ( void )
}
```

■ **Tip**   These methods can be very useful for logging the error.

Errors

In older versions of PHP, errors were treated very differently from exceptions. An error was something produced in the engine and so long as it was not fatal it could be handled by a user-defined function.

The problem was that there were several errors that were fatal and could not be handled by a user-defined error handler.

This meant that you couldn't handle fatal errors in PHP5.6 gracefully. There were several side-effects that were problematic—such as the loss of runtime context, destructors would not be called, and dealing with them was cludgy.

In PHP 7, fatal errors are now exceptions and are a lot easier to deal with.

■ **Note**   Only fatal errors result in an error exception being thrown. You need to handle non-fatal errors with an error-handling function.

Here is an example of catching a fatal error in PHP 7.1. Notice how the non-fatal error is not caught.

```
<?php
try {
    // generates a notice error (not caught)
    echo $thisVariableIsNotSet;
```

---

[1]https://php.net/manual/en/class.throwable.php

```
    // this would be a fatal error (is caught)
    badFunction();
} catch (Error $e) {
    echo "Error caught: " . $e->getMessage();
}
```

This script will output a notice error for the attempt to access an invalid variable. Trying to call a function that does not exist would result in a fatal error in earlier versions of PHP, but in PHP 7.1, you can catch it.

Here is the output for the script:

```
Notice: Undefined variable: thisVariableIsNotSet in /in/1QC3F on line 5
Error caught: Call to undefined function badFunction()
```

Error Constants

PHP has a lot of constants[2] that are used in relation to errors. These constants are used when configuring PHP to hide or display errors of certain classes.

Here are some of the more commonly seen error codes:

Code	Description	Script	Throws Error?
E_DEPRECATED	The interpreter will generate warnings of this type if you use a language feature that is deprecated.	Continues to run	No
E_STRICT	Similar to E_DEPRECATED, this indicates that you are using a language feature that is not currently standard and might not work in the future.	Continues to run	No
E_PARSE	Your syntax could not be parsed and so your script won't start.	Won't run at all	No
E_NOTICE	An informational message.	Continues to run	No
E_WARNING	These are non-fatal warnings.	Continues to run	No
E_ERROR	The script cannot continue to run and is being terminated.	Aborts unless you handle it with an error handler	Yes
E_RECOVERABLE_ERROR	The error was probably dangerous enough to be fatal but the engine is not in a state where it cannot continue.	Aborts unless you handle it with an error handler	Yes

---

[2]https://php.net/manual/en/errorfunc.constants.php

Using an Error-Handler Function

The set_error_handler() function[3] is used to tell PHP how to handle standard engine errors that are not instances of the Error exception class. You cannot use an error-handler function for fatal errors; you must catch them as Error exceptions.

set_error_handler() accepts a callable[4] as its parameter. Callables in PHP can be specified in two ways: Either by a string denoting the name of a function, or by passing an array that contains an object and the name of a method (in that order).

■ **Note** You can specify protected and private methods in an object as the callable.

You can also pass null to tell PHP to revert to using the standard error-handling mechanism.

If your error handler does not terminate the program and returns, then your script will continue executing at the line after where the error occurred.

PHP passes parameters to your error-handler function. You can optionally declare these in the function signature if you want to use them in your function.

```php
<?php

function myHandler(int $errNo, string $errMsg, string $file, int $line) {
    echo "Error #[$errNo] occurred in [$file] at line [$line]: [$errMsg]";
}

set_error_handler('myHandler');

try {
    // This does not throw an Error
    5 / 0;
} catch ( Throwable $e ) {
    echo 'Caught error : ' . $e->getMessage();
}

/*
   Error #[2] occurred in [/in/XaOTd] at line [11]: [Division by zero]
*/
```

In the preceding example, we divide the number five by zero. In PHP this results in a warning so an Error is not thrown. We have, however, set the function myHandler() up as the customer error handler and so it is invoked when PHP encounters the warning.

Errors that cause the script to terminate cannot be caught with a user error handler; these include E_ERROR, E_PARSE, E_CORE_ERROR, E_CORE_WARNING, E_COMPILE_ERROR, and E_COMPILE_WARNING.

---

[3]https://php.net/manual/en/function.set-error-handler.php
[4]https://php.net/manual/en/language.types.callable.php

Displaying or Suppressing Non-Fatal Error Messages

Generally, you want to hide all system error messages while in production and your code should run without generating warnings or messages. If you are going to show an error message, make sure that it is one that you've generated and that does not include information that could help an attacker break into your system.

In your development environment, you want all errors to be displayed so that you can fix all the issues that they relate to, but while in production you want to suppress any system messages being sent to the user.

To accomplish this, you need to configure PHP using the following settings in your php.ini file:

- display_errors can be set to false to suppress messages

- log_errors can be used to store error messages in log files

- error_reporting can be set to configure which errors trigger a report

The best practice is to gracefully handle errors in your application. In production, you should rather log unhandled errors instead of allowing them to be displayed to the user.

■ **Note** We looked at the error suppression operator @ in the first chapter. Remember that it's best to avoid using it.

The error_log() function[5] can be used to send a message to one of the systems error-handling routines. You shouldn't confuse it with the error_log configuration option. The configuration option specifies how to deal with logs, whereas the function is used to send a message.

You can also use the error_log() function to send e-mails, but personally I would not do so and would rather do this in code or use a service like Rollbar.[6]

Error-Handling Functions

PHP has many functions[78] that relate to error handling. This table provides a summary of them. We'll be looking at most of them in this chapter.

---

[5]https://php.net/manual/en/function.error-log.php
[6]https://rollbar.com/
[7]https://php.net/manual/en/errorfunc.configuration.php#ini.error-log
[8]https://php.net/manual/en/ref.errorfunc.php

Function	Purpose
debug_backtrace	Generates a backtrace.
debug_print_backtrace	Prints a backtrace. Be careful when using this function because it can generate a lot of output!
error_clear_last	Clears the most recent error.
error_get_last	Gets the last occurred error.
error_log	Sends an error message to the defined error-handling routines.
error_reporting	Sets which PHP errors are reported.
restore_error_handler	Restores the previous error-handler function.
restore_exception_handler	Restores the previously defined exception-handler function.
set_error_handler	Sets a user-defined error-handler function.
set_exception_handler	Sets a user-defined exception handler function.
trigger_error	Generates a user-level error/warning/notice message.
user_error	Alias of trigger_error.

Exceptions

Exceptions are a core part of object-oriented programming and were first introduced in PHP 5.0. An exception is a program state that requires special processing because it's not running in the expected manner.

You can use an exception to change the flow of your program, for example, to stop doing something if certain preconditions are not met.

An exception will bubble up through the call stack if you do not catch it. Let's look at an example:

```php
<?php
function A() {
  // The exception thrown in C will bubble up to A
  // because it is not handled in C or B
  try {
    B();
  } catch (Exception $e) {
    echo "Caught exception in " . __METHOD__;
  }
}

function B() {
  // we're not catching exceptions in B
  C();
}
```

```php
function C() {
    // we do not catch the exception where it is thrown
    throw new Exception('Bubble');
}
A();
/*
Outputs:
    Caught exception in A and the program ends successfully
*/
```

This program calls function A, which calls B, which then calls C. Function C throws an exception but we don't catch it in C. The exception bubbles to B, but it's not caught there either. The exception continues to bubble up to A, where we do catch it.

If we hadn't caught the exception in A then it would have bubbled to the global scope where we would have one final chance at catching it. If an exception is not caught then PHP looks for a default exception handler, and eventually if there is no handler, it will result in a fatal error.

Extending Exception Classes

PHP includes several standard exception types, and the standard PHP library (SPL) includes a few more. Although you don't have to use these exceptions, doing so means you can use more fine-grained error detection and reporting.

The Exception and Error classes both implement the Throwable interface[9] and, like any other classes, can be extended. This allows you to create flexible error hierarchies and tailor your exception handling.

Only a class that implements the Throwable class can be used with the throw keyword. In other words, you can't declare your own base class and then throw it as an exception.

As an example, let's create an exception class that we can use to signal that there has been a form validation problem:

```php
<?php
class ValidationException extends Exception { }

function myValidation() {
    if (empty($_POST)) {
        throw new ValidationException('No form fields entered');
    }
}
```

---

[9]https://php.net/manual/en/class.throwable.php

Let's look at the syntax and then discuss exceptions in more detail:

```php
<?php
class ParentException extends Exception {}
class ChildException extends ParentException {}

try {
    // some code
    throw new ChildException('My Message');
} catch (ParentException $e) {
    // matches this class because of inheritance
    echo "Parent Exception :" . $e->getMessage();
} catch (ChildException $e) {
    // matches this class exactly
    echo "Child Exception :" . $e->getMessage();
} catch (Exception $e) {
    // matches this class because of inheritance
    echo "Exception :" . $e->getMessage();
}
```

The output of this example is Parent Exception :My Message.

In the example, we are throwing a ChildException, which inherits from ParentException, which in turn extends the base Exception class.

The blocks are evaluated in order from top to bottom. The first block that is matched will be executed.

The class of the exception being thrown is matched against the name of the class given as a parameter to the catch clause.

The matching criteria are that the classes are either:

- Exactly the same, or

- The thrown exception is an ancestor of the exception in the catch statement

In this example, we threw an exception of the ChildException, which inherits from the ParentException. The exception is therefore matched against the first catch block and the code is executed.

I put the base Exception at the bottom of the list of catch blocks because all custom exceptions inherit from it, which makes it a catchall.

The Exception Hierarchy

So far, we've understood that Errors and Exceptions both implement the Throwable interface. We've just seen that both the Error and Exception class can be extended.

The built-in PHP 7 exception hierarchy looks like this:

```
interface Throwable
    |- Exception implements Throwable
        |- ...
    |- Error implements Throwable
        |- TypeError extends Error
            |- ArgumentCountError
        |- ParseError extends Error
        |- ArithmeticError extends Error
            |- DivisionByZeroError extends ArithmeticError
        |- AssertionError extends Error
```

As you can see, there are several predefined error classes that form a hierarchy underneath Error. The following table summarizes their purpose:

Class	Purpose
TypeError	A TypeError is thrown when the argument passed to a function does not match its corresponding declared parameter type, or when the function does not return the expected type.
ArgumentCountError	ArgumentCountError is thrown when too few arguments are passed to a user-defined function or method.
ParseError	A ParseError is thrown when there is an error parsing PHP code, for example, when you call eval() or include a file.
ArithmeticError	An arithmetic error occurs when you try to bitshift by a negative amount or make a call to intdiv() that would result in a value outside the limits of an integer on the current system.
DivisionByZeroError	A DivisionByZeroError occurs if you try to divide by zero.
AssertionError	An AssertionError is thrown when an assertion made with the assert() language construct fails.

Handling Exceptions

Robust code can encounter an error and cope with it.[10] Handling exceptions in a sensible way improves the security of your application and makes logging and debugging easier. Managing errors in your application will also allow you to offer your users a better experience. In this section, we cover how to trap and handle errors that occur in your code.

---

[10]https://en.wikipedia.org/wiki/Robustness_(computer_science)

Catching Exceptions

Remember that earlier in the chapter, we defined a ValidationException like this:

```php
<?php
class ValidationException extends Exception { }

function myValidation() {
    if (empty($_POST)) {
        throw new ValidationException('No form fields entered');
    }
}
```

Let's continue from there and imagine that we are calling the myValidation()
function and want to catch exceptions. The syntax to catch the exception is as follows:

```php
<?php
try {
    // assume that if there is validation problem this throws a
    ValidationException
    myValidation();
} catch (ValidationException $e) {
    echo "Validation exception caught ";
    echo $e->getMessage();
} catch (Exception $e) {
    echo "General exception type caught";
}
```

Note that there are two catch clauses. Exceptions will be matched against the clauses
from top to bottom until the type of the exception matches the catch clause.

■ **Note** The matching criteria are that the classes are either exactly the same or the
thrown exception class is an ancestor of the Exception class in the catch statement.

Since myValidation throws a ValidationException, we would expect it to be caught
in the first block, but if any other type of exception is thrown in the function, then it will
be caught in the second catch block.

Note also the method getMessage() is being called on the exception object. Other
methods in the basic Exception class will give error codes, stack traces, and other
information. The PHP manual on Exceptions[11] is the best reference for the prototype for
the exception object.

It is possible to throw an exception in a catch block. This lets you catch an exception
and then rethrow it, perhaps as a different type, if need be.

---

[11]https://php.net/manual/en/language.exceptions.php

■ **Tip** You should always order your `catch` blocks from most specific at the top to the most general at the bottom—remember that `catch` blocks are greedy!

A `catch` block can specify multiple exception classes by separating them with a pipe (|) character.

In the following example, the `catch` block will match exceptions that are of the `MyException` class or of the `AnotherException` class.

```php
<?php

class MyException extends Exception {}
class AnotherException extends Exception {}

try {
    throw new AnotherException;
} catch (MyException | AnotherException $e) {
    echo "Caught : " . get_class($e);
}
/*
Caught : AnotherException
*/
```

■ **Note** A `try` block must have at least one `catch` block.

The finally Block

The last clause that we will look at is `finally`. This block of code will always be executed, whether an exception is thrown or not. It is executed either after the try block completes or after the exception block has completed.

One common use for the `finally` block is to close a file handle, but `finally` can be used wherever you want code to always be executed.

```php
<?php
try {
  // perform some functions
} catch (Exception $e) {
  // handle the error
} finally {
  // always run these statements
}
```

Setting the Default Exception Handler

Any exception that is not caught results in a fatal error. If you want to respond gracefully to exceptions that are not caught in catch blocks, then you'll need to set a function as the default exception handler.

To do so, you use the set_exception_handler() function, which accepts a callable as its parameter. Your script will terminate after the callable has executed.

The function restore_exception_handler() will revert the exception handler to its previous value.

CHAPTER 11 QUIZ

Q1: What will this code output?

```php
<?php
$handler = function($errorNumber, $errorMessage, $file, $line) {
  echo "Error [$errorNumber] in [$file] at line [$line]:
  '[$errorMessage]'\r\n";
};
set_error_handler($handler);
try {
    echo $a;
    session_start();
    echo session_id();
} catch (Throwable $e) {
    echo "Error caught!";
}
```

Error caught!

A random string which is the session ID

A notice error and a warning

Two formatted lines each containing information about the error

Q2: What will this code output?

```php
<?php
$handler = function($errorNumber, $errorMessage, $file, $line) {
  echo "Error [$errorNumber] in [$file] at line [$line]: '[$errorMessage]'\
  r\n";
};
set_error_handler($handler);
this_function_is_not_defined();
```

Nothing, this runs without error

A normal fatal error PHP message

A formatted line of information about the error

None of the above

Q3: What will this code output?

```php
<?php
class IndianaError extends ArithmeticError {}
define('PI', 3);
try {
    if (is_int(PI)) {
        throw new IndianaError('Oops');
    }
} catch (Exception $e) {
    echo $e->getMessage();
}
```

Nothing, this code runs without error

Oops!

A PHP fatal error

None of the above

Q4: What will this code output?

```php
<?php
set_error_handler(function($errorNumber, $errorMessage, $file, $line) {
  debug_print_backtrace();
});
trigger_error('Hello world', E_USER_WARNING);
```

Hello world

Two lines of information

A PHP fatal error

None of the above

Q5: What will this code output?

```php
<?php
try {
    echo 50/0;
} catch (Exception $e) {
    echo "Exception caught!";
} catch (Throwable $e) {
    echo " Throwable caught!";
} catch (Error $e) {
    echo "Error caught!";
} catch (DivisionByZeroError $e) {
    echo "DivisionByZeroError caught!";
}
```

_____

Exception caught!

Throwable caught!

Error caught!

DivisionByZeroError caught!

None of the above

_____

CHAPTER 12

Exercises

This chapter is just about questions. The aim of all these questions is to help you to identify areas that you need to review. The exam includes questions that are very detail oriented and you need to make sure that you're familiar with the functions in common use.

I have not grouped the questions by chapter. The real exam has questions that focus on knowledge from multiple areas of the syllabus.

Q1: What will happen when you run this code?

```php
<?php
class CustomException { }
throw new CustomException('Error!');
```

A fatal error will occur because the exception is not being caught

A fatal error will occur when you try to throw the exception

The script will run without any output because you're not using getMessage() on the exception

None of the above

Q2: What will this script output?

```php
<?php
function addOne($arg) {
$arg++;
}

$a = 0;
addOne(&$a);
echo $a;
```

Syntax error; it won't run at all

It depends on what version of PHP you're using

A fatal error

1

Q3: What will the output of this script be?

```php
<?php
$a = function($a) {
return is_callable($a);
};
$b = function($b) use ($a) {
return $a($b);
};
echo $b($a) ? 'True' : 'False';
```

Syntax error; it will not run

True

False

None of the above

Q4: What is the output of this script?

```php
<?php
$a = 3;
echo $a >> 1;
```

Syntax Error

0

1

2

9

Q5: The recommended production setting for the display_error configuration setting is On.

True

False

Q6: The `session_generate_id()` function is used to create a session identifier and should be called when a person logs in to help mitigate session fixation attacks.

True

False

Q7: When you call the `json_encode` function on an object to serialize it, which magic method will PHP call?

__sleep

__wake

__get

__clone

None of these

Q8: What will this script output?

```php
<?php
$emptyArray = [];
$encode = json_encode($emptyArray, JSON_FORCE_OBJECT);
$decode = json_decode($encode);
echo gettype($decode);
```

Syntax error; it won't run at all

array

object

string

None of the above

Q9: What is the output of the following script?

```php
<?php
$arr1 = [1,2,3];
$arr2 = array("1" => 2, 0 => "1", 2 => 3 );
$equal = $arr1 == $arr2 ? 'Equal' : 'Not Equal';
$identical = $arr1 === $arr2 ? 'Identical' : 'Not Identical';
echo "The arrays are [$equal] and [$identical]";
```

Syntax error; this won't run

The arrays are [Equal] and [Identical]

The arrays are [Equal] and [Not Identical]

The arrays are [Not Equal] and [Not Identical]

The arrays are [Not Equal] and [Identical]

None of the above

Q10: What will the output of this function be?

```php
<?php
$number = 1234.5678;
echo number_format($number, 2, ',', '.') . PHP_EOL;
```

1,235

1,234.568

1.234,57

None of the above

Q11: You should escape strings before passing them into the database with a function like addslashes() so that it is not possible to use the SQL injection attack on your site.

True

False

Q12: What is the output of this code?

```php
<?php
class A
{
    public $name = '0';
    private $surname = '0';
    public function __isset($property)
    {
        return true;
    }
}
$a = new A;
$empty = empty($a->name);
$set = isset($a->surname);
```

266

```php
if ($empty === $set) {
   echo "Yes";
} else {
   echo "No";
}
```

Yes

No

Syntax error; this won't run

Q13: If you do not specify a visibility modifier, PHP chooses private by default so that your code is secure.

True

False

Q14: You can use the _____ function to make sure that a variable is suitable to display and doesn't contain any spaces.

---

ctype_alpha

ctype_print

ctype_graph

filter_var

Q15: What will this code output?

```php
<?php
function bird($message) {
    function nest($string) {
        echo $string;
    }
    nest($message);
}
bird('hello');
echo " ";
nest('world');
```

Syntax error; it won't run

It will never finish running

It will generate an error because the function nest() does not exist in the global scope

hello world

None of the above

Q16: What will the code output?

```php
<?php
$a = 0;
$b = $a++;
$a = $a + 1;
echo --$a;
```

An error will occur

0

1

2

Q17: You can use the _____ function to make sure that a file was actually uploaded and is not a different file on your OS.

```php
check_file_uploaded()
finfo_file()
is_uploaded_file()
```
None of the above

Q18: What is the output of this PHP code?

```php
<?php
echo (isset($a)) ? "A is set" : "A is not set";
echo " and ";
echo (empty($b)) ? "B is not set" : "B is set";
```

Syntax error

A is not set and B is set

A is not set and B is not set

A is set and B is set

A warning will be produced and it will output "A is not set and B is not set"

It will have a fatal error saying variable not found

Q19: Both PUT and POST are idempotent.

True

False; POST is idempotent but PUT is not

False; PUT is idempotent but POST is not

False; neither are idempotent

False; REST is stateless so nothing is idempotent

Q20: You are able to instantiate a class before it is defined, as in this example:

```php
<?php
$foo = new ExampleClass();
echo $foo;
class ExampleClass {}
```

True

False

Q21: If you're not using prepared statements and want to escape strings when using the MySQL database, you can use the _____ function.

mysql_real_escape_string()

real_escape_string()

mysqli_real_escape_string()

addslashes()

mysqli_escape_string()

None of the above

Q22: What will this script output?

```php
<?php
$a = "foo";
$$a = "bar";
$a = "Hello world";
echo ${"foo"};
```

Syntax error; this won't run

foo

bar

Hello world

Q23: Considering the following code, what will the output be?

```php
<?php
$a = "0.0";
$b = (int)$a;
if ( (boolean)$a === (bool)$b) {
echo "True";
} else {
echo "False";
}
```

Syntax error; this won't run

True

False

Q24: What will this script output?

```php
echo "Apples"<=>"bananas" ? 'foo' : 'bar';
```

---

foo

bar

None of the above

Q25: This is a tricky question, so go through it carefully and predict the output of the code. Remember that the second parameter of md5() causes the hash to be returned in RAW binary format instead of as a hex string.

```php
<?php
namespace A;
function md5($value) {
return \md5($value . ' Extra saltiness');
}
echo strlen(md5('Hi', true));
```

Syntax error; this won't run

16

32

This causes an error because you can't define a function with the same name as a PHP function name

None of the above

Q26: Which of the following types of error will prevent the script from executing?

Notice

Warning

Syntax error

Fatal error

Q27: What is the output from this script?

```php
<?php
$a = true;
$b = false;
$truth = $a && $b;
$pravda = $a and $b;
var_dump($truth == $pravda);
```

bool(true)

bool(false)

Q28: If you want PHP to display all errors except notices, which setting in php.ini would you use?

```
error_reporting= -E_NOTICE
error_reporting=E_ALL - E_NOTICE
error_reporting= ~E_NOTICE
error_reporting= E_ALL & ~E_NOTICE
```

Q29: Private methods are only accessible by the class in which they are defined, so this code will output an empty array.

```php
<?php
class Mirror {
    private function showMeGorgeous($me) {
        echo $me;
    }
}
$refObj = new ReflectionClass('Mirror');
print_r($refObj->getMethods());
```

```
True

False
```

Q30: Assume that you are running this script from the command line, and not in a web-browser. What will the output be?

```php
<?php
class SetMissing {
    public function __set($name, $value) {
        $this->$name = filter_var($value, FILTER_SANITIZE_STRING);
    }
}
$obj = new SetMissing();
$obj->example = "<strong>hello</strong>";
echo $obj->example . PHP_EOL;
$obj->example = "<strong>hello</strong>";
echo $obj->example;
```

```
hello
<strong>hello</strong>
```

```
<strong>hello</strong>
<strong>hello</strong>
```

```
hello
hello
```

None of the above

Q31: If you implement the __sleep() function, you need to make sure that it returns an associative array containing the names and values of the instance variables you want to be serialized.

True

False

Q32: What will the output of this code be?

```php
<?php
trait Dog {
public function makeNoise() {
echo "Woof";
}
  public function wantWalkies() {
echo "Yes please!";
}
}

trait Cat {
public function makeNoise() {
echo "Purr";
  }
public function wantWalkies() {
    echo "No thanks!";
}
}

class DomesticPet
{
use Dog, Cat {
Cat::makeNoise insteadof Dog;
Cat::wantWalkies as kittyWalk;
Dog::wantWalkies insteadof Cat;
}
```

```php
}
$obj = new DomesticPet();
$obj->kittyWalk();
```

Yes please!

No thanks!

Woof

Purr

None of the above

Q33: What is the output of this code?

```php
<?php
class A
{
    public $name = '0';
    private $surname = '0';
    public function __isset($property)
    {
        return true;
    }
}
$a = new A;
$empty = empty($a->name);
$set = isset($a->surname);
if ($empty === $set) {
  echo "Yes";
} else {
  echo "No";
}
```

Syntax error; this won't run

Yes

No

Fatal error

Q34: Are PHP keys case sensitive? What will the output of this script be?

```php
<?php
$arr1 = ["A" => "apple", "B" => "banana"];
$arr2 = ["a" => "aardvark", "b" => "baboon"];
echo count($arr1 + $arr2);
```

They are not case sensitive; this will output 2

They are case sensitive; this will output 4

PHP keys are converted to integers; this outputs 2

None of the above

Q35: What will this script output?

```php
<?php
$a = "0";
$c = $b = empty($a);
$d = ++$b + $a;
echo $d;
```

0

1

2

Syntax error; you can't assign two variables on one line

None of the above

Q36: What will this code output?

```php
<?php
$a = 1.23;
$b = 4.56;
$c = (int)$a + (int)$b;
echo (double)$c;
```

5

6

5.79

None of the above

Q37: What will this script output?

```php
<?php
$arr = ["one", "two", 1.5 => "three"];
echo $arr[1];
```

one

two

three

None of the above

Q38: Interfaces can only specify public methods, but your class can implement them however you like.

True

False

Q39: You can force sessions to be contained exclusively in cookies by using the _____ configuration setting.

session.cookie_secure

session.use_cookies

session.use_trans_sid

None of the above

Q40: What is the output of this code?

```php
<?php
define('PI', 3.14159625);
define('_PI', "3.1459625");
$radius = 10;
if (PI == _PI) {
    $area = (int)PI * $radius ** 2;
    echo $area;
} else {
    echo "Indiana";
}
```

Indiana

300

900

986.962699801

400

1600

Q41: What is the output of this script?

```php
<?php
function HelloWorld() {
echo HELLO;

}
const HELLO = "Hello World!";
HelloWorld();
```

Syntax Error

Hello World!

PHP Notice: Use of undefined constant HELLO

None of the above

Q42: What will this code output?

```php
<?php
function add(int $a, int $b): integer {
    return $a + $b;
}
echo add(5.7, -4.6);
```

Syntax error

1

1.1

None of the above

Q43: What is the output of this script?

```php
<?php
$a = 0b0010;
$b = 0b0001;
echo gettype($a & $b);
```

Syntax error; this won't run

undefined

integer

double

boolean

Q44: What will the output of this code be?

```php
<?php
$result = echo print("Hello world!");
var_dump($result);
```

NULL

1NULL

Hello world!NULL

A syntax error

Q45: You have invoked PHP on the command line and want to access the arguments you passed in your PHP script. Which superglobal will contain these?

$GLOBALS

$_ARGV

$_SERVER

$_ARGUMENTS

Q46: The function gc_collect_cycles() is used to do which of the following?

There is no such function

Pause the script for a certain number of processor cycles

Initiate garbage collection to free up memory

Flush the opcode cache

Q47: What will this code output?

```php
<?php
try {
    // generates a notice error (not caught)
    echo $thisVariableIsNotSet;
} catch (Error $e) {
    echo "Error caught";
}
```

This produces a notice error

This produces a fatal error

Error caught

None of the above

Q48: What will this code output?

```php
<?php
$emotion = "loves";
$theBeeb = function($name) use ($emotion) {
    echo "$name $emotion Justin";
};
$emotion = "adores";
$theBeeb("Ron");
```

Ron loves Justin   *

Ron adores Justin

$name $emotion Justin

None of the above

Q49: Assume that the Pluto and Grumpy classes are both declared in the class.
definitions.php file, which is in the same directory as this script. What will happen
when you run this script?

```php
<?php
$a = function() {
include('class.definitions.php');
};
spl_autoload_register($a);
// Class Pluto is defined in class.definitions.php
$planet = new Pluto;
// Class Grumpy is defined in class.definitions.php
$dwarf = new Grumpy;
```

The script will generate a fatal error because you need to put brackets after the class
name

The script will generate an error when you try to include the script a second time

The file will be included once and the script won't output anything

The script will fail because you cannot use a variable for spl_autoload_register; only
a string literal

None of the above

Q50: Which of the following pieces of information associated with the request cannot be easily changed by the client?

Remote IP address

Session data

Cookie data

User agent

All of these are easily changed by the client

■ ■ ■

Quiz Answers

Chapter 1: PHP Basics

Question	Answer
1	None of the above, these are all fine
2	Class name and functions
3	https://3v4l.org/rSi4Q
4	https://3v4l.org/C9WG7
5	https://3v4l.org/D9u6l
6	https://3v4l.org/JZ9s9
7	memory_limit and max_execution_time
8	https://3v4l.org/UjSh6
9	https://3v4l.org/Knvvd
10	https://3v4l.org/XQ9ob

Chapter 2: Functions

Question	Answer
1	https://3v4l.org/qoNo4
2	I disagree because echo is a language construct and not a function. All PHP functions require you to use brackets when calling them.
3	True
4	https://3v4l.org/IQ17h
5	https://3v4l.org/gqEH9
6	https://3v4l.org/QI1Ri
7	https://3v4l.org/dhkSW
8	https://3v4l.org/rDOoB
9	https://3v4l.org/WSbld
10	https://3v4l.org/ZYJLj

Chapter 3: Strings and Patterns

Question	Answer
1	False
2	strcasecmp
3	$haystack, $needle
4	Returns the maximum length of a string in $subject that contains only letters contained in $mask
5	It returns the portion of the $haystack that occurs after the first instance of $needle
6	https://3v4l.org/tnqpL
7	All of them, except the first
8	https://3v4l.org/WMueT
9	https://3v4l.org/hhrjW
10	Use a callback function to supply the replacement string instead of a static string

Chapter 4: Arrays

Question	Answer
1	https://3v4l.org/INLuB
2	https://3v4l.org/HlDFv
3	https://3v4l.org/NLtbg
4	https://3v4l.org/T5pLI
5	https://3v4l.org/1cUvs
6	https://3v4l.org/LpV7o
7	https://3v4l.org/HbY1Y
8	https://3v4l.org/C16lb
9	https://3v4l.org/oTRIs
10	https://3v4l.org/ESFFL

Chapter 5: Object-Oriented PHP

Question	Answer
1	1_Example_Class
2	https://3v4l.org/Pfu42
3	https://3v4l.org/nshfi
4	No
5	False, you can declare them in different namespaces False, you can declare them in different scopes
6	None of these
7	False, you cannot change the visibility when you implement
8	https://3v4l.org/cYI5A
9	CLASS MEMBERS ➤ TRAIT METHODS ➤ INHERITED METHODS
10	False

Chapter 6: Security

Question	Answer
1	False
2	False. It will not help with session fixation, as the mechanism of tricking the user to supply a token known to the attacker will still work. It will help with session hijacking because it will make it harder to read the token while it is carried over the network.
3	None of the above
4	False. The token will be predictable so the attacker would have a good chance of being able to include it in a request.
5	False. crypt() does not generate a salt. As of PHP 5.6 it will generate a notice warning if you do not specify a salt. The intended use of password_hash() is to allow PHP to generate the salt because it uses a cryptographically secure way to do so.
6	False. The browser doesn't check the file type and you cannot trust what it tells you either.
7	False. You must use move_uploaded_file() and not copy() to maintain security.
8	True
9	False. You need to use different methods of escaping depending on the context of what you're outputting. strip_tags() will not work to escape all parts of a document and so is not sufficient by itself.
10	False

Chapter 7: Data Structures

Question	Answer
1	False, they are fitted into the encoding scheme (converted to question marks).
2	False
3	https://3v4l.org/p5NYT
4	Editing php.ini
5	See https://3v4l.org/8Ij53
6	Nothing is wrong, this will work
7	https://3v4l.org/K1otJ (Note: xpath is not zero based so team[1] is the first team (not the second))
8	dom_import_simplexml()
9	https://3v4l.org/jItbF
10	https://3v4l.org/1lBtt

Chapter 8: Input-Output

Question	Answer
1	string(0) ""
2	6,7,8 1,2,3,4,5
3	Read the php://input stream
4	a
5	GIF image data, version 89a, 400x400

Chapter 9: Web Features

Question	Answer
1	Ronald
2	`<input type="text" name="justin[numberonefan]">`
3	No, they are not reliable.
4	A notice because $a is undefined (this outputs content), and a warning because $a is undefined (because headers were sent with the notice message).
5	Prevent the browser from sending this cookie to other web sites.

Chapter 10: Databases and SQL

Question	Answer
1	`http_build_query()`
2	There is no such PHP function
3	They can be more secure than using normal queries and they are faster for repeated queries
4	`SELECT `postcode` FROM `accounts` AS `a`` `JOIN `customers` as `c` ON `c.account_id` = `a`.`id`` `WHERE `c`.id = 123`

Chapter 11: Error Handling

Question	Answer
1	`https://3v4l.org/poDFC`
2	`https://3v4l.org/4XK2R`
3	`https://3v4l.org/4KoKF`
4	`https://3v4l.org/q2K52`
5	`https://3v4l.org/ru5gu`

Chapter 12: Exercises

Question	Answer
1	https://3v4l.org/HWd8N
2	https://3v4l.org/itFYF
3	https://3v4l.org/suCYR
4	https://3v4l.org/bZJ7h
5	False
6	False. The function should be session_regenerate_id().
7	None of these
8	https://3v4l.org/iSeQU
9	https://3v4l.org/UWMp8
10	https://3v4l.org/8vIFB
11	False
12	https://3v4l.org/i4Goi
13	False. It's public by default and visibility has nothing to do with code security.
14	ctype_graph
15	https://3v4l.org/N27Ao
16	https://3v4l.org/vaRbT
17	is_uploaded_file()
18	https://3v4l.org/2J18W
19	False; PUT is idempotent but POST is not.
20	True
21	mysqli_real_escape_string()
22	https://3v4l.org/JG42J
23	https://3v4l.org/vPhFh
24	None of the above; there is no <?php so it won't be parsed as PHP.
25	https://3v4l.org/kOEeM; sending TRUE as the second parameter of \md5 (in the global namespace) would result in the md5 digest being returned in RAW binary format with a length of 16. However, we are calling the function A\md5(), which only has one parameter and so the TRUE is ignored. We are not passing it to the md5() function in the global namespace. Adding a salt string to the value before hashing will not impact the length of the hash. So, the answer is 32.
26	Syntax error

(continued)

Question	Answer
27	If the answer is surprising to you, make sure you run the code at https://3v4l.org/5ZOqI.
28	error_reporting= E_ALL & ~E_NOTICE
29	False. https://3v4l.org/ES7ve
30	https://3v4l.org/1803k
31	False
32	https://3v4l.org/F7vve
33	https://3v4l.org/i4Goi
34	They are case sensitive; this will output 4 (https://3v4l.org/INLuB).
35	https://3v4l.org/k2hOf
36	https://3v4l.org/FSOOD
37	https://3v4l.org/1IR8b
38	False
39	None of the above; the setting is session.use_only_cookies.
40	https://3v4l.org/cQir5
41	https://3v4l.org/1FrCQ
42	https://3v4l.org/B3l86
43	https://3v4l.org/8m5F4
44	A syntax error, because echo does not return any value (not even NULL). Also, remember that print() returns 1 if it is successful.
45	$_SERVER
46	Initiate garbage collection to free up memory
47	https://3v4l.org/g5NnV
48	https://3v4l.org/oXFau
49	The file will be included once and the script won't output anything
50	Session data

Index

■ O

■ P, Q

■ R

Get the eBook for only $5!

Why limit yourself?

With most of our titles available in both PDF and ePUB format, you can access your content wherever and however you wish—on your PC, phone, tablet, or reader.

Since you've purchased this print book, we are happy to offer you the eBook for just $5.

To learn more, go to http://www.apress.com/companion or contact support@apress.com.

Apress®

Printed in the United States
By Bookmasters